Behavioral Strategy

Emerging Perspectives

A volume in
Research in Behavioral Strategy
T. K. Das, *Series Editor*

RESEARCH IN BEHAVIORAL STRATEGY

T. K. Das, *Series Editor*

Published

Behavioral Strategy: Emerging Perspectives
Edited by T. K. Das

Forthcoming volumes

The Practice of Behavioral Strategy
Edited by T. K. Das

Economic Perspectives on Behavioral Strategy
Edited by T. K. Das

Decision Making in Behavioral Strategy
Edited by T. K. Das

Behavioral Strategy

Emerging Perspectives

edited by

T. K. Das

City University of New York

IAP

INFORMATION AGE PUBLISHING, INC.
Charlotte, NC • www.infoagepub.com

Library of Congress Cataloging-in-Publication Data

A CIP record for this book is available from the Library of Congress
http://www.loc.gov

ISBN: 978-1-62396-711-6 (Paperback)
978-1-62396-712-3 (Hardcover)
978-1-62396-713-0 (ebook)

Printed and bound by CPI Group (UK) Ltd, Croydon, CR0 4YY

CONTENTS

ABOUT THE BOOK SERIES

Behavioral strategy continues to attract increasing research interest within the broader field of strategic management. Research in behavioral strategy has clear scope for development in tandem with such traditional streams of strategy research that involve economics, markets, resources, and technology. The key roles of psychology, organizational behavior, and behavioral decision making in the theory and practice of strategy have yet to be comprehensively grasped. Given that strategic thinking and strategic decision making are importantly concerned with human cognition, human decisions, and human behavior, it makes eminent sense to bring some balance in the strategy field by complementing the extant emphasis on the "objective' economics-based view with substantive attention to the "subjective" individual-oriented perspective. This calls for more focused inquiries into the role and nature of the individual strategy actors, and their cognitions and behaviors, in the strategy research enterprise. For the purposes of this book series, behavioral strategy would be broadly construed as covering all aspects of the role of the strategy maker in the entire strategy field. The scholarship relating to behavioral strategy is widely believed to be dispersed in diverse literatures. These existing contributions that relate to behavioral strategy within the overall field of strategy has been known and perhaps valued by most scholars all along, but were not adequately appreciated or brought together as a coherent sub-field or as a distinct perspective of strategy. This book series on *Research in Behavioral Strategy* will cover the essential progress made thus far in this admittedly fragmented literature and elaborate upon fruitful streams of scholarship. More importantly, the book series will focus on providing a robust and comprehensive forum for the growing

Behavioral Strategy: Emerging Perspectives, pages vii–viii scholarship in behavioral strategy. In particular, the volumes in the series will cover new views of interdisciplinary theoretical frameworks and models (dealing with all behavioral aspects), significant practical problems of strategy formulation, implementation, and evaluation, and emerging areas of inquiry. The series will also include comprehensive empirical studies of selected segments of business, economic, industrial, government, and non-profit activities with potential for wider application of behavioral strategy. Through the ongoing release of focused topical titles, this book series will seek to disseminate theoretical insights and practical management information that will enable interested professionals to gain a rigorous and comprehensive understanding of the subject of behavioral strategy.

—T. K. Das
City University of New York
Series Editor
Research in Behavioral Strategy

CHAPTER 1

COGNITIVE BIASES AND STRATEGIC DECISION PROCESSES

T. K. Das
Bing-Sheng Teng

ABSTRACT

Previous studies have not adequately addressed the role of cognitive biases in strategic decision processes. In this article we suggest that cognitive biases are systematically associated with strategic decision processes. Different decision processes tend to accentuate particular types of cognitive bias. We develop an integrative framework to explore the presence of four basic types of cognitive bias under five different modes of decision making. The cognitive biases include prior hypotheses and focusing on limited targets, exposure to limited alternatives, insensitivity to outcome probabilities and illusion of manageability. The five modes of strategic decision making are rational, avoidance, logical incrementalist, political and garbage can. We suggest a number of key propositions to facilitate empirical testing of the various contingent relationships implicit in the framework. Lastly, we discuss the implications of this framework for research and managerial practice.

Behavioral Strategy: Emerging Perspectives, pages 1–26

INTRODUCTION

Cognitive biases are an ever-present ingredient of strategic decision making. Clearly, a better understanding of how biases influence strategic decision processes should help managers in becoming more effective in achieving their goals. There has been a growing recognition among scholars of the importance of cognitive biases in strategic decision making. Nevertheless, little effort has been made to integrate cognitive biases with various modes of decision making beyond the early attempt by Lyles and Thomas (1988) to study biases in problem formulation. In fact, many scholars assume that some cognitive biases are "strong tendencies" that are present in various situations (Zajac & Bazerman, 1991, p. 52). It is as if these cognitive biases apply equally to all strategic decision situations. In our view, such a monolithic assumption does disservice to our understanding of cognitive biases in strategic decision making, as contingent relationships exist between major biases and particular kinds of strategic decision processes. Schwenk (1984, p. 124) argues for such relationships, stating that researchers are yet to specify the conditions under which each cognitive bias may be prevalent.

Thus, our purpose here is to outline a contingency framework of cognitive biases in strategic decision processes. We propose that not all basic types of bias are robust across all kinds of decision processes; rather, their selective presence is contingent upon the specific processes that decision makers engage in. By examining these contingent relationships we not only clarify the domain and the role of key cognitive biases in strategic decision making, but also better differentiate various strategic decision processes.

We divide the article into three sections. First, we discuss five modes of strategic decision processes. We next identify four major types of cognitive bias. In the third section, we examine these cognitive biases in terms of their roles in the five modes of strategic decision processes. We also develop propositions for empirical testing (and discuss the practical implications) of the more significant relationships between particular types of cognitive bias and specific kinds of strategic decision processes.

STRATEGIC DECISION PROCESSES

Strategic decision making is the process by which top management makes its most fundamental decisions. Strategic decisions are "important, in terms of the action taken, the resources committed, or the precedents set" (Mintzberg, Raisinghani, & Theoret., 1976, p. 246). Research on strategic decision processes has been fairly extensive, and the literature reveals a large number of decision modes (Cohen, March, & Olsen, 1972; Cyert & March, 1963; Das, 1986; Mintzberg et al., 1976; Quinn, 1980; Schwenk, 1995;

Weick, 1979). Each of them denotes a different perspective for the decision process and highlights particular aspects of the process. Considerable empirical evidence has been found to support a number of these modes (see Eisenhardt & Zbaracki, 1992; Hart & Banbury, 1994; Schwenk, 1995). Since the coexistence of many seemingly contradictory decision modes generates much confusion, researchers have often felt the need to classify various modes (Cowan, 1986; Cyert & Williams, 1993; Eisenhardt & Zbaracki, 1992; Hart, 1992; Hickson, 1987; Hitt & Tyler, 1991; Lyles & Thomas, 1988; Shrivastava & Grant, 1985).

Eisenhardt and Zbaracki (1992) propose three dominant paradigms of strategic decision processes: rationality and bounded rationality, politics and power, and garbage can. The rational and boundedly rational paradigm is concerned with the degree to which decision makers have purposes, and describes strategic decision making as a rather purposive, systematic, and comprehensive process (Allison, 1971). In this process, decision makers are supposed to start with known objectives, then collect information and develop alternatives, and finally identify the optimal course of action (Simon, 1955). The politics and power mode posits that the emergence, competition, and resolution of conflicting interests are the essence of strategic decision processes (Baldridge, 1971; March, 1962; Pfeffer & Salancik, 1974). As decision makers harbor different and often conflicting goals in organizations, decision making often becomes a political operation whose ultimate result reflects the preference of the most powerful coalition. Finally, the garbage can mode (Cohen et al., 1972) portrays decision making processes as organized anarchies, in which a decision is largely dependent on chance and timing. In this kind of process, decision makers do not know their objectives *ex ante*, but merely look around for decisions to make.

Similarly, Hickson (1987) identifies three basic modes of decision making: dual rationality, incrementalism, and garbage can. The dual rationality mode posits that "decision making is a process of handling both problems and politics" (Hickson, 1987, p. 185), so that it could be viewed as an integration of the rational mode and the political mode. Incremental decision making is a step-by-step process, and the strategy is always amenable to adjustment. A series of incremental actions is adopted to ensure that "large, complex strategic problems are factored into smaller, less complex, and hence more manageable increments for implementation" (Joyce, 1986, p. 44). There is some distinction to be made between logical incrementalism (Quinn, 1980) and disjointed incrementalism (Lindblom, 1959), the difference being in whether there is consistency among the increments toward a broad (rather than local) objective (Joyce, 1986). The garbage can mode is the same one as in Eisenhardt and Zbaracki's (1992) study.

Finally, Lyles and Thomas (1988) list five primary modes of strategic decision making: rational, avoidance, adaptive, political, and decisive. Four of these are similar to the modes identified by Hickson (1987) and Eisenhardt and Zbaracki (1992). For example, the adaptive mode is largely based on logical incrementalism, and the garbage can mode is the key constituent of the decisive mode. On the other hand, the avoidance mode (Cyert & March, 1963)—which delineates strategic decision making as a systematic process aimed at maintaining the status quo—appears to be an important supplement. In essence, the avoidance mode is about avoiding the identification of new problems so that strategic changes can be rendered unnecessary (Janis & Mann, 1977).

An examination of the above typologies indicates a considerable degree of consensus regarding what the major modes of strategic decision making are. Hence, rather than attempting to propose yet another typology, we essentially adopt Lyles and Thomas' (1988) typology and examine the following five primary modes of strategic decision making: (a) rational mode (Allison, 1971; March & Simon, 1958); (b) avoidance mode (Cyert & March 1963; Janis & Mann, 1977); (c) logical incrementalist mode (Quinn, 1980); (d) political mode (Baldridge, 1971; March, 1962; Pfeffer & Salancik, 1974); and (e) garbage can mode (Cohen et al., 1972). The slight modification in naming the decision modes is to conform to the way the major decision modes are generally known in the literature.

We recognize, of course, that there are various other frameworks of strategic decision making in the literature (e.g., Hart & Banbury, 1994; Nutt, 1984). For instance, Shrivastava and Grant (1985) suggest four prototypical patterns of strategic decision making: autocracy, bureaucracy, adaptive, and political. However, we prefer Lyles and Thomas' list because it covers the most important modes of strategic decision making. Another reason is that this list of five modes seems to capture an underlying continuum: from the most systematic and structured decision processes at one end to the most ill-structured and anarchical decision processes at the other. We should note, though, that none of these five modes have explicitly incorporated cognitive biases into the strategic decision processes. Thus, the bias related aspects in these decision processes remain largely unexplored. In the next section we cover the major types of cognitive biases.

COGNITIVE BIASES

Decision makers are known to rely on a few judgmental rules, or heuristics, to simplify complex decision situations. Although these "rules of thumb" are often necessary and useful, they also introduce cognitive biases that can lead to severe and systematic errors in decision making (Kahneman, Slovic, & Tversky, 1982). Thus, cognitive biases can be viewed as a negative consequence of adopting heuristics. Biases entice decision makers away from making optimal decisions in terms of utility maximization.

Scholars in cognitive psychology identify a number of heuristics and biases that individuals are subject to in making judgments under uncertainty (Bazerman, 1994; Hogarth, 1980; Slovic, Fischhoff, & Lichtenstein, 1977; Taylor, 1975; Tversky & Kahneman, 1973, 1974; Walsh, 1995). Decision makers also differ in terms of their individual temporal orientations, so that they tend to be more cognizant of either the near future or the distant future (Das, 1987, 1991). Based on extensive lab experiments, Tversky and Kahneman (1974) report that biases may result from three major heuristics: representativeness, availability, and adjustment and anchoring. Whereas representativeness refers to the tendency to "imagine that what we see or will see is *typical* of what can occur," availability refers to the condition where "[w]hen imagining what could happen, we remember similar past situations" (Hogarth, 1980, p. 217). Decision makers also tend to make judgments based on an initial assessment as anchor, but fail to make sufficient adjustments later on. According to Tversky and Kahneman (1974), each heuristic may lead to several cognitive biases. For example, availability gives rise to the bias of retrievability, the bias of imaginability, and so on. In addition, researchers have also called attention to some other cognitive biases, such as illusion of control (Langer, 1975), hindsight (Fischhoff, 1975), and overconfidence (Fischhoff, Slovic, & Lichtenstein, 1977). Kahneman & Lovallo (1993) use the term "inside view" to describe decision makers' proneness to treat their problems as unique so that they can ignore historical statistics. Hogarth (1980) summarizes the various research findings and identified 29 separate biases that are likely to occur in decision making, while Bazerman (1994) discusses 13 types of cognitive biases found in managerial decision making.

Based on these findings, strategy scholars highlight the issue of cognitive simplification and bias in strategic decision making. Since strategic decisions are characterized by ambiguities, uncertainty and a lack of structure, there seems to be no reason to expect strategists being exempt from various cognitive biases (Schwenk, 1984). Support for this position is also derived from field studies that suggest the prevalence of these biases (Barnes, 1984). Recent research challenging the dominant strategy paradigms also highlights the importance of cognitive biases (Levy, 1994; von Krogh & Roos, 1996). For example, Levy (1994) applies chaos theory to strategy and suggests that long-term planning is essentially impossible, since industries, as chaotic systems, are extremely sensitive to initial conditions. It would thus seem that entertaining only a few possible scenarios is both practical and justified. Other researchers extend the concept of autopoiesis to strategic management. In autopoiesis, knowledge is not merely representations of the world, but rather is developed and is "highly dynamic as managers make new observations, talk, use their imaginations to envision possible futures and courses of action" (von Krogh, Roos, & Slocum, 1994, p. 58). Thus, managers' own experiences and dispositions help create knowledge that is potentially biased. Strategy scholars identify several biases they believe most likely to occur in strategic decision processes. Schwenk (1984, 1985), for example, identifies 11 cognitive biases, including prior hypothesis bias, single outcome calculation, illusion of control, and so on. He then classified and mapped these biases onto the three specific decision stages (i.e., goal formulation, alternative generation, and alternative selection), according to their respective relevancy. Barnes (1984) also discusses five judgmental biases common to both managers and strategic planners, which he termed availability, hindsight, misunderstanding the sampling process, judgments of correlation and causality, and representativeness.

In recent years, a considerable number of empirical studies have been carried out (Bateman & Zeithaml, 1989; Bukszar & Connolly, 1988; Golden, 1992; Lant, Milliken, & Batra, 1992), providing further support to the prominence of cognitive biases in strategic decision making. According to Schwenk (1995), there is considerable research potential in this area. Following this cue, we believe that one important aspect that needs attention is the interactions between cognitive bias and strategic decision processes. Schwenk's studies (1984, 1985) provide insights about biases present in various stages of a general process of strategic decision making. However, given that not all strategic decision processes are the same, we need to explore in some detail the presence of various biases in different situations.

In order to do so, the first step seems to be the identification of a few key biases. March and Shapira (1987) describe three major heuristics (or biases in our terminology) that managers use in making strategic decisions. First, managers are insensitive to estimates of the outcome probabilities. Secondly, they tend to focus on several performance targets and a relatively small number of alternatives. And thirdly, decision makers think that decision outcomes are subject to their control. As this list of biases is more succinct than other elaborate lists (e.g., Bazerman, 1994; Hogarth, 1980; Schwenk, 1985), we adopt it here with some modifications. We present the following four basic forms of cognitive bias: (1) prior hypotheses and focusing on limited targets; (2) exposure to limited alternatives; (3) insensitivity to outcome probabilities; and (4) illusion of manageability. Essentially, we have divided the second bias in March and Shapira (1987), that is, focusing on several performance targets and a small number of alternatives, into two biases (#1 and #2 in our list). The reason is that targets (ends) and alternatives (means) represent two very different aspects in the decision process, and thus should be examined separately. Furthermore, the sequence of the biases has been reordered for increased clarity. Fredrickson (1984) notes that a strategic decision process consists of four sequential steps: situation diagnosis, alternative generation, alternative evaluation, and decision integration. Thus, the four biases are now ordered keeping in mind a one-to-one correspondence with the four sequential steps (e.g., "a" is related more to situation diagnosis, and so on). Although in spirit Fredrickson's sequence may be compatible only with a rational mode, we feel that this correspondence makes the list of biases easily comprehensible. Of course, we do not imply that other biases do not exist; rather, our intention here is to concentrate on those key biases which seem to be generally present in strategic decision processes. We now discuss these four cognitive biases.

Prior Hypotheses and Focusing on Limited Targets

Research shows that decision makers are likely to bring their previously formed beliefs or hypotheses into decision making situations. For example, they may have prior perceptions about the relationships of salient variables, so that they may overlook information and evidence that may prove the opposite (Schwenk, 1984). At the same time, managers have been found to focus on selected targets, rather than on broad objectives (March & Shapira, 1987). Their attention focuses on those key objectives that appeal to their interests, and therefore they tend to ignore information about other worthwhile objectives. Hoskisson, Hitt, and Hill (1991) observe that the use of budgetary controls leads managers to focus on selected critical performance targets. In sum, bringing prior hypotheses to decision making and attention to selected targets together result in a biased perception of the environment and the problem at hand.

Exposure to Limited Alternatives

Strategic decision makers also expose themselves to only a limited number of alternatives that can achieve a goal (March & Shapira, 1987). Information is usually incomplete in decision making situations, so that decision makers tend to focus on a relatively small number of options (March & Simon, 1958; Simon, 1955). Decision makers are found to adopt sequential attention to alternatives (Anderson, 1983) and to use intuition to supplement rational analysis (Fredrickson, 1986). As a result, "rather than attempting to specify all relevant values and goals and generate a number of alternative courses of action as normative theory would suggest," decision makers are exposed to limited options (Schwenk, 1984, p. 119).

Insensitivity to Outcome Probabilities

Research has shown that decision makers do not trust, do not understand, and usually do not use estimates of outcome probabilities (Kunreuther,

1976; Slovic, 1967). Managers tend to be influenced more by the value of possible outcomes than by the magnitude of the probabilities (Shapira, 1995). Managers are more likely to use a few key values to describe a situation, rather than to compute or use standard statistics based on probabilities (March & Shapira, 1987). Another reason decision makers do not use estimates of probability is that they see problems as unique (Kahneman & Lovallo, 1993). Thus, probability estimates and statistics from comparable events in the past become irrelevant. In addition, decision makers are also characterized by their insensitivity to the validity of estimates (Tversky & Kahneman, 1974).

Illusion of Manageability

Developing an illusion of manageability is yet another type of cognitive bias, which manifests itself in two ways. First, decision makers may inappropriately perceive a success probability higher than the objective probability would warrant (Langer, 1975; Langer & Roth, 1975; Lefcourt, 1973), and then have an illusion of control. In this case, although they are concerned with outcome probabilities, they tend to form overly optimistic estimates. They do not accept the fact that a fair amount of risk is inherent in any decision situation. In a contrasting way, managers tend to overestimate the extent to which an outcome is under their control, believing that risk can be reduced by using their professional skills (Shapira, 1995).

Second, managers have the illusion that consequences of decisions are manageable (Vlek & Stallen, 1980). They mistakenly assume that should problems arise they would be able to fix them. Decision makers tend to believe that outcomes can be contained, corrected, or reversed, given some extra efforts. Shapira (1995) found that managers believe in "postdecisional control," which allows them "to influence whatever goes on *after* the moment of choice" (p. 80). The illusion of manageability of bad outcomes eases managers' anxiety over such outcomes.

COGNITIVE BIASES IN STRATEGIC DECISION PROCESSES

So far, we have discussed four key types of cognitive bias and have identified five basic modes of strategic decision making. We will now discuss the more salient relationships among these biases and decision processes. As mentioned earlier, the literature has generally deemed cognitive biases as prevailing across situations (Zajac & Bazerman, 1991). This may lead one to believe that these biases are equally manifested under all conditions. To this point, few studies have explicitly questioned the plausibility of such an assumption. Schwenk (1984, 1985) only explored the contingent relationship between biases and stages of decision making through his classification of different biases into three decision stages. Lyles and Thomas (1988) list different biases in five strategic decision modes, but fall short of making the point that the presence of a specific bias is contingent upon the particular decision process. We assert that, because strategic decision processes can be significantly different, there is a need to examine the contingencies between the biases and various decision processes. It would thus seem that different modes of strategic decision making will attract different combinations of the basic types of cognitive bias (see Table 1.1). In some decision modes more types of cognitive bias may be present, while in others fewer types will be evident. We now discuss each of the five modes of strategic decision making in terms of the four types of cognitive bias, and develop testable propositions for the more significant of these relationships.

Rational Mode

The rational mode is the benchmark, against which all the others are considered because it is based on the assumption that human behavior is rational or boundedly rational (Eisenhardt & Zbaracki, 1992; March & Simon, 1958). In this mode, the decision makers are assumed to enter decision situations with known objectives, and that in the process managers diligently analyze both the external environment and internal operations. Therefore, decision making is a comprehensive, normative process in which top managers gather information, develop alternatives, and then objectively select the optimal alternative (Anderson, 1983; Nutt, 1984). Following this mode, organizations employ formal, comprehensive analyses to deal with uncertainties in decision making. These formal decision making systems quantify and specify goals and alternatives, and then choose the one with best values.

Some theorists, however, suggest that the process can be only boundedly rational, due to decision makers' limited cognitive capabilities. In this view, although decision makers attempt to enhance the rationality of their decisions by engaging in exhaustive processes, their cognitive limitations preclude the possibility of a truly comprehensive process. Researchers note that executives can perceive only a selected portion of the environment (e.g., Beyer, Chattopadhyay, George, Glick, ogilvie, & Pugliese, 1997). Significant evidence also indicates that the degree to which executives accurately perceive their external environment may vary greatly (Bourgeois, 1985; Sutcliffe, 1994; Thomas, Clark, & Gioia, 1993; Thomas & McDaniel, 1990). Despite the difference between the truly rational and the boundedly rational, the consensus seems to be that decision making consists of a series of sequential, analytical processes (Dean & Sharfman, 1993; Huff & Reger, 1987). In fact, Simon (1978) proposes the term "procedural rationality"—that is, the extent to which a decision process reflects decision makers' intention and efforts to make the best decision possible. Thus, Fredrickson and his associates (Fredrickson, 1984, 1986; Fredrickson & Mitchell, 1984) argue that the most basic characteristic of rational decision making is its "comprehensiveness" (i.e., the degree of exhaustiveness and inclusiveness in making and integrating strategic decisions).

When strategic decision making processes follow the rational mode, cognitive biases are still inevitable. In terms of the four basic types of bias, two are highly likely in the rational mode. First, according to the rational mode, decision makers enter decision situations with known objectives (Allison, 1971; Simon, 1955). These a priori hypotheses, objectives, and goal consensus lead decision makers to focus on particular parts of the environment and problems (Bourgeois & Eisenhardt, 1988). Therefore, Cell 1 (in Table 1.1) exemplifies a likely situation. The emphasis in rational decision making is not on extensive search for objectives; rather, it highlights the value of gathering information about alternatives and outcomes. Referring to the Machine Bureaucracy, Mintzberg (1983) asserts that much of the information generated by its management information system is of the wrong kind (p. 184). In the same vein, Baird and Thomas (1985) posit that the major drawbacks of formal analyses, such as risk analysis, decision analysis, and cost-benefit analysis, are "their lack of openness and explicit recognition of the different value systems implicit in strategic decisions" (p. 240). Therefore, rational decision making may create an "error of the third kind" (Raiffa, 1968)—that is, solving the wrong problem. Hence:

TABLE 1.1 Cognitive Biases and Strategic Decision Process Modes

Cognitive Biases	Strategic Decision Process Modes: Rational	Avoidance	Logical incrementalist	Political	Garbage can
Prior hypotheses and focusing on limited targets	1 P1	5 P3	9	13 P7	17
Exposure to limited alternatives	2	6 P4	10	14	18 P8
Insensitivity to outcome probabilities	3	7 P5	11	15	19 P9
Illusion of manageability	4 P2	8	12 P6	16	20

> **Proposition 1:** *The more rational and systematic the strategic decision process, the more likely the managers will bring prior hypotheses to decisions.*

On the other hand, exposure to limited alternatives (Cell 2) is not likely to occur in the rational mode. In fact, the essence of the rational approach is to systematically develop and consider strategic alternatives. Comprehensiveness is what decision makers in the rational mode endeavor to achieve (Fredrickson, 1984). Thus, even though a rational process may not exhaust all possible strategic options, decision makers should have access to reasonably broad alternatives.

Similarly, in the rational mode being insensitive to outcome probabilities (Cell 3) is not a likely occurrence. Systematic evaluation of alternatives is important in the rational mode. The value of the possible consequences of each alternative is gauged, based on the known objectives. As a result, accurate estimates of outcome probabilities become the prerequisite for the evaluation process, and managers are supposed to pay close attention to these estimates.

In Cell 4, the illusion of manageability could be present in rational decision making. After gathering information, developing and evaluating alternatives, decision makers tend to be confident that they have selected the optimal alternative. Oftentimes, merely by going through this process effectively generates confidence about results instead of actually coming up with suitable options. In other words, the process itself is believed to provide justification and rationality. Lyles and Thomas (1988) suggest that wishful thinking and rationalization are possible biases in the rational mode. Furthermore, decision makers may also believe that they have managed the risks by employing their skills, so that nothing really bad could happen. In essence, decision makers in the rational mode tend to perceive the risk inherent in an action somewhat lower than its actual level (March & Shapira, 1987). Thus:

> **Proposition 2:** *The more rational and systematic the strategic decision process, the more likely the managers will have an illusion of manageability.*

Avoidance Mode

The avoidance mode is concerned with the fact that strategic decision making processes often lead to a resistance to strategic change (Janis & Mann, 1977, Mintzberg, Brunet, & Waters, 1986). The avoidance mode is based on Cyert and March's (1963) observation that organizations tend to avoid uncertainty. Therefore, maintaining the status quo is a highly desirable objective. Studies on upper echelons (e.g., Hambrick, Geletkanycz,

& Fredrickson, 1993) confirm that commitment to the status quo is a significant executive orientation, and it is common for managers to be overly committed to the status quo. Furthermore, according to Miles and Snow's (1978) strategic typology—that is, Reactors, Defenders, Analyzers, and Prospectors—one type of firm can be classified as Reactors because they usually fail to adapt to environmental changes. These firms are likely to follow an avoidance mode in their decision processes.

Prospect theory of risk taking (Kahneman & Tversky, 1979) provides an alternative rationale for the avoidance mode. According to prospect theory, decision makers are loss averse, weighing losses and disadvantages more than gains and advantages. Therefore, they favor "inaction over action and the status quo over any alternatives" (Kahneman & Lovallo, 1993, p. 18). Hickson (1987) confirms that executives take risk only when they have to. One way to avoid substantive decision making is to suppress issues that then do not become matters for decision. Mintzberg (1978) observes that organizations prove highly resistant to strategic change when the market environment undergoes major change. Organizations may choose to ignore symptoms of a problem, hoping the problem will eventually go away. On the other hand, Butler, Astley, Hickson, Mallory, and Wilson (1979/80) suggest that avoidance of strategic change occurs when there is no pressure for new activities or no competition for resources. Though there is disagreement regarding the context of strategic avoidance, it seems clear that strategic decision making sometimes becomes a process to justify the necessity of maintaining the status quo. As Mintzberg et al. (1986) argues, formal strategic planning could be a mechanism that curbs strategic change.

Decision makers who value the status quo highly, and therefore try to avoid strategic change, actually harbor considerable biases in their decision making. In this mode, managers tend to avoid the identification of new problems (Janis & Mann, 1977), but problems not being recognized will not go away. Existing problems may well accumulate as time passes, until a crisis happens. The risk of adopting an avoidance approach seems to be serious, as three out of the four types of cognitive bias can be present.

In Cell 5, it is evident that (in the avoidance mode) the prior hypothesis is that maintaining the status quo is important. The sole objective of the decision process is to justify this position, even when change appears warranted. Such highly focused attention often leads to irrational decisions, owing to the well-known phenomenon of escalating commitment (Staw, 1981). Clearly, here the prior hypotheses are that quitting is undesirable and that persistence will ultimately pay off. Thus:

> **Proposition 3:** *The more emphasis on maintaining the status quo in a strategic decision making process, the more likely the managers will bring prior hypotheses to decisions.*

other alternatives. To move slightly toward one direction does not mean that one has to stick to it. In fact, while at any given time decision makers are able to examine only a few alternatives, over time they would go through a fairly exhaustive list of options (Hickson, 1987). The step-by-step approach gives an organization the flexibility to consider emerging alternatives. Because strategists do not make drastic decisions, they keep the company open to options. Also, since they keep getting information and keep conducting global analyses, they do not unduly miss an alternative.

Furthermore, decision makers must be very sensitive to the estimates of outcome probabilities (Cell 11), according to the incremental mode. Trusting the estimates, being sensitive to the estimates, and acting on the basis of the estimates are prerequisites for logical incrementalism. Quinn's (1980) insistence that incrementalism employs formal analysis of the situation reflects the attention paid to outcome probabilities.

Finally, the adoption of the logical incrementalist mode tends to encourage the development of an illusion of manageability (Cell 12). By emphasizing its "logic" and its "incrementalism," decision makers have the false impression that everything is under control. Managers may perceive that the inherent risks facing them could be controlled by moving slowly and carefully. Since they move only one small step at a time, they are likely to believe that even if some unexpected outcomes were to materialize, they would be able to manage or control the situation. This leads us to:

> **Proposition 6:** *The more logical incrementalist the strategic decision process, the more likely the managers will have an illusion of manageability.*

Political Mode

Different from the incremental mode, decision makers in the political mode are often unable to attain even a broad consensus on organizational objectives (Pettigrew, 1973). The political mode of decision making assumes that groups of organizational members with competing interests fight for a decision favorable to them. The outcome is therefore decided by those who can form the most powerful coalition. Each party perceives the problem in the light of its own domain of interests (Simon & Hayes, 1976). People tend to be politically biased, and full information is never available. Each group attempts to protect and maximize its own interests through political activities. As Eisenhardt and Zbaracki (1992) put it, "people are individually rational, but not collectively so" (p. 23). Inevitably, strategic decision making becomes a process of power struggle, and the most powerful people win the game. Scholars note (e.g., Amason, 1996) that in strategic decision processes there are both cognitive conflicts—that is, judgmental differences—and affective conflicts—that is, personal incompatibilities or disputes. Thus, the political decision mode would tend to create affective conflicts among different camps.

Decision makers in the political mode bring prior hypotheses to the decision situation and focus on limited targets (Cell 13). Groups of people can only perceive limited targets as related to their own interests, which are constant across decisions (Hickson, Butler, Cray, Mallory, & Wilson, 1986). Studies (e.g., Taylor, 1975) show that coalitions within an organization tend to use their past experience and histories to construct a problem perception. Many coalitions simply take the same position every time, never bothering to examine their hypothesized values. Therefore:

> **Proposition 7:** *The more political the strategic decision process, the more likely the managers will bring prior hypotheses to decisions.*

Regarding the biases arising from exposure to limited alternatives (Cell 14) and insensitivity to outcome probabilities (Cell 15) in a political decision process, the literature offers two competing views. On the one hand, it has been argued that most political processes are static, and that decision makers tend to be embedded in their positions and interests. Browne (1992) points out that decision makers in a political process not only consider a small number of alternatives, but also a limited number of consequences. Following this view, decision makers in a political process are defined by, restrained, and attached to their predetermined interests and positions. The level of flexibility would be significantly limited in a political process as compared with that in a non-political process. Therefore, it seems logical to assume that coalitions would not comprehensively develop all possible alternatives. Even though different coalitions may each provide a different alternative, the total range of alternatives is unlikely to be sufficiently broad.

On the other hand, however, it has also been argued that the political process can be fluid and that decision makers may easily shift their positions if necessary (March, 1962; Pfeffer, 1981). According to this view, decision makers would be flexible regarding their stance (e.g., being willing to trade between short term and long term interests). As Eisenhardt and Zbaracki observe, the traditional view assumes politics as fluid, and "they [decision makers] vary their political tactics like teenagers change radio stations" (1992, p. 26). The political process is characterized by a determination to realize one's best interests, no matter what route one may have to take. Hence, besides the target itself, there is hardly anything static in a political process. Actors in a political process are required to be skillful in making compromises, horse-trading, shifting positions, and repackaging proposals.

Taking this more dynamic view of political processes, it seems that exposure to a few selected alternatives would not be a likely occurrence (Cell 14). Nemeth's (1986) work on the influence of minority opinions lends considerable support for this position. According to this line of research (Nemeth & Kwan, 1987; Peterson & Nemeth, 1996), exposure to minority viewpoints stimulates decision makers to consider a problem from multiple perspectives. That is, a minority viewpoint unfreezes people's convergent thought and opens up new approaches to the issues. The result is that decision makers go beyond both the majority view and the minority view. Applying this finding to the political mode of strategic decision making, it seems that opposing views offered by various groups activate decision makers to think creatively and develop additional solutions to an issue. Thus, as compared to many other modes of operating, under circumstances in which the political mode prevails, decision makers are less likely to fall prey to cognitive biases arising from an exposure to limited alternatives.

Using a similar logic, it seems that in the political mode, decision makers would be quite sensitive to outcome probabilities (Cell 15). Of course, one may argue that decision makers in a political process are supposed to take a stand at the very beginning of the decision process and fiercely resist others. Since everyone is supposed to have a definite view, probability estimates just cannot rock anyone's beliefs. Again, this view may be exaggerating the robustness of the political process (March, 1962). In fact, managers engaged in political behavior need to be highly attuned to outcome probabilities, or they would become more vulnerable. The importance of outcome probabilities in a political process is underlined by the heavy reliance on information about evolving trends and changes in the environment. In organizational politics, decision makers also frequently shift their positions based on their best estimate of outcome probabilities. Since the goal is to bring about the outcome that best serves one's interest, decision makers in a political process simply cannot afford to ignore outcome probabilities.

Finally, developing an illusion of manageability (Cell 16) is not to be expected in this mode. Political processes are characterized by a high level of uncertainty. Pfeffer (1981) and Pettigrew (1973) emphasize the tactical aspects of politics. For example, information may be manipulated to favor a particular alternative. Thus, when a strategic decision is made through a political process, oftentimes it is hard to foresee which party's intentions would prevail. In addition, defeated coalitions are often able to come back later and reverse a situation. Thus, in a political process, decision makers understand that a winning course of action may not be the result of being the best on grounds of merit; rather, it could be only a temporary victory in a continuing series of battles. If that is the case, an illusion of manageability is unlikely to be fostered.

Garbage Can Mode

The most uncertain and fluid mode of strategic decision making is the garbage can mode (Cohen et al., 1972; Kreiner, 1976; Padgett, 1980). The garbage can mode of strategic decision making has no inherent consistencies. As organizations are viewed as "organized anarchies," there is no particular rationale for making a strategic choice. The decision process consists of four components: (1) choice opportunities; (2) solutions; (3) participants; and (4) problems. Decision making is conceived in terms of problems looking for a choice opportunity, solutions looking for problems to address, and decision makers looking for a job (Cohen et al., 1972). What accounts for the outcome is only timing and chance. However, although managers have little control over the process, some of their cognitive biases may still be prevalent in that process.

The first bias (i.e., prior hypotheses and limited targets) is not prominent in this mode (Cell 17). Managers are not committed to any objective; they do not hold any prior hypothesis regarding the situation. They "wander in and out of the decision" (Eisenhardt & Zbaracki, 1992, p. 27), not knowing what they want and often changing their minds. The reason they enter the decision making process is just to look for jobs to do (Cohen et al., 1972).

On the other hand, decision makers in the garbage can mode do limit themselves to selected alternatives only (Cell 18). First, in the garbage can mode, solutions exist only from trial-and-error learning, rather than being actively developed. In this mode, existing solutions look for appropriate problems that can be addressed. Decision makers have particular expertise and predilections, and they are constantly looking to act upon them. As solutions need to be already in existence, the stream of solutions for any particular problem is unlikely to be rich. Second, since the key to decision making is a timing match among problems, choice opportunities and solutions, even existing solutions may not all have been approached before a decision is made. That is, decisions are made when decision makers first see an existing solution matching a problem. Thus, other alternatives may not be developed or considered. Therefore:

> **Proposition 8:** *The more disorderly and anarchical the strategic decision process, the more likely the managers will be exposed to limited alternatives.*

Moreover, decision makers would be insensitive to outcome probabilities (Cell 19) in this mode. Actually, what they are looking for is just something to decide, no matter what kind of consequences the option may carry. Therefore, estimates of probabilities do not catch decision makers' attention at all. Indeed, probability estimates are not one of the components in the garbage can mode. If only chance matters, why bother about outcome probabilities? Consequently:

> **Proposition 9:** *The more disorderly and anarchical the strategic decision process, the more likely the managers will be insensitive to outcome probabilities.*

Lastly, in the garbage can mode, managers usually do not develop an illusion of manageability (Cell 20). The outcome of such decision making processes is random and not subject to any effective control, and managers do not even know what their desirable outcome is (Cohen et al., 1972). How could they in such circumstances have confidence in the results? They would not bother to think about any outcome probability or about managing possible consequences. In this mode, the role of managers seems to be diminished to the minimum.

DISCUSSION AND CONCLUSION

It is evident from our discussion in the previous section that none of the five modes of strategic decision making explicitly consider the role of cognitive biases. Bias is treated as something inherent but unremarkable in the process and effectively assumed away, so that cognitive bias is not addressed at all. As a result, we do not at present have an adequate understanding about what cognitive biases mean to strategic decision processes.

On an overall basis, our analysis revealed that the four types of cognitive bias, taken together, have a substantive role in all the five modes of strategic decision making (see Table 1.1). As it turns out, each cognitive bias has some role in differing subsets of the five decision processes. This would indicate that the four types of cognitive bias identified in this article have sufficient relevance individually and in combination for all the five decision processes.

Furthermore, while three cognitive biases are present in the avoidance mode, only two are present in the rational and garbage can modes, and only one each in the logical incrementalist and political modes. If we look at the differences of cognitive biases among the various strategic decision making modes, it is not hard to see that the rational mode and the garbage can mode complement each other. The reason for the pairing is that the garbage can mode and the rational mode represent two poles in terms of the degree of rationality and control (Das, 1989, 1993). Decision makers in the rational mode emphasize a strict control over the process, so that they take risks by having predetermined objectives and by being overly confident. In contrast, decision makers in the garbage can mode give up control totally and let everything be fluid in the process. As a result, it suffers from inadequate alternatives and insensitivity to outcome probabilities. By the same token, the match between the avoidance mode and the logical incrementalist mode reveals their inherent similarity as well as contrast. None of them are about dramatic strategic change. However, what makes them different is that the incremental process moves slowly, while the avoidance process leads to no change at all. Since these two modes exhibit seemingly similar characteristics, although driven by somewhat different motivations, it is evident that they mutually share those four basic types of cognitive bias.

Examining the framework (Table 1.1) horizontally, two types of cognitive bias (namely, exposure to limited alternatives and insensitivity to outcome probabilities) seem to follow a similar pattern. When a decision process is characterized by exposure to limited alternatives, managers can also be expected to be insensitive to outcome probabilities. Contrariwise, if one type is absent, the other type tends to be absent too. The explanation is that the presence of both types of cognitive bias is determined by the rationality consideration. If the process involves a rational and logical development of strategic choices, as the rational and the incremental modes do, these two types of cognitive bias would be absent. On the other hand, if factors other than rationality consideration, such as power, undergird the process, then managers would be more likely to ignore some options and probabilities. Hence, these two types of cognitive bias would tend to appear in tandem. The other two biases are also present in various decision processes. For example, the illusion of manageability is expected to occur in both the rational mode and the logical incremental mode. This seeming contradiction is due to the fact that both modes help decision makers believe that the probability of success is high, and that potential problems can be fixed. Apparently, although the rational mode and the logical incremental mode are different in many respects (e.g., regarding prior hypotheses), they are similar in terms of generating the illusion of manageability.

We examined the contingent relationships between cognitive biases and strategic decision processes. By proposing an integrative framework, we sought to make two theoretical contributions. First, we attempted to show that the prevalence of cognitive biases is contingent upon the nature of the particular decision process. Extant research explores only various types of cognitive bias, without specifying the conditions under which each type may be evoked in practice. We proposed that the presence and nature of cognitive bias is contingent upon the character of the specific strategic decision making process. Not all of the four basic types of cognitive bias are present in every specific decision process. Certain modes of decision process seem to elicit particular combinations of cognitive bias. However, we need to recognize that other factors are also involved in determining the presence of specific types of cognitive bias. In particular, it would be useful to study the roles of various individual, organizational, environmental, and cultural variables as they relate to the presence of managerial cognitive biases in strategic decision processes.

The second contribution here is that we provide an additional perspective for understanding various kinds of strategic decision processes. Theorists have often stressed the need to better differentiate various strategic decision processes found in the literature. In our view, the ambiguities in our understanding stem partially from the failure to incorporate cognitive biases into these decision modes. The critically relevant cognitive biases have not been systematically included or examined in previous writings on most modes of strategic decision making. We demonstrate in our framework that cognitive biases provide a meaningful perspective for evaluating different kinds of strategic decision processes.

We show that managers involved in different decision processes exhibit different combinations of four basic types of cognitive bias. For example, managers in the avoidance mode are likely to engage in most of the basic types of cognitive bias. In contrast, managers subscribing to the logical incrementalist mode and political mode tend to adopt only one type of cognitive bias. By taking cognitive biases into account, various strategic decision processes can now be better differentiated and understood. The list of propositions we developed here has as its eventual purpose the empirical testing of the contingent relationships between the four types of cognitive bias and the five modes of strategic decision processes.

Finally, the integrative framework we proposed here also has implications for managerial practice. Heuristics and biases are often valuable and indispensable for effective decision making. This may be particularly relevant for strategic decisions, which are highly uncertain and need to be made in a timely fashion. Clearly, in order to avoid systematic errors arising from biases, managers need to be keenly aware of the assumptions, heuristics and biases employed in their decision making. Thus, they ought to examine their own cognitive biases, which may be more easily identified and appreciated than one might think possible. For example, managers could check if they have a tendency to reject alternatives without carefully weighing them. They could also review whether they make decisions based on rigorous estimates of probability. Such procedures would enable managers to reveal for themselves any cognitive biases inherent in their decision making, and thereby be in a position to make appropriate adjustments.

ACKNOWLEDGMENT

This chapter, save some minor changes, was earlier published as Das, T. K., & Teng, B. (1999). Cognitive biases and strategic decision processes: An integrative perspective. *Journal of Management Studies, 36*, 757–778.

REFERENCES

Allison, G. T. (1971). *Essence of decision: Explaining the Cuban missile crisis.* Boston, MA: Little, Brown.

Amason, A. C. (1996). Distinguishing the effects of functional and dysfunctional conflict on strategic decision making: Resolving a paradox for top management teams. *Academy of Management Journal, 39,* 123–148.

Anderson, P. A. (1983). Decision making by objection and the Cuban missile crisis. *Administrative Science Quarterly, 28,* 201–222.

Baird, I. S., & Thomas, H. (1985). Toward a contingency model of strategic risk taking. *Academy of Management Review, 10,* 230–243.

Baldridge, J. V. (1971). *Power and conflict in the university.* New York, NY: Wiley.

Barnes, J. H., Jr. (1984). Cognitive biases and their impact on strategic planning. *Strategic Management Journal, 5,* 129–137.

Bateman, T. S., & Zeithaml, C. P. (1989). The psychological context of strategic decisions: a model and convergent experimental findings. *Strategic Management Journal, 10,* 59–74.

Bazerman, M. H. (1994). *Judgment in managerial decision making* (3rd ed.). New York, NY: Wiley.

Beyer, J. M., Chattopadhyay, P., George, E., Glick, W. H., ogilvie, dt, & Pugliese, D. (1997). The selective perception of managers revisited. *Academy of Management Journal, 40,* 716–737.

Bourgeois, L. J. (1985). Strategic goals, perceived uncertainty, and economic performance in volatile environments. *Academy of Management Journal, 28,* 548–573.

Bourgeois, L. J., & Eisenhardt, K. M. (1988). Strategic decision processes in high velocity environments: four cases in the microcomputer industry. *Management Science, 34,* 816–835.

Browne, M. (1992). *Organizational decision making and information.* Norwood, NJ: Ablex.

Bukszar, E., & Connolly, T. (1988). Hindsight bias and strategic choice: Some problems in learning from experience. *Academy of Management Journal, 31,* 628–641.

Butler, R. J., Astley, W. G., Hickson, D. J., Mallory, G. R., & Wilson, D. C. (1979/80). Strategic decision making: Concepts of content and process. *International Studies of Management and Organization, 9,* 4, 5–36.

Cohen, M. D., March, J. G., & Olsen, J. P. (1972). A garbage can model of organizational choice. *Administrative Science Quarterly, 17,* 1–25.

Cowan, D. A. (1986). Developing a process model of problem recognition. *Academy of Management Review, 11,* 763–776.

Cyert, R. M., & March, J. G. (1963). *A behavioral theory of the firm.* Englewood Cliffs, NJ: Prentice-Hall.

Cyert, R. M., & Williams, J. R. (1993). Organizations, decision making and strategy: Overview and comment. *Strategic Management Journal, 14* (Special Winter Issue), 5–10.

Das, T. K. (1986). *The subjective side of strategy making: Future orientations and perceptions of executives.* New York, NY: Praeger.

Das, T. K. (1987). Strategic planning and individual temporal orientation. *Strategic Management Journal, 8,* 203–209.

Das, T. K. (1989). Organizational control: An evolutionary perspective. *Journal of Management Studies, 26,* 459–475.

Das, T. K. (1991). Time: The hidden dimension in strategic planning. *Long Range Planning, 24*(3), 49–57.

Das, T. K. (1993). A multiple paradigm approach to organizational control. *International Journal of Organizational Analysis, 1,* 385–403.

Das, T. K., & Teng, B. (1999). Cognitive biases and strategic decision processes: An integrative perspective. *Journal of Management Studies, 36,* 757–778.

Dean, J. W., Jr., & Sharfman, M. P. (1993). Procedural rationality in the strategic decision-making process. *Journal of Management Studies, 30,* 587–610.

Eisenhardt, K. M., & Zbaracki, M. J. (1992). Strategic decision making. *Strategic Management Journal, 13,* 17–37.

Festinger, L. (1954). A theory of social comparison. *Human Relations, 7,* 117–140.

Fischhoff, B. (1975). Hindsight & foresight: The effect of outcome knowledge on judgment under uncertainty. *Journal of Experimental Psychology: Human Perception and Performance, 1,* 288–299.

Fischhoff, B., Slovic, P., & Lichtenstein, S. (1977). Knowing with certainty: The appropriateness of extreme confidence. *Journal of Experimental Psychology: Human Perception and Performance, 3,* 552–564.

Fredrickson, J. W. (1984). The comprehensiveness of strategic decision processes: Extension, observations, future directions. *Academy of Management Journal, 27,* 445–466.

Fredrickson, J. W. (1986). An exploratory approach to measuring perceptions of strategic decision constructs. *Strategic Management Journal, 7,* 473–483.

Fredrickson, J. W., & Mitchell, T. R. (1984). Strategic decision processes: Comprehensiveness and performance in an industry with an unstable environment. *Academy of Management Journal, 27,* 399–423.

Golden, B. R. (1992). The past is past—or is it? The use of retrospective accounts as indicators of past strategy. *Academy of Management Journal, 35,* 848–860.

Hambrick, D. C., Geletkanycz, M. A., & Fredrickson, J. W. (1993). Top executive commitment to the status quo: Some tests of its determinants. *Strategic Management Journal, 14,* 401–418.

Hart, S. L. (1992). An integrative framework for strategy-making processes. *Academy of Management Review, 17,* 327–351.

Hart, S. L., & Banbury, C. (1994). How strategy-making processes can make a difference. *Strategic Management Journal, 15,* 251–269.

Hickson, D. J. (1987). Decision-making at the top of organizations. *Annual Review of Sociology, 13,* 165–192.

Hickson, D. J., Butler, R. J., Cray, D., Mallory, G. R., & Wilson, D. C. (1986). *Top decisions: Strategic decision-making in organizations.* San Francisco, CA: Jossey-Bass.

Hitt, M. A., & Tyler, B. B. (1991). Strategic decision models: integrating different perspectives. *Strategic Management Journal, 23,* 327–351.

Hogarth, R. M. (1980). *Judgment and choice: The psychology of decision.* Chichester, UK: Wiley.

Hoskisson, R. E., Hitt, M. A., & Hill, C. W. (1991). Managerial risk taking in diversified firms: An evolutionary perspective. *Organization Science, 2*, 296–314.

Hrebiniak, L. G., & Joyce, W. F. (1985). Organizational adaption: Strategic choice and environmental determinism. *Administrative Science Quarterly, 30*, 336–349.

Huff, A. S., & Reger, R. K. (1987). A review of strategic process research. *Journal of Management, 13*, 211–36.

Janis, I. L., & Mann, L. (1977). *Decision-making: A psychological analysis of conflict, choice and commitment.* New York, NY: Free Press.

Joyce, W. F. (1986). Towards a theory of incrementalism. *Advances in Strategic Management, 4*, 43–58.

Kahneman, D., & Lovallo, D. (1993). Timid choices and bold forecasts: A cognitive perspective on risk taking. *Management Science, 39*, 17–31.

Kahneman, D., Slovic, P., & Tversky, A. (Eds.). (1982). *Judgement under uncertainty: Heuristics and biases.* New York, NY: Cambridge University Press.

Kahneman, D., & Tversky, A. (1979). Prospect theory: An analysis of decision under risk. *Econometrica, 47*, 263–291.

Kreiner, K. (1976). Ideology and management in a garbage can situation. In J. G. March & J. P Olsen (Eds.), *Ambiguity and choice in organizations* (pp. 156–173). Bergen, Norway: Universitetsforlaget.

Kunreuther, H. (1976). Limited knowledge and insurance protection. *Public Policy, 24*, 227–261.

Langer, E. J. (1975). Illusion of control. *Journal of Personality and Social Psychology, 32*, 311–328.

Langer, E. J., & Roth, J. (1975). The effect of sequence of outcomes in a chance task on the illusion of control. *Journal of Personality and Social Psychology, 32*, 951–955.

Lant, T. K., Milliken, F. J., & Batra, B. (1992). The role of managerial learning and interpretation in strategic persistence and reorientation: an empirical exploration. *Strategic Management Journal, 13*, 585–608.

Lefcourt, H. M. (1973). The function of the illusions of control and freedom. *American Psychologist, 28*, 417–425.

Levy, D. (1994). Chaos theory and strategy: Theory, application, and managerial implications. *Strategic Management Journal, 15* (Summer Special Issue), 167–178.

Lindblom, C. E. (1959). The science of muddling through. *Public Administration Review, 19*, 79–88.

Lyles, M. A., & Thomas, H. (1988). Strategic problem formulation: Biases and assumptions embedded in alternative decision-making models. *Journal of Management Studies, 25*, 131–145.

March, J. G. (1962). The business firm as a political coalition. *Journal of Politics, 24*, 662–678.

March, J. G., & Shapira. Z. (1987). Managerial perspectives on risk and risk taking. *Management Science, 33*, 1404–18.

March, J. G., & Simon, H. A. (1958). *Organizations.* New York, NY: Wiley.

Miles, R. E., & Snow, C. C. (1978). *Organizational strategy, structure and process.* New York, NY: McGraw-Hill.

Mintzberg, H. (1978). Patterns in strategy formation. *Management Science, 24*, 934–948.

Mintzberg, H. (1983). *Structure in fives: Designing effective organizations.* Englewood Cliffs, NJ: Prentice-Hall.

Mintzberg, H., Brunet, J. P., & Waters, J. A. (1986). Does planning impede strategic thinking? Tracking the strategies for Air Canada from 1937–1976. *Advances in Strategic Management, 4,* 3–41.

Mintzberg, H., Raisinghani, D., & Theoret, A. (1976). The structure of unstructured decision processes. *Administrative Science Quarterly, 21,* 246–275.

Nemeth, C. J. (1986). Differential contributions of majority and minority influence. *Psychological Review, 93,* 23–32.

Nemeth, C. J., & Kwan, J. L. (1987). Minority influence, divergent thinking and detection of correct solutions. *Journal of Applied Social Psychology, 17,* 788–799.

Nutt, P. C. (1984). Types of organizational decision processes. *Administrative Science Quarterly, 29,* 414–450.

Padgett, J. F. (1980). Managing garbage can hierarchies. *Administrative Science Quarterly, 25,* 583–604.

Peterson, R. S., & Nemeth, C. J. (1996). Focus versus flexibility: Majority and minority influence can both improve performance. *Personality and Social Psychology Bulletin, 22,* 14–23.

Pettigrew, A. M. (1973). *Politics of organizational decision-making.* London, UK: Tavistock.

Pfeffer, J. (1981). *Power in organizations.* Marshfield, MA: Pitman.

Pfeffer, J., & Salancik, G. R. (1974). Organizational decision making as a political process: The case of a university budget. *Administrative Science Quarterly, 19,* 135–151.

Quinn, J. B. (1980). *Strategies for change: Logical incrementalism.* Homewood, IL: Irwin.

Raiffa, H. (1968). *Decision analysis.* Reading, MA: Addison-Wesley.

Schwenk, C. R. (1984). Cognitive simplification processes in strategic decision-making. *Strategic Management Journal, 5,* 111–128.

Schwenk, C. R. (1985). Management illusions and biases: Their impact on strategic decisions. *Long Range Planning, 18*(5), 74–80.

Schwenk, C. R. (1995). Strategic decision making. *Journal of Management, 21,* 471–493.

Shapira, Z. (1995). *Risk taking: A managerial perspective.* New York, NY: Russell Sage Foundation.

Shrivastava, P., & Grant, J. H. (1985). Empirically derived models of strategic decision-making processes. *Strategic Management Journal, 6,* 97–113.

Simon, H. A. (1955). A behavioral model of rational choice. *Quarterly Journal of Economics, 69,* 99–118.

Simon, H. A. (1978). Rationality as process and product of thought. *Journal of the American Economic Association, 68,* 1–16.

Simon, H. A., & J. R. Hayes (1976). The understanding process: Problem isomorphs. *Cognitive Psychology, 8,* 165–190.

Slovic, P. (1967). The relative influence of probabilities and payoffs upon perceived risk of a gamble. *Psychonomic Science, 9,* 223–224.

Slovic, P., Fischhoff, B., & Lichtenstein, S. (1977). Behavioral decision theory. *Annual Review of Psychology, 28,* 1–39.

Staw, B. M. (1981). The escalation of commitment to a course of action. *Academy of Management Review, 6*, 577–587.

Sutcliffe, K. M. (1994). What executives notice: Accurate perceptions in top management team. *Academy of Management Journal, 37*, 1360–1378.

Taylor, R. (1975). Concepts, theory and techniques, psychological determinants of bounded rationality: Implications for decision-making strategies. *Decision Science, 6*, 409–29.

Thomas, J. B., & McDaniel, R. R., Jr. (1990). Interpreting strategic issues: Effects of strategy and the information-processing structure of top management teams. *Academy of Management Journal, 33*, 286–306.

Thomas, J. B., Clark, S. M., & Gioia, D. A. (1993). Strategic sensemaking and organizational performance: Linkages among scanning, interpretation, action, and outcomes. *Academy of Management Journal, 36*, 239–270.

Tversky, A., & Kahneman, D. (1973). Availability: A heuristic for judging frequency and probability. *Cognitive Psychology, 4*, 207–32.

Tversky, A., & Kahneman, D. (1974). Judgement under uncertainty: Heuristics and biases. *Science, 185*, 1124–31.

Vickers, G. (1965). *The art of judgment: A study of policy making*. New York, NY: Basic Books.

Vlek, C., & Stallen, P. J. (1980). Rational and personal aspects of risk. *Acta Psychologica, 45*, 273–300.

von Krogh, G., & Roos, J. (Eds.). (1996). *Managing knowledge: Perspectives on cooperation and competition*. London, UK: Sage.

von Krogh, G., Roos, J., & Slocum, K. (1994). An essay on corporate epistemology. *Strategic Management Journal, 15*(Summer Special Issue), 53–71.

Walsh, J. P. (1995). Managerial and organizational cognition: Notes from a trip down memory lane. *Organization Science, 6*, 280–321.

Weick, K. E. (1979). *Social psychology of organizing*. 2nd ed., Reading, MA: Addison-Wesley.

Wrapp, H. E. (1967). Good managers don't make policy decisions. *Harvard Business Review, 45*(5), 91–99.

Zajac, E. J., & Bazerman, M. H. (1991). Blind spots in industry and competitor analysis: Implications of interfirm (mis)perceptions for strategic decisions. *Academy of Management Review, 16*, 37–56.

CHAPTER 2

EXPLORATION VERSUS EXPLOITATION

The Differential Impact of Historical and Social Comparison Performance Feedback on Executives' Cognitive Orientation

Tine Buyl
Christophe Boone

ABSTRACT

In this study, we relate to the growing research interest for integrating assumptions on managerial cognition in organizational research by examining the effect of performance feedback on executives' cognitive orientations. We furthermore extend prior performance feedback literature by explicitly distinguishing between (1) the effects of performance feedback on two types of cognitive orientations—exploratory and exploitative; and (2) the influence of two types of performance feedback—historical and social comparison. We propose that historical performance feedback—as an internal, self-reflective type of feedback—stimulates executives' exploitative cognitive orientation,

Behavioral Strategy: Emerging Perspectives, pages 27–54

but discourages their exploratory cognitive orientation. In contrast, social comparison performance feedback—which refers to the organization's position in the social ranking—is anticipated to engender exploratory, but hamper exploitative cognitive orientations.

We use an initial empirical study including longitudinal data of 35 U.S. industrial organizations (2000–2009) to test these propositions. In general, the pattern of our results provides support for our anticipations, as we find that executives' exploratory orientation is affected positively by social comparison performance feedback, and negatively by historical performance feedback. Furthermore, but to a lesser extent, executives' exploitative orientation appears to be stimulated only by historical performance feedback.

With this study, we do not only contribute to the emerging research stream on behavioral strategy and the integration of cognitive assumptions into organizational research, but also to the extant literature on exploration and exploitation and on the effects of performance feedback.

INTRODUCTION

Increasingly, scholars underscore the relevance of executives' cognition and cognitive frames in explaining organizational behavior (e.g., Eisenhardt, Furr, & Bingham, 2010; Gavetti, Levinthal, & Ocasio, 2007; Ocasio, 1997, 2011). For instance, the emerging "behavioral strategy" stream (e.g., Powell, Lovallo, & Fox, 2011) aims to integrate assumptions on human cognition and social psychology into strategic management and practice. In their extensive review of the cognitive perspective in strategy, Narayanan, Zane, and Kemmerer (2011, p. 337) highlight an apparent gap in this literature stream: they indicate that the patterns of executive cognition, organizational learning, and frame-breaking are "areas that cry out for theoretical and empirical works, given the current paucity" and that works such as March's (1991) distinction between exploratory and exploitative processes "offer convenient starting points for this line of research." In keeping with this appeal, we study the antecedents of patterns of executives' exploratory and exploitative cognitive orientation. An exploratory orientation is about flexibility, innovation, and embracing variation, while an exploitative orientation focuses on efficiency, control, and variance reduction (March, 1991).

Narayanan et al. (2011, p. 338) furthermore suggest that a theoretical puzzle in cognition literature could be elucidated by studying how *organizational performance* affects executive cognition and cognitive frames. While the extant literature generally views organizational performance as an outcome of executive cognition, feedback on performance can in turn also alter executive cognition. Grounded in the behavioral theory of the firm

(BTF) (Cyert & March, 1963), scholars have explored backward-looking search behavior—i.e., search behavior as a result of performance feedback (e.g., Greve, 2003). We build on this stream of research and focus on search behavior that is encapsulated in executives' cognitive orientations (cf. Eggers & Kaplan, 2009; Walsh, 1995). To be precise, we examine the effect of performance feedback on executives' exploratory and exploitative cognitive orientations. Gavetti et al. (2007) explicitly call for such an integration of traditional ideas of the BTF with better insights of how cognitive processes shape organizational behavior and strategy.

Inspired by the BTF and prospect theory (Kahneman & Tversky, 1979), scholars mostly assume that performance feedback is negatively related to search behavior. However, we build new theory by explicitly distinguishing between (1) two types of search behavior—executives' exploratory (i.e., search inducing flexibility and innovation) and exploitative (i.e., search for efficiency and refinement) cognitive orientation, e.g., Lavie, Stettner, & Tushman, 2010; March, 1991); and (2) two types of performance feedback—historical (i.e., internal feedback; performance compared to the organization's own historical performance) and social comparison (i.e., external feedback; performance compared to that of their peer organizations, e.g., Greve, 2003). Though both the distinction between exploratory and exploitative search (Greve, 2007) and that between historical and social comparison feedback (Chen, 2008; Iyer & Miller, 2008; Washburn & Bromiley, 2012) have been made before in research on performance feedback, prior studies (implicitly) assume that the effects of both types of feedback (historical vs. social comparison) on both types of search (exploratory vs. exploitative) are analogous (i.e., following the BTF's and prospect theory's assumptions). However, we exactly argue that these distinctions determine the situations in which the BTF's and prospect theory's assumptions are applicable or not.

We propose that historical feedback—as an internal type of feedback—focuses executives' attention on its existing internal processes, by discouraging exploratory search and stimulating exploitative search. For social comparison feedback, which is an external type of feedback associated with the organization's relations to its peers and its position in the social ranking, we expect the opposite effects to hold, as this type of feedback represents an indication for organizations of both their capability to explore (Chatterjee & Hambrick, 2011) and their external legitimacy to pursue deviant strategies (Desai, 2008). These opposing forces of historical and social comparison feedback imply that it will be very difficult for executives to obtain a balance between both cognitive orientations.

We empirically investigate our anticipations using a longitudinal dataset of 35 U.S. companies from the industrial machinery and equipment industry (2-digit SIC code 35) for 10 years (2000–2009). In companies in this industry, which generally execute the whole production process—from initial conception of an idea to finished product—in-house, high emphasis is placed on the "engineering" problem (cf. Miles & Snow, 1978), which implies that efficiency is of utmost importance. Due to the strong pull towards efficiency, these organizations often run the risk of becoming trapped into a stream of endless incremental refinements (exploitation) of the existing products and processes (March, 1991). Nevertheless, renewal and innovation (exploration) are also needed to attain organizational success. Recombination of technologies represents the main type of innovation in this industry (for a description of innovation as a process of technological recombination, see Fleming, 2001). Because of these industry characteristics, including the strong trend towards exploitation and the need for more innovation and exploration, this industry is particularly appropriate for studying the patterns of executives' exploratory and exploitative cognitive orientations. Overall, our findings provide support for our anticipations.

THEORY AND HYPOTHESES

Probably the most used theoretical frames in studying feedback reactions to organizational performance are those inspired by prospect theory and the BTF (e.g., Greve, 2003), which typically hypothesize a negative relationship between organizational performance and consecutive search behavior. According to these theories, organizations which perform well (i.e., above their aspiration levels) are less likely to engage in search processes because they are satisfied with their current performance. On the contrary, organizations that perform below their aspiration levels are motivated to search for solutions (problemistic search) to improve their performance (Cyert & March, 1963; Greve, 2003). A recent meta-analysis, however, reveals a more complicated pattern (Bowen, Rostami, & Steel, 2010). Several other theoretical frames (e.g., performance as a "capability cue," Chatterjee & Hambrick, 2011) or "organizational slack" (Daniel, Lohrke, Foraciari, & Turner, 2004), and the "threat-rigidity" perspective (Staw, Sandelands, & Dutton, 1981) contradict the prior theories' propositions and predict a positive association between organizational performance and subsequent search behavior.

In studying the effects of performance feedback on executives' cognitive orientations, we attend to this issue in two ways. First, we argue that executives have different foci of search and differentiate between two: exploratory and exploitative search. The distinction between exploratory and exploitative processes is common in organizational research (see Lavie et al., 2010 for a review). Both exploratory and exploitative orientations entail search processes to ameliorate the organization's performance, but through different processes and mechanisms: an exploratory orientation relates to search for new and innovative solutions, while an exploitative orientation involves search for efficiency and refinement (March, 1991). Though Greve (2007) also studies the effects of performance feedback on both exploratory and exploitative innovation, he assumes that the effects of performance feedback are in a similar direction for both types of outcomes. The results of his study reveal a rather puzzling pattern. We explicitly argue that the effects of performance feedback diverge for exploratory as compared to exploitative orientations, given that they entail divergent types of search behavior.

Second, we propose that the direction of the effect of performance feedback on executives' cognitive orientation depends upon the type of feedback. Scholars generally assume that organizational performance is compared with two types of aspiration levels in assessing performance feedback. The first is a comparison of the organization's performance with its own performance history (Cyert & March, 1963, i.e., historical performance feedback). In this case, an organization's prior performance represents a benchmark against which it evaluates its current performance (Baum et al., 2005). Second, organizations also use external comparison (Argote & Greve, 2007). Social comparison performance feedback compares the organization's performance against that of its reference or peer group (Baum et al., 2005). As historical feedback irrevocably entails some kind of internal reflection, while social comparison feedback focuses executives' attention to the external environment and the organization's position on the social ladder (cf. Boksem, Kostermans, Milivojevic, & De Cremer, 2012), we expect them to have diverging effects on executives' exploratory and exploitative orientations. Chen (2008, p. 619) specifically calls for research in this matter: "An implication for future research is to separate the historical and social comparison models in testing the effects of aspirations on firm behaviors and to identify factors that differentiate the effects of social and historical aspirations."

Historical Performance Feedback

Historical performance feedback can be regarded as an internal, self-reflective type of feedback, as organization's performance is compared to their history (Short & Palmer, 2003). It "indicates a trend—whether an organization's performance is improving, worsening, or stable over time" (Baum et al., 2005, p. 543). Hence, it gives an indication of how the organization is currently doing, whether it is "on track." Positive historical performance feedback is seen as a signal that the organization is doing well and that its current activities, processes, and routines pay off (Short & Palmer, 2003). This organization's executives will, therefore, not feel the urge to change their ongoing activities and they are not motivated to search for activities and processes that diverge from the extant organizational routines (Cyert & March, 1963; Greve, 2003). At the same time, positive historical feedback encourages them to refine and elaborate on the current,—apparently successful—activities and processes (Gupta, Smith, & Shalley, 2006; Levinthal & March, 1993). Put differently, positive historical performance feedback engenders executives to adjust their exploratory orientation downwards, but their exploitative orientation upwards.

On the contrary, if an organization's performance is below its historical aspiration levels, managers consider this as a signal that the organization's current activities and processes are not successful (Cyert & March, 1963). Therefore, management is stimulated to on the one hand break through the current activities and processes by pursuing deviant strategies (Greve, 2003) and on the other hand decrease the refinement and further development of these current activities and processes, which obviously do not yield the expected results (Short & Palmer, 2003). In other words, we expect that negative historical performance feedback encourages executives to decrease their exploitative, but increase their exploratory orientation. Hence, we expect that for historical performance feedback, the BTF's and prospect theory's anticipations will hold. In sum, we hypothesize:

> **Hypothesis 1a:** *Positive historical performance feedback decreases executives' exploratory cognitive orientation.*

> **Hypothesis 1b:** *Positive historical performance feedback increases executives' exploitative cognitive orientation.*

Social Comparison Performance Feedback

Organizations generally also compare their performance levels to those of other organizations in their vicinity (Short & Palmer, 2003). "Social aspiration performance feedback, in contrast, provides a benchmark level—whether an organization's performance is currently above, below, or similar to its peers" (Baum, Rowley, Shipilov, & Chuang, 2005, p. 543). Whereas historical performance feedback provides internal feedback on whether the organization is "on track," social comparison feedback presents the organization's managers with information on how the organization is doing in comparison to the other organizations in the industry (Short & Palmer, 2003). It can thus be regarded as external feedback on the organization's position in the social comparison ranking.

An organization that receives positive social comparison performance feedback performs well compared to its peers. Its high position in the social comparison ladder gives this organization the legitimacy to follow deviant strategies (Desai, 2008). Furthermore, more than performance compared to the organization's own history, performance compared to the organization's peers indicates a level of slack or excess resources, which the organization is able to build (cf. Bowen et al., 2010; Short & Palmer, 2003). These resources can both be tangible (e.g., cash) and intangible (e.g., network opportunities, reputation). Moreover, Chatterjee and Hambrick (2011) found that managers consider their performance relative to their peers to be a strong "capability cue," instigating exploratory search. Such capability cues, or signals of efficacy, affect executives' confidence and color their interpretation of the riskiness of current decisions: positive cues induce boldness, while negative cues provoke timidity (Sitkin & Weingart, 1995).

In sum, organizations that obtain positive social comparison feedback feel capable and have the resources, slack, and legitimacy to pursue exploratory strategies (Short & Palmer, 2003). Refinement of their current activities and processes is not needed to improve their position. Labianca, Fairbank, Andrevski, and Parzen (2009) refer to the "temporal competitive advantages theories" to argue that organizations that perform well as compared to their peers will have greater financial power to initiate change, to experiment, and to explore. As they want to stay ahead of their competitors, these well-performing organizations use their financial power to continuously undertake such change and exploration efforts (Covin & Slevin, 1991; D'Aveni, 1994).

On the contrary, organizations that perform worse than their peers, may want to climb up to a higher social position, but they lack the resources and legitimacy to do this via strategies that deviate from their ongoing processes and activities (Desai, 2008). They are therefore forced to shift their focus toward internal factors (i.e., refinement of internal processes) to increase their profitability and enhance their social position (Baum et al., 2005; Short & Palmer, 2003). Furthermore, because they feel threatened by their low social position, "bottom-of-class" organizations generally react in a conservative, treat-rigidity instigated way (Jordan & Audia, 2012; Staw et al., 1981). This argument is supported by evidence from social psychology research; Boksem et al. (2012) found that people with a low position in the social ranking are more likely to display inhibitory processes, because they experience social evaluative threat causing them to monitor and self-reflectively adjust their own behavior frequently. Our hypotheses run as follows:

Hypothesis 2a: *Positive social comparison performance feedback increases executives' exploratory cognitive orientation.*

Hypothesis 2b: *Positive social comparison performance feedback decreases executives' exploitative cognitive orientation.*

METHODS

Sample

We test our hypotheses on a dataset of publicly-traded US companies from the "industrial machinery and equipment" industry (2-digit SIC code 35). We chose this industry as it seemed particularly suited to study exploratory and exploitative patterns, given the high pull towards efficiency (exploitation) combined with the need for innovation (exploration).

Companies were included if (1) their headquarters were based in the United States; (2) they were quoted on the New York Stock Exchange or the NASDAQ for the period 2000-2009; (3) in the period 2000-2009 they did not experience any change in name due to a merger or acquisition; and (4) they published annual reports with letters to shareholders on a regular basis. This selection left us with a sample of 54 companies. Of these companies, we collected annual reports (with letters to shareholders), form 10-K's and proxy statements via corporate websites, the U.S. Securities and Exchange Commission's website, or mail request. Nineteen companies were dropped from the sample because we were not able to retrieve an adequate amount of letters to shareholders (as these letters formed the basis of our dependent variables). Our final working sample comprises 35 companies and 338 letters to shareholders (allowing a maximum of two missing letters per company). The average size of the companies in our sample was 10,255 employees (with a minimum of 136 and a maximum of 65,000), while the average TMT in our sample comprises 7 members (with a minimum of 2 and a maximum of 19). Net sales average at 2,617 million U.S. dollars (with a minimum of 21 million and a maximum of 28,400 million U.S. dollars).

Measuring Executives' Cognitive Orientation

Content Analysis of Letters to Shareholders

The measurement of managerial orientations and cognitions presents a major challenge for researchers (Cho & Hambrick, 2006; Lant & Shapira, 2001). Qualitative research methods such as interviews are not only difficult to realize for large-scale studies, they also often suffer from low reliability and replicability (Osborne, Stubbart, & Ramaprasad, 2001). Surveys of executives are impractical for assessing past cognitions as they often suffer from retroactive sensemaking and are generally restricted by low response rates from top managers in major companies (Cho & Hambrick, 2006).

We therefore chose to use automated text analysis of company documents, and in particular the letters to shareholders found in companies' annual reports, to gauge TMT's cognitive patterns. Building on the Sapir-Whorf hypothesis on linguistic relativity, this method assumes that words are not used coincidentally, but that they reflect the writer's world view (Short, Broberg, Cogliser, & Brigham, 2010). Though text or content analysis of company's letters to shareholders is a relatively new research method in upper echelons research, it has already been used in various organizational studies (e.g., Bowman, 1984; Cho & Hambrick, 2006; Kabanoff & Brown, 2008; Kaplan, 2008; Levy, 2005; Short et al., 2010). Prior research revealed that such letters to shareholders are "excellent sources of managerial cognitions" (Short et al., 2010, p. 334). They provide a forum for executives to voice their perceptions, beliefs, and thoughts on important issues affecting the organization and signal the major topics and themes executives believe to be salient.

Evidently, the latter method has also been the target of criticism. For instance, critics have argued that annual reports, and in particular the letters to shareholders, are usually written aiming at impression management (Yadav, Prabhu, & Chandy, 2007) and that they might display self-serving biases in attributions for past performance (Barr, 1998; Salancik & Meindl, 1984). Nevertheless, though these letters to shareholders are usually written for multiple purposes, including impression management and self-serving issues, research shows that they still reflect key managerial initiatives, concerns, and points of view (Barr, 1998; Cho & Hambrick, 2006). Further on, Abrahamson and Hambrick (1997) have established that, though professional writers are often involved in the formulation of the letter, the CEO and the other executives will direct the writers and carefully assess and refine their work (Abrahamson & Hambrick, 1997). This is illustrated by Eggers and Kaplan's (2009) finding that changes in the executive team had a dramatic impact on the style, length, and content of the letters. Numerous researchers (e.g., Bowman, 1984; D'Aveni & MacMillan, 1990; Kaplan, 2008; Yadav et al., 2007) have found that the cognitions embodied in letters to shareholders do have systematic effects on firm actions, consistent with theoretical expectations. These findings further suggest the soundness and appropriateness of the method. Moreover, the accuracy and completeness of annual reports' content is attested because of laws such as Sarbanes-Oxley (Mckenny, Short, & Payne, 2013).

Several tests have provided empirical evidence supporting the validity of the method to capture executive cognitions (e.g., Fiol, 1995; Michalisin, 2001). For example, D'Aveni and MacMillan (1990) showed that measures of the executives' cognition drawn from letters to shareholders demonstrated high correlations with measures obtained from other data sources. In addition, Huff and Schwenk (1990) found that, especially in turbulent times, patterns of executives' attributions in letters to shareholders are rather accurate translations of their attempts at sensemaking. Finally, by comparing the information comprised in letters to shareholders with boardroom agendas, Yadav et al. (2007) assert that letters to shareholders reliably reflect how senior managers allocate their attention.

More generally, other attempts at quantifying cognition are sensible to the same criticism as the managerial cognition measures derived from letters to shareholders (Abrahamson & Hambrick, 1997). "Thus, any critique must consider the relative advantages this method provides over other methods for studying top management cognition. Clearly, using letters to shareholders provides an unobtrusive access to managerial cognition and allows testing theoretical propositions containing longitudinal aspects" (Levy, 2005, p. 804).

Measures of Executives' Cognitive Orientation

We used the open-source "Yoshikoder" software (the former Vbpro) to calculate our variables. The first step in this type of content analysis involves the development of word lists (dictionaries) of the constructs of interest, in our case exploratory and exploitative orientations. In developing these dictionaries, we followed Short et al.'s (2010) suggestions to improve construct validity. In particular, to ensure deductive content validity, we firstly developed exhaustive word lists based on working definitions of the constructs drawn from theory (e.g., Lavie et al., 2010; March, 1991) and dictionaries used by other scholars to gauge comparable constructs (e.g., Michalisin's (2001) dictionary of "innovativeness" and Uotila, Maula, Keil, and Zahra's (2009) dictionary of "exploratory action" for exploration, and Cho and Hambrick's (2006) "engineering issues" and Uotila et al.'s (2009) "exploitative action" for exploitation). Thesauruses were used to include as many synonyms in the initial word lists as possible. To enhance the inductive content validity, we then complemented these initial theoretical word lists with other words from the letters to shareholders (deriving from a full list of all words in the letters) that could be associated with the constructs (cf. Short et al., 2010). Lastly, two independent expert raters assessed the word lists. The raters were unaware of the hypotheses. Inter-rater agreement was .78 for the word list on and .72 for the one on exploitation.

In line with Eggers and Kaplan's (2009) work, "*Exploratory orientation*" is operationalized as the proportion of words (relative to the total number of words), in percentage, in the letter to shareholders indicating an exploratory orientation (e.g., breakthrough, newness, proactive) and "*exploitative orientation*" as the proportion of words, in percentage, in the letter to shareholders indicating an exploitative orientation (e.g., cost-reducing, efficiency, incremental).[1]

Validity of the Measures

In this study, we use executives' exploratory and exploitative cognitive orientations as dependent variables. Implicitly, we consider these cognitive measures to be related to actual organizational behavior. However, numerous scholars (e.g., Abrahamson & Hambrick, 1997; Levy, 2005) have already argued that executives' cognition only represents a first step in a tripartite information processing sequence that involves attention, interpretation, and action (Daft & Weick, 1984). Narayanan et al. (2011) also emphasize that executive cognition and organizational behavior are related, but not equivalent. Just like there are often differences between a firms's intentional versus realized strategies (Mintzberg, 1978), cognition does not always materialize in observable organizational behavior. The bottom line is that a strong relationship between cognition and actual organizational behavior is not a necessary condition per se to establish the former's validity (Mckenny et al., 2013). We are particularly interested in the firm's intentions (i.e., executive cognition) apart from the firm's realized strategy (i.e., actual firm behavior), as we want to find out how performance feedback affects executives' cognitive orientations.

To assess the validity of the used measures for executive cognition, we undertook two actions. First, to ensure that we are not simply measuring the organization's strategy but the executives' actual cognitive orientation as driven by performance feedback, we controlled for three strategy variables in our analyses: *"R&D intensity,"* measured as the organization's annual R&D expenses divided by sales (Cohen & Levinthal, 1990), *"internationalization,"* operationalized as the average of the percentage of sales abroad and the proportion of foreign subsidiaries related to the total number of subsidiaries (cf. Jaw & Lin, 2009), and *"current ratio."* Both R&D intensity and internationalization have been used in past research to indicate the organization's innovative and deviant strategies (Cohen & Levinthal, 1990; Li, 2010). Current ratio can be considered as the excess, slack resources, which can both be seen as an asset and as an obstruction for exploratory strategies, as it both increases the organization's capabilities and decreases the organization's incentives to pursue deviant strategies (Lavie et al., 2010). By including these strategy variables as controls, we ensure that our measures of executive cognition are not simply an epiphenomenon of the organization's ongoing strategy, but that they truly capture executives' forward-looking cognitive orientation.

Our second effort to assess the validity of our measures for executives' cognitive orientation was aimed at ensuring that the measures truly capture the executives' intentions. For this purpose, we collected information on executive compensation for all organizations in the sample for the period 2006–2009 (we were not able to find consistent compensation data for the period 2000–2005) and we used a cross-lagged panel correlation approach

(Kenny, 1975) to examine whether compensation packages might affect executives' cognitive orientation or vice versa. As executives' intentions are generally found to be driven by compensation structures (the "incentive effect"; Gerhart & Rynes, 2003), our guiding assumption was that our measures of executive cognition should be correlated by their compensation structure in prior periods more than in consecutive periods. Based on Sanders' (2001) finding that stock options favor risk-seeking, while stocks induce risk-averse strategies, we proposed that there would be a positive correlation between the percentage executives are paid in stock options (relative to their total compensation) and their subsequent exploratory orientation, and between the percentage executives are paid in stocks and their subsequent exploitative orientation. Table 2.1 displays the cross-lagged correlations of stock options and exploratory orientation on the one hand and stocks and exploitative orientation on the other hand. It appears that, for both exploratory and exploitative orientation, the correlations with stock options and stocks, respectively, are higher for their orientation in later periods ($t + 1$).

Organizational Performance Feedback

To measure previous organizational performance, many variables might have been used (Short & Palmer, 2003). Following the lead of other scholars (e.g., Chen, 2008; Roberts, 2002; Tuggle, Schnatterly, & Johnson, 2010), we use a standard accounting measure: return on assets (ROA). "*ROA*" is defined as the operating income (i.e., operating revenue minus operating expenses) divided by the organization's total assets. We prefer to use ROA over return on equity (ROE) as the latter can be distorted because of differences in financial leverage across firms (Chen, 2008; Iyer & Miller, 2008). Greve (2007) indicates that ROA is the preferred measure in studies on performance feedback effects on search and risk-taking.

Two measures of performance feedback are created: historical performance feedback and social comparison performance feedback. "*Historical performance feedback*" is measured as ROA minus ROA in $t - 1$ (cf. Iyer &

TABLE 2.1 Cross-Lagged Correlations of Executive Compensation and Executives' Cognitive Orientation

	Executives' Cognitive Orientation		
	$t - 1$	t	$t + 1$
Stock options—exploratory orientation	.22*	.29*	.33*
Stocks—exploitative orientation	–.04	.07	.09

Miller, 2008). Hence, we use the organization's lagged performance as an aspiration level to calculate historical performance feedback.[2] In line with scholars such as Harris and Bromiley (2007), Desai (2008), and Iyer and Miller (2008), we calculated *"social comparison performance feedback"* as the firm's ROA minus the mean ROA for the firm's industry in the same year, retrieved from Census databases.

Control Variables

We include control variables at different levels of analyses. Firstly, we control for the yearly "*GDP growth*" in the United States, as a measure for the yearly economic climate the organizations operate in, which is found to affect the organizations' level of exploratory and exploitative behavior (cf. Lavie et al., 2010). We also incorporate four firm-level control variables. "*Organization age*" (in years) is included as it has been linked to exploratory and exploitative behavior in previous studies (e.g., Lavie et al., 2010).[3] As outlined above, we also control for three strategy-related organizational variables: *"R&D intensity,"* *"internationalization,"* and *"current ratio."*

At the top management team (TMT) level, we use two control variables, the TMT's size and the entry of new members into the TMT. Information in the form 10-K's and proxy statements is used to operationalize these control variables. *"TMT size"* (total number of executives in the TMT) is included as it represents an important covariate of the TMT's cognitive patterns (Cho & Hambrick, 2006). "*TMT entry*" is calculated as the number of new TMT members (excluding the CEO) that entered the TMT in the year under review. This variable, which is an indicator of the turnover in the TMT, is also expected to have an impact on executives' exploratory and exploitative orientation, as the entry of new executives inevitably introduces new perspectives and knowledge bases into executive decision-making processes (March, 1991).

Finally, we control for two CEO-level variables, CEO organizational tenure and CEO duality. "*CEO organizational tenure*" is measured as the number of years the CEO has been part of the organization.[4] As longer-tenured CEOs are usually expected to be more wedded to status-quo situations and to be reluctant to pursue deviant strategies (Hambrick & Fukutomi, 1991), the CEO's tenure might be a significant driver of exploratory and exploitative orientation. "*CEO duality*" is a dummy variable which equals 1 if the CEO is also the chairman of the organization's board of directors. This control variable can be considered as an indicator of the CEO's power to drive executive cognition (Tuggle et al., 2010).

Modeling Drivers of Executives' Cognitive Orientation

To accurately operationalize the effects of performance feedback on executives' exploratory and exploitative cognitive orientation into regression analyses, we have to move away from cross-sectional methods and towards a method that captures the intertemporal behavior of cognitive orientations. Inspired by studies on the persistence of firm profitability (e.g., Roberts, 1999; Roberts & Dowling, 2002), we use first-order autoregressive models with lagged dependent variables. Equation (2.1) depicts the model that we use to estimate our hypotheses:

$$\begin{aligned} \text{Cognitive orientation}_{it} = \alpha_0 &+ \alpha_1 \times \text{historical performance feedback}_{i(t-1)} \\ &+ \alpha_2 \times \text{social comparison performance feedback}_{i(t-1)} \\ &+ \alpha_3 \times \text{controls}_{i(t-1)} \\ &+ \beta_0 \times \text{cognitive orientation}_{i(t-1)} + \varepsilon_{it} \end{aligned} \tag{2.1}$$

With the inclusion of a lagged dependent variable, we follow the example of prior studies on executive cognition (e.g., Cho & Hambrick, 2006) and performance feedback (e.g., Chatterjee & Hambrick, 2011). For the analyses, our sample size drops to 298 because of missing observations in the (lagged) dependent variables.

RESULTS

Table 2.2 shows the means, standard deviations, and correlations of the variables included in the analyses. We chose to use a random-effects in favor of a fixed-effects approach, as the latter is a very conservative method that does not take into account the variance between the organizations in the dataset. A fixed-effects approach might obscure some of the effects under study in the present setting and is therefore not be the best way to estimate our models.[5] Furthermore, the Hausman specification test indicates that the differences in coefficients for random- versus fixed-effects are not systematic. Hence, we can use the random-effects models, which produce more efficient results. We accounted for clustering of observations within firms and we used the Huber/White/sandwich estimator of variance to ensure standard errors that are robust to cross-sectional heteroskedasticity and within-panel (serial) correlation. Since we have two dependent variables, we executed two sets of analyses, one for "exploratory orientation" (Table 2.3, models 1–2) and one for "exploitative orientation" (Table 2.3, models 3–4).

Models 1 and 3 include the lagged dependent and control variables only for exploratory and exploitative orientation, respectively. It appears that both exploratory and exploitative orientations are co-determined by their

TABLE 2.2 Means, Standard Deviations, and Correlations

	Mean	S.D.	1	2	3	4	5	6	7	8	9	10	11	12	13	14
Dependent variables																
1 Exploratory orientation	.92	.44	—													
2 Exploitative orientation	.89	.45	–.01	—												
3 Exploratory orientationt-1	.92	.43	.35*	–.09	—											
4 Exploitative orientationt-1	.90	.45	–.02	.50*	.00	—										
Independent variables																
5 Historical perf. feedback	–.00	.11	–.07	.04	.01	–.04	—									
6 Social comparison perf. feedback	.04	.10	.07	–.00	.06	–.07	.56*	—								
Control variables																
7 GDP growth	1.82	1.76	.07	–.12*	.00	–.10*	.22*	.10*	—							
8 Organization age	63.66	38.96	–.14*	.14*	–.13*	.14*	–.04	.08	–.04	—						
9 R&D intensity	.03	.05	.21*	–.05	.24*	–.03	–.05	–.18*	–.07	–.29*	—					
10 Internationalization	.53	.23	.11*	–.09	.09*	–.09*	.05	.07	–.04	–.12*	.23*	—				
11 Current ratio	2.51	1.48	–.00	.02	–.02	–.02	–.04	–.00	–.07	–.18*	.29*	–.15*	—			
12 TMT size	7.38	3.52	.05	.03	.06	–.02	.00	.16*	–.02	.13*	–.16*	.30*	–.32*	—		
13 TMT entry	.92	1.15	.12*	–.06	.07	–.04	–.03	.06	–.08	–.03	–.00	.20*	–.09*	.47*	—	
14 CEO org. tenure	17.70	11.10	–.28*	–.18*	–.27*	–.21*	–.03	–.00	–.05	.25*	–.14*	–.13*	.22*	–.20*	–.15*	—
15 CEO duality	.71	.46	–.16*	.04	–.18*	–.04	.00	–.14*	.07	–.07	–.08	–.12*	–.05	.09*	.01	.21*

TABLE 2.3 Effects of Historical and Social Comparison Performance Feedback on Executives' Exploratory and Exploitative Orientation; Random Effects

	DV: Exploratory orientation		DV: Exploitative orientation	
	1	2	3	4
Constant	.69***	.66***	.47***	.48***
	(.12)	(.12)	(.11)	(.12)
Exploratory orientation$_{t-1}$	.26***	.25***	–.11*	–.11*
	(.06)	(.06)	(.06)	(.07)
Exploitative orientation$_{t-1}$	–.03	–.01	.43***	.43***
	(.06)	(.06)	(.04)	(.04)
Historical perf. feedback	—	–.73**	—	.42*
		(.26)		(.25)
Soc. comp. perf. feedback	—	.77*	—	–.18
		(.40)		(.21)
GDP growth	.03#	.04*	–.04*	–.05*
	(.02)	(.02)	(.02)	(.03)
Organization age	–.00	–.00	.00*	.00**
	(.00)	(.00)	(.00)	(.00)
R&D intensity	1.12#	1.31*	–.17	–.17
	(.71)	(.70)	(.50)	(.52)
Internationalization	.02	.03	–.04	–.05
	(.08)	(.07)	(.12)	(.12)
Current ratio	–.00	–.01	.03#	.04#
	(.02)	(.01)	(.02)	(.02)
TMT size	–.00	–.01	.01	.01
	(.01)	(.01)	(.01)	(.01)
TMT entry	.04#	.03#	–.04*	–.04*
	(.02)	(.02)	(.02)	(.02)
CEO org. tenure	–.01**	–.01**	–.01**	–.01**
	(.00)	(.00)	(.00)	(.00)
CEO duality	–.08#	–.06	.04	.04
	(.06)	(.06)	(.06)	(.06)
R^2	.19	.22	.30	.31
Wald χ^2	189.32***	204.89***	289.82***	280.55***

Note: $N = 298$
Robust standard errors are shown in parentheses
# $p < .10$; * $p < .05$; ** $p < .01$; *** $p < .001$ (one-tailed)

prior levels, as indicated by the highly significant coefficients of the lagged dependent variables. In line with our expectations, exploratory orientation is furthermore positively affected by GDP growth, the organization's level of R&D intensity and the entry of new executives into the TMT, and negatively by CEO duality and the CEO's tenure (see Model 1). Model 3 suggests that executives' exploitative orientation is higher when GDP growth is low, when the organization is older and has a higher current ratio, when there is less entry of new executives into the TMT, and when the CEO's tenure is shorter. Furthermore, we also find that the direct effect of executives' exploratory orientation on their subsequent exploitative orientation is negative and significant.

Hypotheses Tests

Hypothesis 1a on the impact of historical performance feedback on exploratory orientation is tested in Model 2. We find that the coefficient of historical performance feedback is negative and highly significant ($B = -.73$; $p < .01$), providing support for Hypothesis 1a. Model 4 indicates that historical performance feedback also drives exploitative orientation, with a positive and significant coefficient ($B = .42$; $p < .05$), supporting Hypothesis 1b. In Model 2, we also test for the effect of social comparison performance feedback on exploratory orientation (Hypothesis 2b). The positive and significant coefficient of social comparison performance feedback ($B = .77$; $p < .05$) allows us to confirm Hypothesis 2a. Hypothesis 2b, on the effect of social comparison performance feedback on exploitative orientation is not supported. Though the regression shows a negative coefficient, it fails to reach significance.

Robustness of the Results

To check for the robustness of the results, we estimated the regressions using different methods. First, we used the (population-averaged) "generalized estimating equations" (GEE; Ballinger, 2004) method, both with an exchangeable within-group correlation structure and with a correlation structure that accounts for autoregression (AR1). The results (available upon request) remained unchanged for the focal variables. Second, we redid the analyses using "seemingly unrelated regressions" (SUR; Zellner, 1962), which account for the fact that the regressions might be related because the errors associated with both dependent variables, exploratory and exploitative orientation, may be correlated. For all models, we found that the correlation in error terms did not significantly differ from zero, leading to SUR models (available upon request) that did not diverge from the reported ones.

As our sample size is rather small, we performed several analyses to check for the sensitivity of the results to influential observations or outliers, such as the Cook's D statistic, the leverage of observations and the dfbeta's.

For historical and social comparison feedback, we found several extreme variables[6] that displayed a high leverage. To check the robustness of the findings, we winsorized the values for these outlier observations (i.e., we replaced their values by the mean plus or minus three standard deviations). This method is commonly used in for instance accountancy research (Lien & Balakrishnan, 2005). We redid the analyses using these new, winsorized variables (see Table 2.4). The results indicate that we should be careful in interpreting the results.

Though the pattern of results still seems to hold, with opposing effects of historical and social comparison feedback on exploratory and exploitative orientation, some of these results fail to reach significance. In particular, whereas historical and social comparison feedback is significantly related to executives' exploratory orientation, they do not appear to drive executives' exploitative orientation. Again, we redid the analyses using different methods, such as GEE and SUR. The results remained the same.

DISCUSSION

Contributions

In this study, we empirically analyze the effects of performance feedback on executives' cognitive orientation patterns concerning search in a sample of 35 U.S. industrial companies over a time-span of 10 years (2000–2009). Our findings suggest that when studying the effect of performance feedback on executives' cognitive orientations, distinctions should be made between on the one hand the type of performance feedback—historical versus social comparison—and on the other the hand type of search—exploratory versus exploitative. Whereas historical—internal—feedback appears to encourage exploitative[7] and discourage exploratory search, social comparison—external—feedback appears to affect exploratory search in the opposite direction.

We contribute to and extend various streams of literature and research. First, we contribute to the stream on executive cognition. Following Narayanan et al.'s (2011) suggestions, we integrate the ideas of the BTF concerning backward-looking (performance feedback induced) adaptation, into the research on executive cognition (cf. Gavetti et al.'s (2007) call to integrate and revisit the BTF's classic ideas) using March's (1991) distinction between exploration and exploitation as a starting point.

Second, we extend the performance feedback literature in at least two ways. First, we contribute by using a proximal measure of executives' search behavior as our outcome variable: executives' (exploratory and exploitative) cognitive orientation. The majority of research on performance

TABLE 2.4 Effects of Historical and Social Comparison Performance Feedback on Executives' Exploratory and Exploitative Orientation; Random Effects; Extreme Values Winsorized

	DV: Exploratory orientation		DV: Exploitative orientation	
	1	2	3	4
Constant	.69***	.65***	.47***	.38**
	(.12)	(.13)	(.11)	(.12)
Exploratory orientation$_{t-1}$	.26***	.24***	–.11*	–.11#
	(.06)	(.06)	(.06)	(.06)
Exploitative orientation$_{t-1}$	–.03	–.01	.43***	.42***
	(.06)	(.06)	(.04)	(.04)
Historical perf. feedback[a]	—	–.84*	—	.29
		(.41)		(.35)
Soc. comp. perf. feedback[a]	—	1.04*	—	–.22
		(.50)		(.30)
GDP growth	.03#	.04*	–.04*	–.04*
	(.02)	(.02)	(.02)	(.03)
Organization age	–.00	–.00	.00*	.00**
	(.00)	(.00)	(.00)	(.00)
R&D intensity	1.12#	1.36*	–.17	–.20
	(.71)	(.71)	(.50)	(.54)
Internationalization	.02	.04	–.04	–.05
	(.08)	(.07)	(.12)	(.12)
Current ratio	–.00	–.01	.03#	.04#
	(.02)	(.01)	(.02)	(.02)
TMT size	–.00	–.01	.01	.01
	(.01)	(.01)	(.01)	(.01)
TMT entry	.04#	.04#	–.04*	–.04*
	(.02)	(.02)	(.02)	(.02)
CEO org. tenure	–.01**	–.01**	–.01**	–.01**
	(.00)	(.00)	(.00)	(.00)
CEO duality	–.08#	–.05	.04	.03
	(.06)	(.06)	(.06)	(.06)
R^2	.19	.22	.30	.30
Wald χ^2	189.32***	216.90***	289.82***	298.45***

Note: $N = 298$

Robust standard errors are shown in parentheses

# $p < .10$; * $p < .05$; ** $p < .01$; *** $p < .001$ (one-tailed)

[a] winsorized

feedback has used rather distal indicators of search behavior, such as R&D expenses (e.g., Chen, 2008), capacity expenditures (e.g., Desai, 2008), and alliances (e.g., Baum et al., 2005). Argote and Greve (2007) already argued that although Cyert and March's theory (1963) can be applied to issues concerning organizational risk-taking, it most directly predicts search. Studying executive cognition also corresponds to Gavetti et al.'s (2007) call to integrate traditional ideas of the BTF with better insights of cognitive processes and to the emerging research stream on behavioral strategy (Powell et al., 2011). Moreover, by explicitly distinguishing between two types of search—exploratory and exploitative—and, in particular, by proposing that performance feedback will drive these two types of search in an opposite way, we extend research on performance feedback substantially (cf. Greve, 2007).

Our second contribution to the performance feedback literature is the explicit distinction between historical and social comparison feedback. Though we by no means want to suggest that we are the first to make this distinction—it is even made in the early work on the BTF (Cyert & March, 1963)—we are the first, as far as our knowledge, to propose that the effects of historical feedback might be in the opposite direction compared to those of social comparison feedback. Some authors (e.g., Baum et al., 2005; Shinkle, 2012; Washburn & Bromiley, 2012) have emphasized that historical and social comparison feedback diverges in importance contingent upon the situation. However, these authors still suggest that both types of feedback have analogous effects on executives' search behavior (i.e., mostly they assume a negative effect, following the BTF and prospect theory). Moreover, scholars tend to combine historical and social comparison aspirations into one aspiration level in determining performance feedback (e.g., Greve, 2007; Hu, Blettner, & Bettis, 2011). With our study, we provide some first empirical evidence that this assumption does not hold in practice. Indeed, we find that the effects of historical performance feedback generally refer to self-reflective adjustment of internal resources (i.e., good performance feedback discourages distal search and encourages incremental refinements). In contrast, the effects of social comparison feedback are related to the organization's behavior associated with its position on the social ladder (i.e., good performance engenders innovative efforts). Insights from research in psychology or neuro-economics on individual-level feedback behaviors (e.g., Boksem et al., 2011; van Noordt & Segalowitz, 2012) might be used to further unravel these divergent effects.

With these two extensions of performance feedback research, we also attend to the more fundamental distinction in this literature stream between the views predicting a negative—the prospect theory and the BTF—or positive effect—such as the organizational slack, capability cues, or threat rigidity perspectives—of performance feedback. Several authors (e.g., Ocasio, 1995; Jordan & Audia, 2012) have argued before that these seemingly contradictory theoretical frames might all hold depending on specific conditions. However, the body of empirical work still considers the negative view of performance feedback to be the baseline model to explain performance feedback effects, while theories predicting a positive effect are generally used to explain "abnormalities," almost in an ad-hoc way (e.g., by explaining the effects of extremely poor performance using the threat-rigidity perspective; cf. Greve, 2003; Hu, Blettner, & Bettis, 2011). This observation aligns with Bowen et al.'s (2010, p. 1184) meta-analysis, which indicates that the current body of performance feedback research appears to display a "publication bias towards studies framed as confirming search (...) within prospect theory or the behavioral theory of the firm." By building new theory concerning the distinct effects of (1) exploratory versus exploitative search; and (2) historical versus social comparison feedback, we unravel some of the seemingly contradictory effects of performance feedback.

Finally, we extend the literature and research on exploration and exploitation (e.g., Lavie et al., 2010) by providing some insights into paths of exploratory and exploitative orientations (cf. Levinthal & March, 1993) and how these paths might be driven by performance feedback. Let us, for example, take a closer look at the top-performers in an industry. Because of positive social comparison feedback, we expect them to be highly exploratory-oriented. It might happen that in some years, they perform a bit worse than the previous year, simply because of regression to the mean. This negative historical feedback even reinforces their exploratory orientation, illustrating why top-performers in an industry are often organizations which remain highly innovative and risk-taking over time. The opposite "path" might occur in bottom-of-class performers. Negative social comparison feedback makes them highly inward-oriented and focused on incremental improvements. If, because of regression to the mean, they perform a bit better than the previous year, they take this as an incentive to even enhance their exploitative orientation. This process provides some explanation of why bottom-performers seldom make it to the top of their respective industry, as they recurrently will refrain from risk-taking and stick to proximal search processes. For organizations in the middle of the social comparison ladder, we expect that the conflicting forces of historical and social comparison performance feedback will render executives to check and balance their orientations repeatedly, resulting in some kind of status-quo balance of both orientations.

This reasoning based on our preliminary results suggests that executives shift their cognitive orientation, based on performance feedback and their organization's position in the social comparison ladder (e.g., top-of-class performers appear to move towards a higher exploratory orientation, bottom-of-class performers towards a higher exploitative orientation, and middle-players towards a more balanced orientation). As such, it gives us a more nuanced understanding of the process of organizational adaptation (through shifts in executives' cognition) as compared to either the classical BTF (e.g., Greve, 2003) or theories supporting performance feedback as slack resources or a capability cue (e.g., Chatterjee & Hambrick, 2011) separately. We emphasize the complementarity between both views and combine them by distinguishing between the different types of feedback and cognitive orientations, enabling us to generate several empirically relevant—and realistic—paths of shifts in cognitive orientations. We strongly encourage additional in-depth research into these paths and how they are driven by performance and organizations' position to further augment integrated insights in organizational adaptation.

Limitations and Future Research Avenues

Evidently, this study has to be seen in the light of its limitations. Its small scale is an obvious first limitation. Though the empirical study includes observations regarding ten consecutive years (2000–2009), the sample only comprises information on 35 individual companies. As the outset of this study is to present some first, preliminary empirical evidence falsifying taken-for-granted assumptions emerging from prior research (e.g., that historical and social comparison feedback affect search in analogous ways) its small scale might not be considered as a large problem. However, it is advisable for future scholars to use larger-scale datasets to explore some of this study's findings in more depth. This also mitigates the problem of sensitivity of the analyses to outliers.

Second, this study was performed using companies from one specific industry. We chose the industrial machinery & equipment sector purposefully, given its apparent focus on both exploratory and exploitative search. However, our restriction to one industry also limits the generalizability of the findings. In fact, we see great value in exploring the industry-specific contingency factors regarding the effects of historical and social comparison performance feedback on exploratory and exploitative search. For instance, in highly dynamic and volatile industries, executives might be less driven by historical feedback, as the high pace in such industries renders historical measures irrelevant. On the contrary, historical feedback might be of utmost importance in stable, capital-intensive industries.

Finally, we consider our focus on executive cognition as an outcome variable as a strength, but it might also be considered as a limitation, because we do not relate performance feedback to actual organizational search behavior, but rather to executives' search intentions. Though we intentionally chose to use this proximal outcome variable, a valuable next step could be to explore the effects of performance feedback on actual organizational search behavior, while using executive cognition as a mediator (cf. Cho & Hambrick, 2006).

Overall, we hope that this study on the effects of historical and social comparison performance feedback on patterns of executives' exploratory and exploitative cognitive orientations represents a source of inspiration to future scholars. We provide first and preliminary empirical evidence that some of the taken-for-granted assumptions in established research appear not to hold in practice, underscoring recent calls (e.g., Gavetti et al., 2007) to revisit some of the Carnegie School's baseline ideas.

NOTES

1. The full dictionaries are available upon request.
2. As some scholars (e.g., Chen, 2008; Harris & Bromiley, 2007) suggest that aspiration levels might be "sticky"—i.e., that they might adapt slowly—we also calculated alternative measures of "historical performance feedback," comparing the organization's ROA with a weighted sum of ROA in t–1 and in t–2 (with weights varying between 0.1 and 0.9). The analyses with these alternative measures (available upon request) did not diverge substantially from the ones reported. For the sake of parsimony, we therefore decided to use the most simple and "clean" measure of "historical performance feedback."
3. We did not control for the organizations' size, because this variable correlated rather highly with several other control variables, such as *"TMT size."*
4. For 14 of the 350 observations the information on the CEO's tenure was missing. We used regression imputation to deal with these missings.
5. For instance, based on our argumentation, we would anticipate that organizations that outperform their peers year after year would continuously build slack resources and legitimacy, allowing them to explore. By introducing firm dummies in a fixed-effects approach one would filter out these absolute differences between firms, which would make it impossible to capture the effects of a continuous stream of positive social comparison feedback. In the same vein, firm dummies would obscure the effects of historical performance feedback if organizations are, for instance, gradually improving their performance and receive a continuous stream of positive historical performance feedback. In short, comparison and variance between firms is essential to estimate the expected feedback effects in a meaningful way.
6. In some cases (6 for historical feedback and 3 for social comparison feedback) the observations exceeded the mean ±3SD.
7. This result should be interpreted cautiously, as in the regression with winsorized observations, this effect did not reach significance.

ACKNOWLEDGMENTS

We wish to thank the participants of the "Governance and Innovation" session of the Academy of Management Meeting in San Antonio (2011) and the members of the Antwerp Centre of Evolutionary Demography for their constructive comments. Furthermore, we gratefully acknowledge financial support from the Research Foundation—Flanders (FWO-Vlaanderen), both through the Odysseus Program and through an individual scholarship for the first author.

REFERENCES

Abrahamson, E., & Hambrick, D. C. (1997). Attentional homogeneity in industries: The effects of discretion. *Journal of Organizational Behavior, 18*, 513–539.

Argote, L., & Greve, H. R. (2007). A behavioral theory of the firm—40 years and counting: Introduction and impact. *Organization Science, 18*, 337–349.

Ballinger, G. A. (2004). Using generalized estimating equations for longitudinal data analysis. *Organizational Research Methods, 7*, 127–150.

Barr, P. S. (1998). Adapting to unfamiliar environmental events: A look at the evolution of interpretation and its role in strategic change. *Organization Science, 9*, 644–669.

Baum, J. A. C., Rowley, T. J., Shipilov, A. V., & Chuang, Y. T. (2005). Dancing with strangers: Aspiration performance and the search for underwriting syndicate partners. *Administrative Science Quarterly, 50*, 536–575.

Boksem, M. A. S., Kostermans, E., Milivojevic, B., & De Cremer, D. (2012). Social status determines how we monitor and evaluate our performance. *Social Cognitive and Affective Neuroscience, 7*, 304–313.

Bowen, F. E., Rostami, M., & Steel, P. (2010). Timing is everything: A meta-analysis of the relationships between organizational performance and innovation. *Journal of Business Research, 63*, 1179–1185.

Bowman, E. (1984). Content analysis of annual reports for corporate strategy and risk. *Interfaces, 14*, 61–71.

Chatterjee, A., & Hambrick, D. C. (2011). Executive personality, capability cues, and risk taking: How narcissistic CEOs react to their successes and stumbles. *Administrative Science Quarterly, 56*, 202–237.

Chen, W. R. (2008). Determinants of firms' backward- and forward-looking R&D search behavior. *Organization Science, 19*, 609–622.

Cho, T. S., & Hambrick, D. C. (2006). Attention as the mediator between top management team characteristics and strategic change: The case of airline deregulation. *Organization Science, 17*, 453–469.

Cohen, W. M., & Levinthal, D. A. (1990). Absorptive capacity: A new perspective on learning and innovation. *Administrative Science Quarterly, 35*, 128–152.

Covin, J. G., & Slevin, D. P. (1991). A conceptual model of entrepreneurship as firm behavior. *Entrepreneurship Theory and Practice, 16*, 7–24.

Cyert, R. M., & March, J. G. (1963). *A behavioral theory of the firm.* Englewood Cliffs, NJ: Prentice Hall.

Daft, R. L., & Weick, K. E. (1984). Toward a model of organizations and interpretation systems. *Academy of Management Review, 9,* 284–195.

Daniel, F., Lohrke, F. T., Foraciari, C. J., & Turner, R. A. (2004). Slack resources and firm performance: A meta-analysis. *Journal of Business Research, 57,* 565–574.

D'Aveni, R. A., & MacMillan, I. (1990). Crisis and the content of managerial communications: A study of the focus of attention of top managers in surviving and failing firms. *Administrative Science Quarterly, 35,* 634–657.

D'Aveni, R. A. (1994). *Hypercompetition: Managing the dynamics of strategic maneuvering.* New York, NY: Free Press.

Desai, V. M. (2008). Constrained growth: How experience, legitimacy, and age influence risk taking in organizations. *Organization Science, 19,* 594–608.

Eggers, J. P., & Kaplan, S. (2009). Cognition and renewal: Comparing CEO and organizational effects on incumbent adaptation to technical change. *Organization Science, 20,* 461–477.

Eisenhardt, K. M., Furr, N. R., & Bingham, C. B. (2010). Microfoundations of performance: Balancing efficiency and flexibility in dynamic environments. *Organization Studies, 21,* 1263–1273.

Fiol, M. (1995). Corporate communications: Comparing executives' private and public statements. *Academy of Management Journal, 38,* 522–536.

Fleming, L. (2001). Recombinant uncertainty in technological search. *Management Science, 47,* 117–132.

Gavetti, G., Levinthal, D., & Ocasio, W. (2007). Neo-Carnegie: The Carnegie school's past, present, and reconstructing for the future. *Organization Science, 18,* 523–536.

Gerhart, B., & Rynes, S. L. (2003). *Compensation: Theory, evidence, and strategic implications.* Thousand Oaks, CA: Sage.

Greve, H. R. (2003). *Organizational learning from performance feedback.* Cambridge, UK: Cambridge University Press.

Greve, H. R. (2007). Exploration and exploitation in product innovation. *Industrial and Corporate Change, 5,* 945–975.

Gupta, A. K., Smith, K. G., & Shalley, C. E. (2006). The interplay between exploration and exploitation. *Academy of Management Journal, 49,* 693–706.

Hambrick, D. C., & Fukutomi, G. D. S. (1991). The seasons of a CEO's tenure. *Academy of Management Journal, 29,* 695–714.

Harris, J., & Bromiley, P. (2007). Incentives to cheat: Influence of executive compensation and firm performance on financial misrepresentation. *Organization Science, 18,* 50–367.

Hu, S., Blettner, D., & Bettis, R. A. (2011). Adaptive aspirations: Performance consequences of risk preferences at extremes and alternative reference groups. *Strategic Management Journal, 32,* 1426–1436.

Huff, A. S., & Schwenk, C. R. (1990). Bias and sensemaking in good times and bad. In A. Huff (Ed.). *Mapping strategic thought.* New York, NY: John Wiley and Sons.

Iyer, D. N., & Miller, K. D. (2008). Performance feedback, slack, and the timing of acquisitions. *Academy of Management Journal, 51,* 808–822.

Jaw, Y. L., & Lin, W. T. (2009). Corporate elite characteristics and firm's internationalization: CEO-level and TMT-level roles. *International Journal of Human Resource Management, 20,* 220–233.

Jordan, A. H., & Audia, P. G. (2012). Self-enhancement and learning from performance feedback. *Academy of Management Review, 37,* 211–231.

Kabanoff, B., & Brown, S. (2008). Knowledge structures of prospectors, analyzers, and defenders: Content, structure, stability, and performance. *Strategic Management Journal, 29,* 149–171.

Kahneman, D., & Tversky, A. (1979). Prospect theory: An analysis of decision under risk. *Econometrica, 47,* 263–291.

Kaplan, S. (2008). Cognition, capabilities, and incentives: Assessing firm response to the fiber-optic revolution. *Academy of Management Journal, 51,* 672–695.

Kenny, D. A. (1975). Cross-lagged panel correlation: A test for spuriousness. *Psychological Bulletin, 82,* 887–903.

Labianca, G., Fairbank, J. F., Andrevski, G., & Parzen, M. (2009). Striving toward the future: Aspiration-performance discrepancies and planned organizational change. *Strategic Organization, 7,* 433–466.

Lant, T., & Shapira, Z. (2001). *Organizational cognition: Compensation and interpretation.* Mahwah, NJ: Lawrence Erlbaum Associates.

Lavie, D., Stettner, U., & Tushman, M. L. (2010). Exploration and exploitation within and across organizations. *Academy of Management Annals, 4,* 109–155.

Levinthal, D. A., & March, J. G. (1993). The myopia of learning. *Strategic Management Journal, 14,* 95–112.

Levy, O. (2005). The influence of top management team attention patterns on global strategic posture of firms. *Journal of Organizational Behavior, 26,* 797–819.

Li, P. P. (2010). Toward a learning-based view of internationalization: The accelerated trajectories of cross-border learning for latecomers. *Journal of International Management, 16,* 43–59.

Lien, D., & Balakrishnan, N. (2005). On regression analysis with data cleaning via trimming, winsorization, and dichotomization. *Communications in Statistics-Simulation and Computation, 34,* 839–849.

March, J. G. (1991). Exploration and exploitation in organizational learning. *Organization Science, 2,* 71–87.

Mckenny, A. F., Short, J. C., & Payne, G. T. (2013). Using computer-aided text analysis to elevate constructs: An illustration using psychological capital. *Organizational Research Methods, 16,* 152–184.

Michalisin, M. D. (2001). Validity of annual report assertions about innovativeness: An empirical investigation. *Journal of Business Research, 53,* 151–161.

Miles, R. E., & Snow, C. (1978). *Organizational strategy, structure and process.* New York, NY: McGraw Hill.

Mintzberg, H. (1978). Patterns in strategy formation. *Management Science, 9,* 934–948.

Narayanan, V. K., Zane, L. J., & Kemmerer, B. (2011). The cognitive perspective in strategy: An integrative review. *Journal of Management, 37,* 305–351.

Ocasio, W. (1995). The enactment of economic adversity: A reconciliation of theories of failure-induced change and threat-rigidity. *Research in Organizational Behavior, 17,* 287–331.

Ocasio, W. (1997). Towards an attention-based view of the firm. *Strategic Management Journal, 18,* 187–206.

Ocasio, W. (2011). Attention to attention. *Organization Science, 22,* 1286–1296.

Osborne, J. D., Stubbart, C. I., & Ramaprasad, A. (2001). Strategic groups and competitive enactment: A study of dynamic relationships between mental models and performance. *Strategic Management Journal, 22,* 435–454.

Powell, T. C., Lovallo, D., & Fox, C. R. (2011). Behavioral strategy. *Strategic Management Journal, 32,* 1369–1386.

Roberts, P. W. (1999). Product innovation, product-market competition and persistent profitability in the U.S. pharmaceutical industry. *Strategic Management Journal, 20,* 655–670.

Roberts, P. W., & Dowling, G. R. (2002). Corporate reputation and sustained superior financial performance. *Strategic Management Journal, 23,* 1077–1093.

Salancik, G. R., & Meindl, J. (1984). Corporate attributions as strategic illusions of management control. *Administrative Science Quarterly, 29,* 238–254.

Sanders, W. G. (2001). Behavioral responses of CEOs to stock ownership and stock option pay. *Academy of Management Journal, 44,* 477–492.

Shinkle, G. A. (2012). Organizational aspirations, reference points, and goals: Building on the past and aiming for the future. *Journal of Management,* 38, 415–455.

Short, J. C., Broberg, J. C., Cogliser, C. C., & Brigham, K. H. (2010). Construct validation using computer-aided text analysis. *Organizational Research Methods, 13,* 320–347.

Short, J. C., & Palmer, T. B. (2003). Organizational performance referents: An empirical examination of their content and influences. *Organizational Behavior and Human Decision Processes, 90,* 209–234.

Sitkin, S. B., & Weingart, L. R. (1995). Determinants of risky decision-making behavior: A test of the mediating role of risk perceptions and propensity. *Academy of Management Journal, 38,* 1573–1592.

Staw, B. M., Sandelands, L. E., & Dutton, J. E. (1981). Threat-rigidity effects in organizational behavior: A multilevel analysis. *Administrative Science Quarterly, 26,* 501–524.

Tuggle, C. S., Schnatterly, K., & Johnson, R. A. (2010). Attention patterns in the boardroom: How board composition and processes affect discussion of entrepreneurial issues. *Academy of Management Journal, 53,* 550–571.

Uotila, J., Maula, M., Keil, T., & Zahra, S. A. (2009). Exploration, exploitation, and organizational performance: Analysis of S&P 500 corporations. *Strategic Management Journal, 30,* 221–231.

Van Noordt, S. J. R., & Segalowitz, S. J. (2012). Performance monitoring and the medial prefrontal cortex: A review of individual differences and context effects as a window on self-regulation. *Frontiers in Human Neuroscience, 6,* 1–16.

Walsh, J. P. (1995). Managerial and organizational cognition: Notes from a trip down memory lane. *Organization Science, 6,* 280–321.

Washburn, M., & Bromiley, P. (2012). Comparing aspiration models: The role of selective attention. *Journal of Management Studies, 49,* 896–917.

Yadav, M. S., Prabhu, J. C., & Chandy, R. K. (2007). Managing the future: CEO attention and innovation outcomes. *Journal of Marketing, 71,* 84–101.

Zellner, A. (1962). An efficient method of estimating seemingly unrelated regressions and test for aggregation bias. *Journal of the American Statistical Association, 57*, 48–368.

CHAPTER 3

COOPERATIVE BEHAVIOR IN STRATEGIC DECISION MAKING

Human Capital and Personality Traits

Gjalt de Jong
Jan Veijer

ABSTRACT

It has often been observed that people cooperate more than they would be expected to according to standard assumptions of individual rationality. In part, this empirical anomaly is due to the unrealistic assumptions concerning human behavior in economic models. Our study aims to offer new foundations for strategic decision-making behavior of individuals. We argue that human capital and personality traits are key in deciding whether or not to cooperate with a counterpart. Furthermore, we argue that the effect of a particular personality trait—that is, locus of control—on cooperative behavior is moderated by the level of human capital. The hypotheses are tested using Prisoner's Dilemma games in an experiment with 182 university students. The results report significant direct effects of human capital and locus of control on cooperation and confirm the moderating relationship between the two.

Behavioral Strategy: Emerging Perspectives, pages 55–78

Internals tend to cooperate more when having high levels of human capital. For externals, the effect is opposite, that is, externals tend to cooperate more when having low levels of human capital. In so doing, we open the black box of individual decision-making behavior and contribute to a growing field of behavioral strategy research that aims to strengthen the empirical relevance and practical usefulness of management theory.

INTRODUCTION

Decisions are the cornerstone of strategy (Powell, 2011). In strategic management, decisions concerning cooperation with counterparts are key. It has often been observed that people cooperate more than they would be expected to according to standard assumptions of individual rationality (Jones, 1999). Evidence from research in the field of psychology reveals that people do not always act as rational like the *homo economicus* in mainstream economic theory (Annen, 2003). This triggered a need to reconsider the foundations with regards to decision-making. Behavioral strategy applies cognitive and social psychology to management challenges in order to overcome the empirical contradictions (see, for example, Powell, Lovallo, & Fox, 2011 for a review of the recent literature). Scholars in this field aim to bring realistic assumptions about human cognition and social behavior to strategic management decision processes. This chapter contributes to this relatively new but fast growing research tradition. We study the relationship between locus of control, human capital, and cooperative behavior in the setting of social dilemma games. Locus of control is among the most important personality traits of top managers. We argue that the relationship between locus of control and cooperative behavior is moderated by human capital. In so doing, we offer an explanation why people in the "real world"—unlike the "rational machines" in many of the economic models—are predisposed towards cooperation.

Economic theory assumes that economic agents behave according two assumptions: (a) they behave according to the normative rational model; and (b) everyone behaves, ceteris paribus, in the same way. With regard to the first assumption, Mason, Philips and Redington (1991) already have shown that people do not always act as rational as predicted by the modeled behavior; a result that has been consistently confirmed in experimental economics (Pothos, Perry, Corr, Matthew, & Busemeyer, 2011). For example, game theory predicts that in finite Prisoner's Dilemma games, people will never cooperate. The reason for this is that players know at the start of the game that the other player will defect in the last period. Given this knowledge, rational players will defect in the last round of the game, because there is no reason to build a reputation of cooperation in this game (Rasmusen, 2001). The same logic can be applied by backward induction to every round of the game, including the first round. Experimental research, however, shows that cooperation does appear in finitely repeated Prisoner's Dilemma games (Pruitt & Kimmel, 1977, Raiffa, 1982). Apparently, not all players act according to the rationale of backward induction.

This chapter aims to explain differences in cooperative behavior (Boone, De Brabander, & Van Witteloostuijn, 1999a, 1999b; Boone & Van Witteloostuijn, 1999). We empirically test whether human capital and personality characteristics matter for cooperative behavior. We use the Prisoner's Dilemma to model cooperative behavior because it offers an ideal context to understand the antecedents of competitive vis-à-vis cooperative behavior (Biermand & Fernandez, 1993; Lefcourt, 1982; Raiffa, 1982). Our key contributions are twofold. First, we include human capital as an explanatory variable for cooperative behavior. Human capital is defined as the accumulation of knowledge and skills as a result of education and experience (Becker, 1975). Human capital is accumulated over time and constitutes an inclination towards particular behavior. Among others, this perspective is part of cognitive economics (Egidi & Rizzello, 2003), which studies how individual and organizational learning shapes social phenomena. Although the concept is well known and appreciated as an important factor that, for instance, predicts corporate success (Ployhart, Van Iddenkinge, & Mackenzie, 2011), little is known as to how human capital adds to the explanation of cooperative behavior. We aim to fill this research gap. We argue that based on accumulated experience people may have developed an inclination towards cooperation (or defection). Over time people can show alternated patterns of behavior due to learning modifications.

Second, we include personality traits in our study of cooperative behavior. In contrast to the concept of human capital—that can be regarded as a nurtured or learned characteristic—personality capital reflects human nature and is relatively stable over time and situations (Brocklebank, Lewis, & Bates, 2011). In recent years, strategy scholars have used a personality capital perspective to explain deviating from predicted behavior. The Big Five trait theory, for example, reveals a positive relationship between extraversion, neuroticism, and cooperative behavior (Hirsh & Petersen, 2009). We contribute to this research by focusing on another personality trait, that is, locus of control. Locus of control is identified as one of the key characteristics differentiating so-called internal from external type of managers. Although locus of control received empirical support in the experimental literature (Cook & Chi, 1984; Cook & Sloane, 1985; Boone et al. 1999a, 1999b, 2002), the role of internals and externals in explaining cooperative behavior is to an important extent still ambiguous (Egidi & Narduzzo, 1997). We aim to address this research gap and suggest that human capital may moderate the effect of locus of control on cooperative behavior. That is, we suggest that the level of human capital serves as an important prerequisite for the effect of personality capital on cooperative behavior. To the best of our knowledge, this perspective has not been addressed in the literature.

The outline of this chapter is as follows. In Section two, we elaborate on the theoretical background of this research and present the hypotheses. Section three explains the methods used to test the hypotheses and provides details of the games, experimental procedures and measures. Subsequently, we present and discuss the results. The chapter ends with conclusions and suggestions for future research.

THEORETICAL BACKGROUND AND HYPOTHESES

Human Capital

Human capital is defined as the accumulation of knowledge and skills as a result of formal education and experience (Becker, 1975; Becker & Murphy, 2000). In mainstream economics, the mechanism of learning is explained as the ability of individuals to make rational decisions (Perez, 2000). In that sense, learning is a mechanism to reduce errors in decision-making. Cognitive economics applies a more general view and argues that learning is a mechanism that explains any modification of individual behavior as a result of experience. These different perspectives are reflected in the experimental approaches. In the mainstream view, learning is used as a solution to *reduce* irrational behavior. The cognitive perspective uses learning to *explain* irrational behavior. When having developed a successful routine, people apply the learned principles in different contexts (Egidi & Narduzzo, 1997), but those routines not necessarily have to be the most optimal ones. Human capital can therefore be viewed as a path dependent process. In the context of this study, some people might have developed a routine of cooperation whereas others might have developed a routine of defection or competition. We label this routine an inclination towards a particular kind of behavior (i.e., an inclination towards cooperation positively formulating in light of cooperative behavior).

Various studies attribute differences in success for an individual, group or population to differences in human capital endowments (Mincer, 1970). Human capital is relevant because persons with superior human capital endowments are more astute in learning complicated situations and are better able to adjust to environmental contingencies (Boone et al., 2002). Given its intangible nature, human capital resources are difficult to imitate and to copy. Given this nature, and given that it is updated adequately; human capital is seen as a strategic resource, leading to improved performance and effectiveness (Ployhart et al., 2011). For this reason, human capital theory has been applied to understanding differences in organizational performance (Ang, Slaughter, & Ng, 2002; Buchholtz, Ribbens, & Haule, 2003; Watson, Steward, & BarNir, 2003), where human capital is regarded as essential for the long-term survival and growth of organizations (Pennings, Lee, & Van Witteloostuijn, 1998). Organizations that possess superior human capital are more able to plan effectively and solve problems (Florin, Lubatkin, & Schultz, 2003), are better able to adapt to environmental contingencies (Snell & Dean, 1992; Youndt, Snell, Dean, & Lepak, 1996), and find innovative ways to increase customer's benefits (Chandler & Hanks, 1998).

Human capital as a learning concept has been linked to various social phenomena. Novarese (2007), for example, studied the effect of learning on individual behavior in a "Sum 10" experiment that made use of cooperation and coordination in teams. In addition, the experiment included different social contexts that served as training situations for artificial agents. The results indicated that different training situations resulted in heterogeneous behavior among participants. Furthermore, participants tended to replicate the choices that initially proved to be successful. Haselhuhn, Pope, Schweiter and Fishman (2012) studied the relationship between personal experiences and behavior in an appealing study with evidence from video rental fines. Using a field setting with longitudinal data, they unraveled the effects of learning new information from the effects of personal experience. Their results indicate that experience with a fine, and controlling for the effect of new information, has a positive effect on future compliance, whereas a large fine has a greater effect than experience with a small fine. These principles of learning are also recently empirically demonstrated in the field of behavioral finance. This literature merely illustrates the reinforcement learning heuristic, which proposes that increased weight is placed on past strategies that have proven to be successful, even if this past success logically does not imply future success. For example, Kaustia and Knüpfer (2008) illustrate that Finnish investors are inclined to subscribe to future Initial Public Offerings (IPOs) if they previously experienced high returns in their IPO subscriptions. Malmendier and Nagel (2007) emphasize low-frequency responses to differences in return experiences across birth cohorts. Their results indicate that cohorts that have experienced relatively high stock market returns hold more stocks, whereas cohorts that have experienced high inflation prefer to hold fewer bonds.

The aforementioned empirical results are exemplary for the relevance of human capital for decision-making behavior. People tend to be biased by their experience and therefore become inclined to show particular behavior that can be related to accumulated human capital. Further, this inclination towards particular behavior does not necessarily lead to the most optimal results. People can make suboptimal decisions based on their accumulated capital. This results in a path-dependent accumulation of human capital that drives particular behavior in social phenomena. In our research setting of Prisoner's Dilemma games, this might be one of the reasons why some people have an inclination towards cooperation or defection, regardless of whether cooperation or defection is the most optimal strategy.

In studies like ours that use students as research subjects, a common applied variable to address human capital is the extent to which participants are exposed to cooperative courses. Courses from economics (such as game theory) often emphasize the self-interest model of economics, whereas business courses (such as organizational behavior) highlight the concepts from cooperation. Experimental research also reveals that economics students, compared to students from other disciplines such as sociology and psychology, tend to be more self-interested and show more free riding behavior in experiments that request for private contributions to public goods (Frank et al., 1993). Furthermore, economics students make generally less cooperative choices in PD-games then students from other disciplines. In line with Boone and Van Witteloostuijn (1999) we argue that not every student is exposed to cooperative courses to the same extent. Therefore, we distinguish between students who attended economic courses emphasizing the self-interest model, and students who attended courses that stress cooperation. We hypothesize that students exposed to cooperative courses tend to reveal more cooperative behavior than students less exposed to cooperative courses. This results in the first hypothesis:

> **Hypothesis 1:** *Prior exposure to cooperative courses is positively related to cooperative behavior.*

Personality Traits

We include personality traits to explain decisions with respect to cooperative behavior. Over the years, psychology has identified a large number of personality traits. Experimental research suggests personality traits should meet the three criteria in order to explain behavior, that is, relevant traits are (i) stable characteristics of human beings that (ii) have a relevant effect on cooperative behavior while, (iii) easily measurable with validated instruments (Boone et al., 1999a). Further, it has also been argued that traits especially become dominant in "weak" situations rather than "strong" situations (Weiss & Adler, 1984). This means that personality can particularly predict behavior when the environment is uncertain or ambiguous or, in other words, weak. When there are enough cues for appropriate behavior, the situation is described as strong, personality traits will have less or even no significant influence on decisions. In this chapter, we study locus of control.

Rotter (1954) developed the locus of control perspective based on social learning theory. Locus of control refers to the individual's belief in internal or external control of reinforcements (Rotter, 1966). People who believe in external control (externals) view themselves as relatively passive agents and believe that the events in their lives are due to relatively uncontrollable external forces. Externals perceive their desired achievements dependent upon luck, chance and powerful persons or institutions. They perceive a low probability of being able to control their lives by their own decisions and efforts. Conversely, people who believe in internal control (internals), see themselves as active agents, and feel that they can master their outcomes and trust their capacity to influence their environment. Internals believe that they control events and are able to influence their lives by effort and skill. In line with this perspective, it can be hypothesized that internals are more likely to cooperate in PD situations because of their inclination to take risk.

This trait has been included in different experiments of cooperative behavior, albeit that mixed findings are reported. Cook and Chi (1984), for instance, studied the relationship between locus of control and cooperative behavior among children. Their results suggest that external children are more cooperative then internal ones. This result is supported by the study of Bialer (1961), who argued that internal children's "greater awareness of their roles in their own success and failures cause them to strive harder. This may be described as growth in competitiveness." Internals, who believe that they can control events, will adopt a more competitive style of play when they think that competitiveness will pay off. On the other hand, externals believe that they have little control over the events and therefore show a dependency on others and cooperate passively (Cook & Sloane, 1985). These findings with children are used as input for hypotheses involving adults. Boone et al. (1999b), for example, found that locus of control correlates negatively with the number of cooperative choices. Since the Rotter index that is used in their study is scored towards externals, this means that on average internal people make more cooperative choices than external people. In a multivariate analysis, the authors find a positive effect for locus of control on the probability of cooperation. This result contradicts the finding of locus of control and cooperation among children as found by Cook and Sloane (1985). However, Boone et al. (1999b) found no evidence that internals are more cooperative than externals or vice versa. They explain this finding by suggesting that internals use both competitive and cooperative behavior to determine the valued outcome of the games. Externals, on the other hand, are less capable of using cooperative behavior as a means towards that end (Boone et al., 2002). Nevertheless, given that the arguments and evidence generally favor a fostering effect of internals on cooperative behavior, we hypothesize:

Hypothesis 2: *Being internal in locus of control is positively related with cooperative behavior.*

Contingency Perspective

While the existing literature thus indicates that human capital and locus of control plays an essential role in cooperative behavior one way or another, no study has addressed human capital as a moderator to explain the locus of control—cooperative behavior relationship. It is likely that human capital and locus of control are contingent, or in other words, one of both might exclude or reinforce the effect of the other on cooperative behavior. As mentioned above, personality traits mainly have an effect on cooperation in weak situations. From that perspective, people who have accumulated much human capital in a particular area might act as in a strong situation in that particular area, compared to people that have accumulated less human capital but who have identical personality traits.

Contemporaneous experimental research focuses on antecedents of cooperative behavior in isolation. We suggest a contingency approach, combining various characteristics in one model to develop a more complete theory of cooperative behavior, following in part the mixed empirical findings reported above. Therefore, we propose that the impact of personality characteristics on cooperative behavior is conditional on other factors (i.e., human capital). Based on the theory of cognitive economics, conceptualized by human capital and the subsequent inclination towards particular strategies, we expect that previous experience and education with respect to cooperative behavior will have a strong effect on the propensity to cooperate or defect in our PD setting.

Human capital is knowledge accumulated from education and experience that shapes future decisions (either optimal or suboptimal). In that sense, people who developed a cooperative attitude through education will have a higher inclination towards cooperation than people who did not develop such attitude or, on the contrary, those who developed an inclination towards competition through competitive experiences. Using human capital as the point of departure, we can further take into account personality traits to find a more comprehensive explanation of decision-making behavior. In particular, this implies that with different levels of human capital, people with an internal or an external locus of control will show different patterns of cooperative behavior. Therefore, we expect that human capital will moderate the relation between locus of control and cooperative behavior.

Previous research reports that overall, internals are more associated with cooperation than externals (Boone et al., 1999a). Our second hypothesis therefore suggests that, ceteris paribus, internals will cooperate more than externals. Boone et al. (2002) discovered a pattern of learning over different rounds of games. It appeared that internals cooperate more than externals, but externals converge to an identical level of cooperation over the course of the game. This is important because it suggests that with playing different PD games over time, human capital (knowledge) with respect to the most profitable strategy (i.e., cooperation) in PD games is developed.

Therefore, we can expect that internals who also have a background in cooperative courses, have a higher inclination towards cooperation then internals who lack a background in cooperative courses. Internals benefit from this background, which implies a default inclination towards cooperation, and take advantage of this by choosing a strategy of cooperation. In that sense, internals are able to put their background into perspective and choose for themselves how to apply these concepts that they have learned or experienced. Internals that lack exposure to cooperative courses will be less able to use their human capital as a means to support their (non) cooperative strategy.

Theoretically, we expect a different effect for externals. Externals are much more expected to rely on their environment than internals. Remember that externals perceive their desired achievements to be dependent upon luck, chance, and powerful persons or institutions. Therefore, they might be more passive in initiating cooperative behavior, fearing that the counterparty will defect (Cook & Sloane, 1985). A precise prediction concerning the moderating effect of human capital on cooperative behavior for externals is challenging. On the one hand, in case of high levels of human capital, externals might cooperate to the same extent as internals, since they both have a strong cooperative inclination, which makes a situation strong and thereby dwindles the role of locus of control. On the other hand, and still taking into account high levels of human capital, externals might be more confused of the possible downsides of cooperative behavior (i.e., the threat of opportunism). As a consequence of this fear, externals can choose to refrain from cooperation and decide to wait for their counterpart to initiate cooperation first.

In sum, we argue that the moderating effect of human capital on the relationship between locus of control and cooperative behavior will have the strongest effects for internals. If we can separate the effects of locus of control from human capital then we expect to see an enlarged effect when a person is internal and has a high level of human capital. Hence, the impact of locus of control on cooperative behavior is contingent on cooperative inclination. Locus of control fosters cooperation for internals with high levels of cooperative education because those people are able to use their background as a means towards an end in that they believe that they can influence their desired outcomes. Therefore, based on their cognitive background, internals choose the strategy that in their judgment is the most effective. Internals with a lower level of human capital, and thus have a lower cooperative inclination, will show a smaller pattern of cooperative behavior because these internals will have less awareness of their abilities to use cooperative behavior and are therefore more prone to strategies that deviate from cooperative behavior. Consequently, our final hypothesis is stated as follows:

> **Hypothesis 3:** *Internals with a high inclination towards cooperation will cooperate more than internals who have a lower inclination towards cooperation.*

METHODS

Games

As is common in experimental research, we used undergraduate students as our study subjects (for a discussion about the use of undergraduate students in research see, for example, Boone et al., 1999a, 1999b, 2002; Frank, Gilovich, & Regan, 1993; Schlenker, Helm, & Tedeschi, 1973). The experiment was conducted during a four-week course on statistical methods for second-year students of management and organization at the Dutch University of Groningen. The four-week course was part of a new curriculum, and only those students who had passed the first-year programme were allowed to participate. At the outset of the experiment students filled out a digital questionnaire, revealing background and personality information. The experiment was conducted during the first week of the course, and saw 182 management and organization students play five different PD games in a row. The average age of the subjects was 19.65 and 66% of the participants were male. We only told the students that the experiment was designed to deepen their and our understanding of behaviour in a game theory setting. The students were promised feedback on the main findings of the research project after completion of the four-week course. We also guaranteed strict confidentiality of the questionnaire information. The five PDs were presented to the subjects in a fixed order for the sake of simplicity. The order of presentation and the main characteristics of the games are summarized in Table 3.1.

Each game consists of 12 rounds of choosing, except for Game III that has an unknown horizon, ending at random after 13 rounds. In the first two games, subjects played against a fictitious party, receiving no information about the choices made by that party in each round. Therefore, these games were essentially "one-shot" or non-interactive games. In the last three games, dyads were randomly formed and the subjects played interactive repeated games. Here, choices were made simultaneously and independently in each round, after which the subjects were informed of the choice made by the

TABLE 3.1 Main Characteristics of Experimental Games

Game #	Type of game	Main characteristics of game
I	"One-shot"	12 choices (low or high price) against fictitious party No information on past behavior of other party Baseline game
II	"One-shot"	12 choices (low or high price) against fictitious party Information on past behavior of other party
III	Repeated	Subjects make independent and simultaneous choices in each round Exchange of choices made by other parties after each round Unknown horizon ("infinite" game) Final payoff equals sum of payoff in each round
IV	Repeated	Same as game III, except horizon that is finite and known (12 rounds)
V	Repeated	Same as game IV, except payoff matrix that is changed to elicit cooperation

other party. Game III has a so-called infinite horizon as the subjects were not informed about the game's end round (i.e., Game III ended at random). The fourth game was similar to Game III, except for our announcing in advance that the game would end in round 12. In the last game, we changed the values of the payoff matrix used in all the other games so that the incentive to cooperate might increase in the eyes of the players. The horizon of game V was, again, finite and known to be 12 rounds. The instructions and game payoff matrices can be found in the Appendix.

The first two non-interactive games can be considered as baseline measures of cooperative behaviour. Both measures give an impression of the subjects' basic inclination to pursue a competitive or a cooperative strategy. In the second game, we manipulated the reputation of the other fictitious party by suggesting that this party was trustworthy because he or she had made cooperative choices in each of the twelve rounds in the previous encounter (i.e., cooperative feedback). We expected baseline cooperation to drop because opportunism is rooted in Western societies. Subsequently, in the last three repeated games, we expected cooperation on average to gradually gain importance. When players are engaged in repeated interaction with another party, they quickly learn to cooperate, and often enter into tacit collusion, irrespective of whether the game's horizon is known or not.

Experimental Procedure

The experiments were conducted in a large room. In the room there were three groups and each group had three rows of paired tables. The pairs of tables were separated by the space of one table. When entering the room, the students were randomly distributed across the three groups and within the three groups using the seats available. Pairs of subjects were formed to play the repeated PD games (i.e., the last three games in Experiments I and II). These dyads consisted of students sitting side-by-side. One experimenter and two assistants, identifiable by their similar shirts, guided each of the three groups. The assistants handed out the various information forms while the experimenter remained in front of the group for the entire experiment. All the groups started the experiment at the same clock time.

The PD was presented as an oligopoly-pricing problem. The experimenter first announced that five games were to be played, and that detailed information about each game would be provided just before that game started. He then presented and explained the general payoff structure of the first game (see the Appendix). The subjects could make two choices: setting a low price (corresponding to a competitive choice) or setting a high price (corresponding to a cooperative choice). The instructional phase fully and redundantly explained the interdependent nature of the payoffs, so that the consequences of different combinations of choices were clearly understood. We avoided the use of terms like "compete," "cooperate," "defect," and "sucker," so as to ensure a neutral instructional setting.

The experimenter, who gave instructions as to when and how to make choices in each game, strictly controlled the pace of the experiment. The subjects received a booklet with the instructions for each game and a corresponding response sheet. With the use of slides, the experimenter clarified each instruction at the beginning of each game. As mentioned above, Games I and II involved making twelve choices in a row against a fictitious party. At the beginning of Game III, the experimenter announced each subject's opponent/partner for the three repeated games. The subjects each received a booklet with small blank sheets of notepaper and were instructed in each round to choose independently and simultaneously. Next, the subjects had to write down their choice on the aforementioned blank paper. Once each subject had written down his or her choice, the experimenter instructed the parties to exchange notes. Following this exchange, the subjects noted their own choice, their opponent's choice and their payoff on a response sheet. This procedure was repeated for each round in the three interactive games. Of course, apart from the exchange of notes, no communication was allowed.

Following standard experimental gaming (e.g., Boone et al., 1999a; Pruitt & Kimmel, 1977; Schlenker et al., 1973), the subjects were instructed to maximize their payoff during the experiment. Additionally, although experimental psychology has repeatedly revealed that subjects take experiments very seriously in any event, we introduced an extra motivational incentive by announcing that the top five players in accumulated payoff terms would receive a music voucher. We also appealed to a social prestige motive by telling the subjects that the ranking of payoffs, including the players' names, would be announced in public in a final plenary session at the end of the four-week course, both on a bulletin board and on the Faculty's student internet homepages.

Measurements

Independent Variable

Following other researchers (Boone et al., 1999a, 1999b; Cox, Lobel, & McLeod, 1991), we computed the total number of cooperative choices in each game as the measure of our independent variable: cooperative behaviour. Recall that 13 rounds were played in Game III. In order to standardize measures over the five games, we multiplied the total number of cooperative choices in Game III by the ratio 12/13.

Human Capital

Three binary indicators were created to capture the respondents' human capital. The first indicator measured whether the respondent attended a science-type high school prior to enrolment at University on a single binary variable (coded as 1, 0 otherwise). Prior knowledge and exposure to competition or cooperation was measured with two variables. The students received a list of nine courses and they were asked to mark the courses they had already followed. Our assessment of the course content revealed that three courses (i.e., economic principles, law principles and transactions) emphasized the self-interest economic model (i.e., competition) whereas three other courses (i.e., organizational behaviour, international transformation processes and communication) also stressed the importance of cooperation in economic life. We used two ordinal measures (ranging from 0 to 3) to measure exposure to competitive or cooperative courses.

Locus of Control

We measured locus of control with an adapted version of Rotter's original scale that contains 37 forced items (23 of those items being designed to measure locus of control expectancies and 14 being filler items that conceal the purpose of the test). Each item consists of a pair of statements where the respondent has to choose between an "internal" and an "external" alternative. A total locus of control score is obtained by counting the number of external alternatives chosen (with minimum 0 and maximum 23). The Cronbach's alpha of 0.65 is well above the lower limits of acceptability in experimental research, generally considered to be in the 0.50 to 0.60 range (Nunnally, 1978; Robinson & Shaver, 1973; Rotter, 1966).

Control Variables

We included several control variables that are widely agreed upon as having an influence on cooperative behavior. One of the variables is age, for which is found that cooperation increases with age (Cook & Sloane, 1985). The older people are, the more likely they believe that others try to be fair and helpful, which makes them more cooperative (Gächter et al., 2004). The other control variable included is gender, because females are generally found to be more cooperative than males (Mason et al., 1991). In this study, males are coded as 0 and females are coded as 1.

Finally, we included various proxies of social capital. Social capital is broadly conceptualized as the benefit that social actors derive from their social structures (Coleman, 1990). From that perspective, social capital refers to trust, concern for one's connections and a motivation to live according to the norms of the community (Bowles & Gintis, 2001). The literature indicates that religious background, family situations and local community types are important dimensions of social capital. We include three dummies to account for this, that is, a dummy for whether the subject is from a religious family or not, a dummy for whether the subject is from a large family or not, and a dummy for whether the subject is from a southern community type or not. Although different religions may have different effects on people's attitudes, on average, religion is associated positively with attitudes that are conducive to cooperative behaviour. It appears that being brought up in a larger family dilutes young people's sense of urgency about playing and associating outside the family group, thereby making young people from large families more parochial and limited in their understanding of a variety of social roles. Various studies have reported the norm-enforcing effects of communities with a strong social closure environment. More specifically, it has been argued that there are important differences between southern and northern European communities. Southern community types are associated with low levels of trust and a less inclination to cooperate.

RESULTS

We interpreted the data as a pool cross-section/time series sample. This results in 6,553 observations. The dependent variable is a dummy variable, representing the choice that each individual makes during the 37 trails of the last three games (0 = competitive choice, 1 = cooperative choice). We performed a logistic regression analysis, to predict the likelihood of cooperation in each trail. To incorporate the dynamics of the game, two additional variables are included in the first model (1), the trail number (TRAIL) and a lag variable for the choice of the opponent in the previous round (LAGALT). The first variable corrects for the increase in the number of cooperative choices over the course of the experiment. The lag variable corrects for the finding that people are inclined to cooperate when the opponent has been proven cooperative (Pruitt & Kimmel, 1977). Having included these variables, we can proceed assessing whether our personality trait of interest and human capital has an effect on cooperation irrespective of learning effects and the strategy of the opponent. A summary with descriptive statistics and correlations among all variables is presented in Table 3.2. The regression results are in Table 3.3.

In the first model, the dependent variable is regressed on the set of control variables. In the second model, the main effects are included, that is, exposition to cooperative courses (EXCOOP), exposition to competitive courses (EXCOMP) and locus of control (LOC). In the third model, the interaction term is added to investigate whether the combination of exposition to cooperative choices and locus of control has a stronger effect on the choice for cooperation. We mean-centered these variables before multiplying them.

The results of Model 1 confirm the importance of including the control variables in our model. For example, Model 1 shows that the likelihood of cooperation increases over the course of the game: the coefficient for TRAIL is positive and significant. Further, the variable LAGALT is also positive and significant, indicating that when the opponent cooperates, the player is inclined to cooperate as well. Model 1 shows that cooperation tends to increase with age and that females are less cooperative than males. The parameter estimates for science education also is positive and significant. All results for the control variables are in line with our expectations. The results for the control variables remain the same in all three models in terms of parameter estimates and significance levels, by and large.

In Models 2 and 3, the parameter estimates for the main effects for human capital (EXCOOP) and our personality trait locus of control (LOC) are significant. Exposure to cooperative courses is positively related to cooperation and locus of control is negatively related to cooperation. These results confirm Hypothesis 1 and Hypothesis 2. In Model 3, the interaction term is significant and negative. This implies that combining the effects of having attended cooperative courses and being internal in locus of control even further contributes to an inclination towards cooperation. A graphical interpretation of the interaction term (Ai & Norton, 2003) confirms Hypothesis 3. Our results show that internals who are exposed to many cooperative courses have a higher probability to cooperate than internals who are less exposed to cooperative courses. For externals the reverse is true: externals with a low inclination towards cooperation have a higher probability of cooperation than externals with a high inclination towards cooperation.

TABLE 3.2 Correlations, Means, and Standard Deviations

Variables	Mean	SD	1	2	3	4	5	6	7	8	9	10
1. Cooperation	5.48	2.24	1.00									
2. Religion	0.67	0.47	0.01	1.00								
3. Family	0.43	0.50	–0.08	0.19	1.00							
4. Southern community	0.26	0.44	–0.06	0.13	–0.05	1.00						
5. Science education exposure	0.30	0.46	0.09	0.02	0.06	0.11	1.00					
6. Cooperative exposure	2.20	0.96	–0.02	0.01	0.05	–0.02	0.10	1.00				
7. Competitive exposure	2.18	0.92	–0.09	–0.02	0.10	0.01	0.01	0.53	1.00			
8. Gender	0.34	0.37	–0.04	0.06	0.07	–0.01	0.02	0.11	0.01	1.00		
9. Age	19.65	1.04	0.05	–0.12	–0.15	–0.15	0.08	–0.10	–0.05	–0.03	1.00	
10. Locus of control	11.51	3.37	–0.04	0.03	–0.06	–0.13	0.08	0.09	–0.02	0.17	–0.07	1.00

[a] Correlation coefficients larger than 0.02 and 0.05 are significant at $p < 0.05$ and $p < 0.01$, respectively.

TABLE 3.3 Human Capital, Personality Traits and Decision-Making Behavior[a]

Variables	Research Model 1	Research Model 2	Research Model 3
Constant	–2.670***	–2.114***	–3.066***
	(0.531)	(0.559)	(0.601)
Trail	0.015***	0.016***	0.016***
	(0.003)	(0.003)	(0.003)
Other person's choice lagged	1.522***	1.513***	1.511***
	(0.054)	(0.054)	(0.055)
Gender	–0.117**	–0.112*	–0.122**
	(0.057)	(0.059)	(0.059)
Age	0.058***	0.072***	0.079**
	(0.026)	(0.027)	(0.027)
Religion	0.166***	0.157***	0.143**
	(0.059)	(0.060)	(0.060)
Large family	–0.265***	–0.245***	–0.273***
	(0.056)	(0.057)	(0.057)
Exposure to science education	0.461***	0.416***	0.403***
	(0.060)	(0.061)	(0.061)
Southern community type	–0.340***	–0.329***	–0.323***
	(0.108)	(0.109)	(0.110)
Exposure to cooperative courses		0.082**	0.478***
		(0.034)	(0.096)
Exposure to competitive courses		–0.220***	–0.202***
		(0.035)	(0.036)
Locus of control		–0.017**	–0.059***
		(–0.008)	(0.019)
Cooperative courses * locus of control			–0.037***
			(0.008)
-2 log likelihood	–4,008	–3,987	–3,977
model chi-square	1,055***	1,098***	1,118***
change chi-square	1,055***	43***	120***

[a] Standard errors in parentheses with $n = 6{,}553$
*** $p < 0.01$; ** $p < 0.05$; * $p < 0.10$

CONCLUSION

Behavioral strategy is concerned with the gap that is observed between management practice and strategy theory (Powell, Lovallo, & Fox, 2011; Elms, BRammer, Harris, & Phillips, 2010). A multidisciplinary approach cross fertilizing psychology and sociology into management and business theories has proven to be a successful path envisioned by behavioral and cognitive theories of the firm (Nooteboom, 2000) and leadership research that accounts for emotions, attribution and attention (Northouse, 2004). This chapter offers new foundations for strategy research by developing realistic assumptions about human cognition and personality and how these independently as well as in combination determine strategic decision-making behavior. In so doing, we answer the call for more research in this direction (Bingham & Eisenhardt, 2011; Powell, 2011).

One intention of this study was to develop hypotheses based on psychology and social research and test these with new data and proceed in further research by combining diverse relevant constitutes of human capital and personality traits into a more comprehensive theory of strategic decision-making. We convincingly found that human capital in the form of exposure to cooperative courses, constituting an inclination towards cooperation, is positively linked to cooperative behavior. Further, we found strong significant results for the relationship between being external in locus of control and cooperative behavior. However, that link is only based on regression estimations based on direct effects. We revealed that it is crucial to consider the variation among observations with respect to human capital. Especially computing the interaction term between exposure to cooperation and locus of control revealed that the relationships found for the first and second hypothesis can be complemented with a more advanced perspective.

Therefore, an important aim and subsequent result of this study is the contribution to a profound understanding of the interaction between human capital and personality traits, or in other words, further unraveling the underlying causal structure of strategic decision-making behavior. The direct relationships between human capital and cooperation and between locus of control and complemented with the combined significant constituents reveal a novel framework of strategic decisions. The combination of human capital (in the form of exposure to cooperative courses), the ensuing implied inclination towards cooperation, and personality traits (represented by locus of control), established a relevant rationale to improve our comprehension of cooperative behavior. The effect of locus of control on cooperative behavior is conditional on the exposure to cooperative courses and hence, the inclination towards cooperation that follows from education with regard to cooperation. In that sense, internals tend to cooperate more when they have a high inclination towards cooperation, benefiting from their background in cooperation and utilizing that background to use it as a means towards their own ends. For externals the results are opposite.

Our study is not without limitations that offer opportunities for future research. It is particularly worthwhile mentioning that we study one personality trait, locus of control. Locus of control is among the most important personality traits but it is acknowledged that individuals differ on other ones. It is a question to what extent our model also applies to other personality traits such as Type A persons or sensation seeking. Future research might continue in our strand of research, proceeding with the role of other personality traits individually as well as the relationship of these with human capital. Additionally, new studies may also analyze the relationship between personality traits and other characteristics of individuals such as gender, age or their family background and how this matter for decision-making processes. Finally, in line with experimental research, we used students as our research subjects. New research may also collect information from senior or junior managers and test whether our results and conclusions concerning personality traits and decision-making behavior also hold for these individuals. Such new efforts also enable to collect information for individual, team or organizational performance and as such test whether the causalities presented in this chapter also explain performance.

APPENDIX—GAME SETTINGS

Two firms operate in the same market: firms I and II. Both firms can choose between two price strategies: setting a low price and setting a high price. The profits depend on the pairs of strategies chosen. In the following payoff matrix, the four possible profit combinations (in thousands of Euros) are reported for Experiment I (P_i stands for the pricing strategy of firm i, with i = I, II).

		Firm II	
		Low price	High price
Firm I	Low price	(–30,–30)	(600,–600)
	High price	(–600,600)	(300,300)

Each cell contains the possible profit combinations (W_I, W_{II}). W_I and W_{II} are the (negative or positive) profits of Firm I and Firm II respectively. The four profit combinations are as follows:

1. P_I low = P_{II} low. Both firms choose to set the same low price. The profit margins are negative. Both firms generate a loss of EUR 30,000.
2. P_I low < P_{II} high. Firm I offers a lower price than Firm II. The Firm II's customers prefer to buy from the "cheaper" Firm I. The profit of Firm I is therefore EUR 600,000, and Firm II's losses amount to EUR 600,000.

3. P_I high > P_{II} low. Firm II undercuts Firm I. The resulting profit combination is the opposite of the second case. Firm I generates a loss of EUR 600,000 and Firm II a profit of EUR 600,000.
4. P_I high = P_{II} high. Both firms choose to set the same high price. The profit margins are positive. Both firms gain a profit of EUR 300,000.

Game I

Imagine you are Chief Executive Officer of Firm I. You decide autonomously on the pricing strategy of your company. You have an appointment with your distributor to fix the future pricing strategy for your product. It is a custom in this industry that contracts with distributors are concluded annually, in which the price level for each month (or round) for the coming year is stipulated in advance. It is impossible to change the terms of the contract afterwards. The Chief Executive Officer of Firm II will simultaneously determine her/his pricing strategy with her/his distributor (a different on from yours) for the following twelve months. You do not know the price intentions of Firm II and vice versa. Indicate your preferred strategy below (L indicates low price; H indicates high price) for each round (month).

Game II

At the end of the contract, you learn that Firm II has consistently chosen to set a high price in each month of the previous contracting period. Now, you have to agree a new contract with your distributor for the next twelve months. Indicate again which pricing strategy you prefer for each month.

Game III

Your information on the past intentions and pricing strategy of Firm II have become irrelevant because Firm II has been taken over by another company, which installed a new Chief Executive Officer. The government has also decided that contracts in which prices are set for more than one month in advance are now illegal. Therefore, for the next year you are only allowed to fix your price level for one month, after which you have to decide again for the next round. Decisions are made simultaneously in each month.

You play the game for an unknown number of months (rounds). You do not know in advance how many times you will have to make a decision on your pricing strategy. The game can end any moment after round 8. The probability that the game ends after round 8 is 20%. The sequence of decisions/activities you have to perform is as follows:

1. At the beginning of each round, the price strategies are set simultaneously and noted on the response sheet
2. Subsequently, swap sheets with your counterpart
3. Finally, calculate your own profit, given the strategy of the other firm.

Indicate for each month on your response sheet: (i) the strategy you prefer, (ii) the strategy of the other firm and (iii) the profit you gained. Except for the exchange of notes after each round, no communication is allowed during the experiment.

Game IV

Repeat Game III, but for 12 months (rounds).

Game V

In the following period of twelve months demand has increased substantially, along with an increased profit potential. This new situation is reflected in the following profit combinations (profits are in thousands of euros).

REFERENCES

Ai, C., & Norton, E. C. (2003). Interaction terms in logit and probit models. *Economic Letters, 80,* 123–129.

Ang, S., Slaughter, S., & Ng., K. Y. (2002). Human capital and institutional determinants of information technology compensation: Modeling multilevel and cross-level interactions. *Management Science, 48,* 1427–1445.

Annen, K. (2003). Social capital, inclusive networks, and economic performance. *Journal of Economic Behavior and Organization, 50,* 449–463.

Becker, G. (1975). *Human capital,* 2nd ed. Chicago: University of Chicago Press.

Becker, G. S., & Murphy, K. M. (2000). *Social economics: Market behavior in a social environment.* Cambridge, MA: Harvard University Press.

Bialer, I. (1961). Conceptualization of success and failure in mentally retarded and normal children. *Journal of Psychology, 29,* 303–320.

Bierman, H. S., & Fernandez, L., (1993). *Game theory with economic applications.* Reading, MA: Addison-Wesley.

Bingham, C. B., & Eisenhardt, K. M. (2011). Rational heuristics: The "simple rules" that strategists learn from process experience. *Strategic Management Journal, 32,* 1437–1464.

Boone, C., De Brabander, B., Carree, M., de Jong, G., van Olffen, W., & van Witteloostuijn, A. (2002). Locus of control and learning to cooperate in a prisoner's dilemma game. *Personality and Individual Differences, 32,* 929–946.

Boone, C., De Brabander, B. & van Witteloostuijn, A. (1999a). The impact of personality on behavior in five prisoner's dilemma games. *Journal of Economic Psychology, 20,* 343–377.

Boone, C., De Brabander, B., & van Witteloostuijn, A. (1999b). Locus of control and strategic behavior in a prisoner's dilemma game. *Personality and Individual Differences, 27,* 695–706.

Boone, C., & van Witteloostuijn, A. (1999). Competitive and opportunistic behavior in a Prisoner's Dilemma game: Experimental evidence on the impact of culture and education. *Scandinavian Journal of Management, 15,* 333–350.

Bowles, S., & Gintis. H. (2001). Economic status, inheritance of: Education, class and genetics. *International Encyclopedia of the Social & Behavioral Sciences,* pp. 4132–4141.

Brocklebank, S., Lewis, G. J., & Bates C. T. (2011). Personality accounts for stable preferences and expectations across a range of simple games, *Personality and Individual Differences, 51,* 881–886.

Buchholtz, A. K., Ribbens, B. A., & Houle, I. T. (2003). The role of human capital in post acquisition CEO departure. *Academy of Management Journal, 46,* 506–514.

Chandler, G. N., & Hanks, S. H. (1998). An examination of the substitutability of founders' human and financial capital in emerging business ventures. *Journal of Business Venturing, 13,* 353–369.

Coleman, J. S. (1990). *Foundation of social theory.* Cambridge, MA: Cambridge University Press.

Cook, H., & Chi, C., (1984). Cooperative behavior and locus of control among American and Chinese-American boys. *Journal of Psychology, 118,* 197–177.

Cook, H., & Sloane, J. (1985). Locus of control and cooperative behavior in 10-year-old children. *Journal of Social Psychology, 125,* 619–630.

Cox, T. H., Lobel, S. A., & McLeod, P. L. (1991). Effects of ethnic group cultural differences on cooperative and competitive behavior on a group task. *Academy of Management Journal, 34,* 827–847.

Egidi, M. & Narduzzo, A. (1997). The emergence of path-dependent behaviors in cooperative contexts. *International Journal of Industrial Organization, 15,* 677–709.

Egidi, M., & Rizzello, S. (2003). *Cognitive economics [two volumes in the series. "The international library of critical writings in economics."* Aldershot, UK: Edward Elgar.

Elms, H., Brammer, S., Harris, J. D., & Phillips, R. A. (2010). New directions in strategic mangement and business ethics. *Business Ethics Quarterly, 20,* 401–425.

Florin, J., Lubatkin, M., & Schultz, W. (2003). A social capital model of high-growth ventures. *Academy of Management Journal, 46,* 374–384.

Frank, R. H. Gilovich, T., & Regan, D. T. (1993). Does studying economics inhibit cooperation? *Journal of Economic Perspectives, 7,* 159–171.

Gächter, S., Herrmann, B., & Thöni, C. (2004). Trust, voluntary cooperation, and socio-economic background: Survey and experimental evidence. *Journal of Economic Behavior and Organization, 55*, 505–531.

Haselhuhn, M. P., Pope, D. G., Schweiter, M. E., & Fishman, P. (2012). The impact of personal experience on behavior: Evidence from video-rental fines. *Management Science, 58(1)*, 52–61.

Hirsh, J. B., & Peterson, J. B. (2009). Extraversion, neuroticism, and the prisoner's dilemma. *Personality and Individual Differences, 46*(2), 254–256.

Jones, B. D. (1999). Bounded rationality. *Annual Review Political Science, 2*, 297–321.

Kaustia, M., & Knüpfer, S. (2008). Do investors overweight personal experience? Evidence from IPO subscriptions, *Journal of Finance, 63*, 2679–2702.

Lefcourt, H. M. (1982). *Locus of control: Current trends in theory and research* (2nd ed.). New York, NY: McGraw-Hill.

Malmendier, U., & Nagel, S. (2007). Depression babies: Do macroeconomic experiences affect risk-taking? Working paper, Stanford University.

Mason, C. F., Philips, O. R., & Redington, D. B. (1991). The role of gender in a non-cooperative game. *Journal of Economic Behavior and Organization, 15*, 215–235.

Mincer, J. (1970). The distribution of labor incomes. *Journal of Economic Literature, 8*, 1–26.

Nooteboom, B. (2000). *Learning and innovation in organizations and economies.* Oxford, UK: Oxford University Press.

Northouse, P. G. (2004). *Leadership theory and practice.* Thousand Oaks, CA: Sage Publications.

Novarese, M. (2007). Individual learning in different social contexts. *The Journal of Socio Economics, 36*, 15–35.

Nunnally, J. C. (1978). *Psychometric theory.* New York, NY: McGraw-Hill.

Pennings, J. M., Lee, K., & van Witteloostuijn, A. (1998). Human capital, social capital, and firm dissolution. *Academy of Management Journal, 41*, 425–440.

Perez, F. 2000. Private experience in adaptive learning models. *Review of Economic Dynamics, 3*(2), 228–310.

Ployhart, R. E., Van Iddekinge, C. H., & Mackenzie, W. I. (2011). Acquiring and developing human capital in service contexts: The interconnectedness of human capital resources. *Academy of Management Journal, 54*, 353–368.

Pothos, E. M., Perry, G., Corr, P. J., Matthew, M. R., & Busemeyer, J. R. (2011). Understanding cooperation in the Prisoner's Dilemma game. *Personality and Individual Differences, 51*(3), 210–215.

Powell, T. C. (2011). Neurostrategy. *Strategic Management Journal, 32*, 1484–1499.

Powell, T. C., Lovallo, D., & Fox, C. R. (2011). Behavioral strategy. *Strategic Management Journal, 32*, 1369–1386.

Pruitt, D., & Kimmel, M. (1977). Twenty years of experimental gaming: Critique, synthesis, and suggestions for the future. *Annual Review of Psychology, 28*, 363–392.

Raiffa, H., (1982). *The art and science of negotiation.* Cambridge, MA: Harvard University Press.

Rasmusen, E. (2001). *Games and information: An introduction to game theory* (3rd ed.). Cambridge, MA: Basil Blackwell.

Robinson, J. P., & Shaver, P. R. (1973). *Measures of social psychological attitudes.* Ann Arbor, MI: University of Michigan, Survey Research Center, Institute for Social Research.

Rotter, J. B. (1954). *Social Learning and clinical psychology.* Englewood Cliffs, NJ: Prentice-Hall.

Rotter, J. B. (1966). A new scale for the measurement of interpersonal trust. *Journal of Personality, 35,* 651–665.

Schlenker, B. R., Helm, B., & Tedeschi, J. T. (1973). The effects of personality and situational variables on behavioral trust. *Journal of Personality and Social Psychology, 25,* 419–427.

Snell, S. A., & Dean, J. W. J. (1992). Integrated manufacturing for human resource management: A human capital perspective. *Academy of Management Journal, 35,* 467–504.

Watson, W., Steward, W. H., & BarNir, A. (2003). The effects of human capital, organizational demography and interpersonal process on venture partner perceptions of firm profit and growth. *Journal of Business Venturing, 18,* 145–164.

Weiss, H. M. & Adler, S. (1984). Personality and organizational behavior. *Research in Organizational Behavior, 6,* 1–50.

Youndt, M. A., Snell, S. A., Dean, J. W. J., & Lepak, D. P. (1996). Human resource management, manufacturing strategy, and firm performance. *Academy of Management Journal, 39,* 836–866.

CHAPTER 4

DYNAMIC CAPABILITIES AND ORGANIZATIONAL CHANGE

An Integration

Sandip Basu
Suresh Kotha

ABSTRACT

Dynamic capabilities enable organizational change, which helps firms adapt better to their changing environments or impact their environments favorably through innovation. However, not much is known regarding the type of organizational changes that dynamic capabilities are more effective in enabling, and when these changes are beneficial for firms. In this conceptual study, we seek to address this important gap in the dynamic capabilities literature. We conceptualize organizational change as involving various degrees of discontinuity and permanence based on the extent to which existing resources are reconfigured and the new resource configurations are retained. We develop distinctions in types of organizational changes based on the extent of discontinuity and permanence that these involve. We first evaluate how the effectiveness of dynamic capabilities is likely to vary in implementing these different types of organizational change. We then elaborate how firms' adaptation requirements and innovative initiatives play a role in determining

Behavioral Strategy: Emerging Perspectives, pages 79–104

when the use of dynamic capabilities is beneficial for them. Subsequently, we argue that use of dynamic capabilities also impacts the capabilities' own evolution and thereby future effectiveness. Finally, we reorganize our theoretical propositions to develop a normative model that could be used to guide managers in the development and use of dynamic capabilities as well as to generate interesting streams of future academic research.

INTRODUCTION

Organizations often need to undertake significant internal changes to respond to opportunities and threats arising from their external environments (Guth & Ginsberg, 1990). Organizational changes are typically initiated in organizations' fundamental internal attributes, namely, their resources and capabilities (Makadok, 2001). Resources are a firm's tangible (e.g., plant and equipment, human capital) and intangible (e.g., reputation, knowledge, culture) assets that form inputs to its processes and eventually its products (Amit & Schoemaker, 1993; Barney, 1991). Capabilities, on the other hand, refer to value-chain activities that help firms achieve desired performance-related objectives. Capabilities are typically created by the retention and replication of specific combinations of resources (Dosi, Nelson, & Winter, 2000; Helfat & Lieberman, 2002).

While changing organizational form and function may be critical for future survival and prosperity (Rindova & Kotha, 2001), it is usually difficult for firms to discard their entrenched approaches to competition (Prahalad & Bettis, 1986). Behavioral strategy researchers have suggested that such organizational resistance to change results from limited cognition of managers about the implications of such changes (Fehr & Tyran, 2005; Thaler & Sunstein, 2008). Research grounded in the resource-based view and evolutionary economics have started focusing on the role of specialized capabilities, termed "dynamic capabilities," in bringing about critical yet difficult organizational changes. Dynamic capabilities, initially described in Teece, Pisano, and Shuen's (1997) seminal article, are distinct from the operating capabilities a firm uses to carry out primary business activities. These capabilities help organizations recognize and respond to emerging opportunities and threats (Helfat, Finkelstein, Mitchell, Peteraf, Singh, Teece, & Winter, 2007; Teece, 2007) and may be present as informal patterns of activity (Rosenbloom, 2000; Teece et al., 1997) or formal processes relating to functional areas (Eisenhardt & Martin, 2000; Zollo & Winter, 2002).

The growing research on dynamic capabilities encompasses three closely-related research streams. The first focuses on how dynamic capabilities bring about organizational change. Evidence from this work suggests that dynamic capabilities help firms configure their resources in novel ways and thereby modify other capabilities (Galunic & Eisenhardt, 2001; Henderson

& Clark, 1994; Karim & Mitchell, 2000, Zahra & George, 2002). The second illustrates how organizations develop effective dynamic capabilities. This work argues that dynamic capabilities are created through an evolutionary cycle of variation-selection-retention (Benner & Tushman, 2003; Zollo & Winter, 2002). The third stream emphasizes how dynamic capabilities benefit organizations. A dynamic capability enables an organization to adapt better to the needs of its changing environment (Eisenhardt & Martin, 2000; Helfat, 1997; Rindova & Kotha, 2001; Rosenbloom, 2000; Zott, 2003) or favorably impact its environment through innovation (Appleyard, Hatch, & Mowery, 2000; Volberda, 1996).

Despite the growing research on dynamic capabilities, important gaps remain in our understanding of the role played by dynamic capabilities in influencing firm performance. As recent reviews highlight (Barreto, 2010; Easterby-Smith, Lyles, & Peteraf, 2009), there is limited understanding of boundaries or contingencies in the utility of dynamic capabilities. In the current state of the literature, virtually any organizational adaptation or innovation is attributed by researchers to some form of dynamic capability. As a result, firm competitive advantages are often automatically associated with the possession and use of dynamic capabilities (Easterby-Smith et al., 2009; Teece, 2007). Such near-tautological assertions do not help clarify when managers should employ a dynamic capability for organizational change, and more fundamentally, when they should purse development of a dynamic capability. Greater understanding is needed of the kinds of organizational changes that dynamic capabilities are more (and less) suited for, and conditions when the changes brought about by dynamic capabilities are more (and less) beneficial to the organization.

Further, despite the wide acceptance that dynamic capabilities help bring about organizational change (Helfat et al., 2007), there is little research that explicitly links the dynamic capability literature to literature on organizational change. Such an approach might yield more insights into the heterogeneous utility of dynamic capabilities in bringing about change, as discussed above. Finally, the dynamic capability literature provides little understanding of how dynamic capabilities can coevolve with the environments they help firms adapt to (Ambrosini & Bowman, 2009). Although, scholars recognize that dynamic capabilities can be developed "equifinally" through diverse approaches (Eisenhardt & Martin, 2000), there is limited understanding of how these differences in origin emerge and influence the effectiveness of particular capabilities.

In a preliminary attempt to address these important gaps, our research conceptually examines the questions of (1) when dynamic capabilities are effective in bringing about organizational changes; (2) how such changes are beneficial for organizations; and (3) how dynamic capabilities coevolve with the changes they effect. To adequately address our research questions and develop our theoretical logic, we integrate the dynamic capabilities literature with research on organizational change. Drawing from the organizational change literature, we specifically focus on two important dimensions of organizational change: discontinuity and permanence. We identify key types of organizational change based on variances in discontinuity and permanence. Using an open system view of organizational change (Boulding, 1956; Scott, 1987), we propose that dynamic capabilities are most effective for organizational changes that involve moderate levels of discontinuity and permanence. However, they may not be as effective in bringing about change that involves high or low levels of either dimension. Therefore, we propose that dynamic capabilities are best-suited to help firms adapt to moderately turbulent and moderately stable environments. However, in combination with other types of changes that need not be dynamic capability driven, dynamic capabilities help transition extremely turbulent environments to moderately turbulent ones and extremely stable environments to moderately stable ones. In doing so, dynamic capabilities themselves co-evolve with firms' changing environments.

Our theoretical examination allows us to develop a normative model that suggests when it is worthwhile to pursue developing dynamic capabilities and when it is beneficial to use dynamic capabilities for organizational change. The various aspects of our model therefore provide promising directions for future research and important guidelines for managers. We believe our work represents a step towards being able to identify *ex-ante* the dynamic capabilities that firms possess and conditions when these capabilities will be beneficial to them.

THEORETICAL BACKGROUND

Dynamic Capabilities

The broad consensus in the growing literature on dynamic capabilities is that such capabilities are developed specifically for the purpose of bringing about organizational change (Helfat et al., 2007). A dynamic capability must therefore have discrete components or elements to undertake the different aspects of change. For example, one element of an organization's dynamic capability must help the organization sense external opportunities and threats while another element helps it respond and adapt to these (Teece, 2007). While some researchers focus on dynamic capabilities that consist of informal patterns of activity (Rosenbloom, 2000; Teece et al., 1997), others highlight dynamic capabilities that are formal processes relating to specific functional areas such as research and development (R&D), mergers and acquisitions (M&A), product development, and alliances (Eisenhardt

& Martin, 2000; Heimeriks, Schijven, & Gates, 2012; Kate & Singh, 2007). Table 4.1 provides illustrative examples of these two broad and contrasting types of dynamic capabilities. However, as we elaborate later, a dynamic capability is likely to consist of *both* formal and informal elements.

The intellectual origins of the dynamic capabilities literature can be found in the resource-based view (RBV) (Helfat & Peteraf, 2003) and the

TABLE 4.1 Two Broad Types of Dynamic Capabilities

DC Type	Citation	Definition/ Examples
Informal patterns of activity	Teece, Pisano & Shuen (1997)	The firm's ability to achieve new forms of competitive advantage by appropriately adapting, integrating and reconfiguring internal and external organizational skills, resources and functional competence.
	Rosenbloom (2000)	The ability to achieve new forms of competitive advantage in the face of disruptive technologies. Leadership is a central element of this DC.
	King & Tucci (2002)	Routines that exist at a higher order and preserve change processes. For example, the ability to respond to a new market or surmount technological change.
	Zott (2003)	Are embedded in routine organizational processes that guide the evolution of a firm's resource configuration and operational routines.
Formal processes in specific functional areas	Eisenhardt & Martin (2000)	The antecedent organizational and strategic routines by which managers alter their resource base—acquire and shed resources, integrate them together, and recombine them. Processes like product development, alliancing and strategic decision-making are examples.
	Zollo & Winter (2002)	A learned and stable pattern of collective activity through which the organization systematically generates and modifies its operating routines in pursuit of improved effectiveness. Examples are process R&D, restructuring and reengineering, and post acquisition integration.
	Galunic & Eisenhardt (2001)	Dynamic capabilities are the organizational and strategic processes by which managers manipulate resources into new productive assets in the context of changing markets.
	Pisano (2000)	Routines that regulate search for improved routines and methods and have an impact on the evolution of future capabilities. Process development projects are an example.

evolutionary economics (Dosi, Nelson, & Winter, 2000) literatures. Consistent with the RBV logic, a stream of research discusses how dynamic capabilities play a role in bringing about organizational change by helping firms reconfigure resources. For example, firms could use dynamic capabilities to recombine their existing resources in new ways. Henderson and Cockburn (1994) show that certain pharmaceutical firms' dynamic capabilities help create unique combinations of their existing knowledge resources in scientific disciplines and disease areas. Firms also employ dynamic capabilities to acquire valuable resources from their external environment. Karim and Mitchell (2000) examine how pharmaceutical firms' dynamic capabilities to manage acquisitions are used to obtain knowledge required for new products. Finally, firms could use dynamic capabilities to divest unproductive resources that generate rents in factor markets. Moliterno and Wiersema (2007) identify such dynamic capabilities among baseball franchises in their transactions involving professional players. In sum, dynamic capabilities can help firms reconfigure resources through recombination, acquisition, or divestment (Zahra & George, 2002).

Another research stream in the evolutionary economics tradition conceptualizes dynamic capabilities as "higher-order" capabilities, influencing and changing operating (or "lower-order") capabilities (Winter, 2003). A firm's operating capabilities are used to carry out primary business activities such as manufacturing, sales, logistics, and service. Research points out several ways in which dynamic capabilities bring about organizational changes in operating capabilities. For example, a firm's dynamic capabilities could expedite the development of new operating capabilities. Danneels (2008) observes the firms' use of dynamic capabilities in building new technology-related and customer-related capabilities. Dynamic capabilities can also help enhance existing operating capabilities. Pisano (2000) shows that the dynamic capability to execute product development projects provides firms with knowledge that enhanced existing operating processes. Moreover, a firm might use dynamic capabilities to adapt existing operational capabilities to a new context, such as a product market or a geographical location. Fladmoe-Lindqvist (1996) shows that franchisors can expand globally because of their dynamic capability to replicate franchising operations across geographical regions. In sum, dynamic capabilities can help firms modify their operating capabilities through building new ones, enhancing existing ones, and adapting them to new contexts (Chen, Williams, & Agarwal, 2012).

Organizational Change

Organizational change involves the discrete modification of organizational structures and systems (Beck, Bruderl, & Woywode, 2008). Organizations are behaviorally resistant to change (Thaler & Sunstein, 2008) because selecting and implementing such change involves challenges to dominant cognitive frameworks and established routines of activity. Organizational resistance to change is therefore scaled from limited individual cognition regarding implications of such changes (Fehr & Tyran, 2005). A key question in behavioral strategy relates to how organizations can overcome their natural resistance to change (Powell, Lovallo, & Fox, 2011).

Any form of organizational change produces a state that is *discontinuous* (even if minutely so) from the firm's previous state. The new state can have varying degrees of *permanence* based on whether the organization returns to its original state and how soon (Amburgey, Kelly, & Barnett, 1993). Studies of organizational change have examined observable events with considerable discontinuity and permanence, such as changes in firms' market niches (Carroll, Dobrev, & Swaminathan, 2002), top management teams (Bigley & Wiersema, 2002), or formal processes (Beck & Kieser, 2003).

Prior research also recognizes that all organizational changes are fundamentally initiated through reconfiguring the organization's resources (Makadok, 2001). The extent to which organizational change is discontinuous and permanent depends on how the particular organization transforms its underlying resource configurations. Greater the novelty with which a firm is able to reconfigure its resources, the further away is the new state from the old one resulting in a more discontinuous change. The observable outputs of change are modifications in the firm's capabilities as these new resource configurations are absorbed into them. The more that new resource configurations are retained within capabilities, the greater is the permanence of the organizational change.

Accordingly, we conceptualize all organizational change as involving varying combinations of discontinuity and permanence. We examine important generalized types of organizational changes, all identified and discussed in prior research, based on whether the discontinuity and permanence involved is low, moderate, or high. Therefore, any organizational change will closely resemble a specific combination of a type of change categorized by permanence and a type of change categorized by discontinuity. Figure 4.1 depicts this typology of organizational change based on the extent of discontinuity and permanence involved.

As Figure 4.1 depicts, organizational changes can have varying levels of permanence. A representative type of change with relatively low permanence is *improvisatory* change. Improvisation involves creation of new and unfamiliar material with minimal design and planning (Baker, Miner, & Eesley 2003; Miner, Bassoff, & Moorman, 2001) and often arises from a burst of intuition and imagination, possibly in response to an atypical problem (Weick, 1998). In its purest form, improvisation does not require any learning to be incorporated into capabilities to create permanent

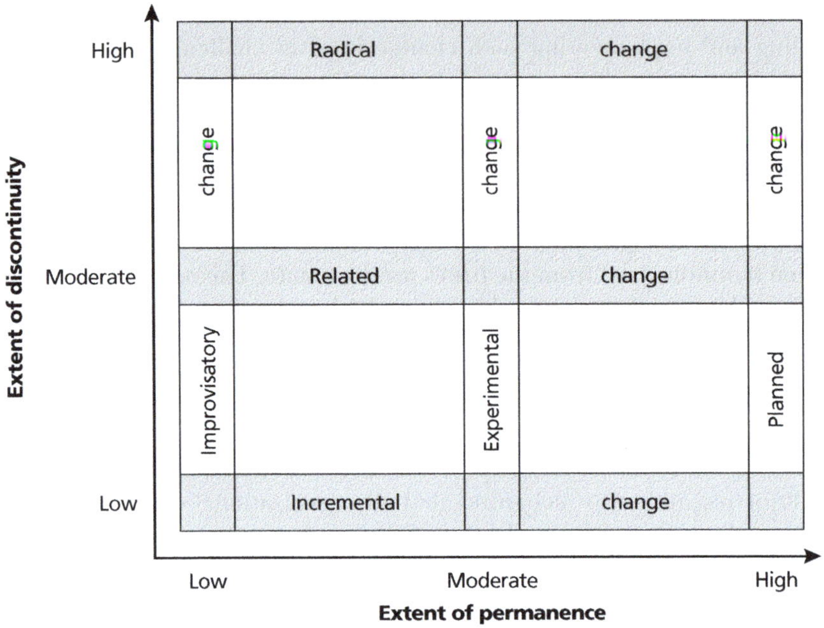

Figure 4.1 Types of organizational change.

modifications in them. For example, a firm may improvise certain activities to respond to a novel problem that is not expected to reoccur in future. Such an improvisation is "ad-hoc," that is, based purely on dealing with the problem at hand (Winter, 2003). Once the contingency has been resolved, the improvising personnel revert to old ways of doing things (Cunha, Cunha, & Kamoche, 1999) and the firm's existing processes and systems settle back to the earlier equilibrium.

In contrast, a type of organizational change with moderate permanence is *experimental* change. This type of change occurs when firms engage in learning-by-doing, through trial and error, often through the initiatives of lower-level employees. If an experiment with a new resource configuration is successful, firm managers may consider absorbing the improvised techniques as a permanent modification to one or more standard capabilities (March, 2006; Zahra, Sapienza, & Davidsson, 2006). Therefore, the results of a large proportion of experiments are discarded while only a small proportion is retained permanently within capabilities. A third type of organizational change with relatively high permanence is *planned* change. Such changes are typically top-down and are outcomes of the strategic planning process (Pearce, Freeman, & Robinson, 1987). Strategic plans for changes in scope, business models, and target markets (Agarwal & Helfat, 2009) are typically accompanied by operational plans to modify or develop relevant operating capabilities, and therefore fall in this category.

Figure 4.1 also depicts organizational changes with varying levels of discontinuity. An example of a change with high discontinuity is *radical* change. We define such changes as new-to-the-world, pioneering changes for which the focal organization is the first mover. Generating such radical changes requires the organization to break away from past precedents, established knowledge, and proven practices (Anderson & Tushman, 1990; Henderson & Clark, 1990), since these are of limited utility in performing novel and unfamiliar tasks. Therefore, attempting to change radically typically involves development of altogether novel configurations of resources and is fraught with considerable risk. In contrast, a type of change with moderate discontinuity is *related* change. In such changes, an organization tries to build on its existing resource base by obtaining or developing certain new resources that can be configured with the existing ones. Examples of such changes are diversification initiatives that are related to the core businesses (Farjoun, 1994; Montgomery, 1982). At the product level, related changes are generally architectural or modular, involving either changes to specific components of a product or the way that components are linked to each other (Henderson & Clark, 1990). Finally, a type of organizational change with low discontinuity is *incremental* change. Such a change occurs by repeated execution of similar tasks, which enables the firm to use its resources more efficiently by riding on the learning curve or experience curve (Amit, 1986; Argote, Beckman, & Epple, 1990). Such types of changes might result in more efficient operations, better product quality, or product-line extensions with improved features (Amit, 1986; Porter, 1996). Incremental change requires very little reconfiguration of resources available to the firm, and too much reconfiguration might actually impede the learning needed for such incremental change (Lapre & Wassenhove, 2001).

INTEGRATIVE FRAMEWORK

Dynamic Capabilities and Organizational Change

As discussed earlier, extant research in a primarily RBV tradition highlights how dynamic capabilities help reconfigure firm resources while extant research from a primarily evolutionary economics perspective highlights how dynamic capabilities modify firm operating capabilities. Employing the open-system view of an organization (Bertalanffy, 1956), discussed earlier, helps integrate these complementary perspectives. In this representation, dynamic capabilities bring about variations by introducing novel resource reconfigurations into the firm. After appropriate selection of certain

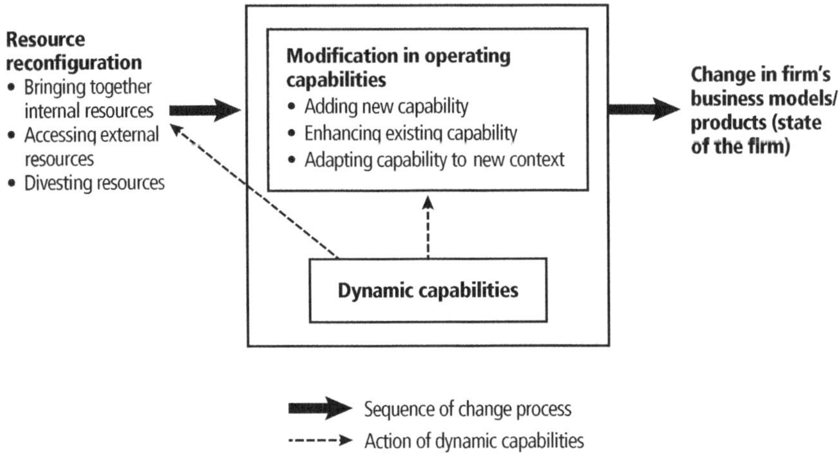

Figure 4.2 Systemic representation of change through dynamic capabilities.

variations, dynamic capabilities then retain these through modifications in the firm's base of operating capabilities. The inputs (resource reconfigurations) and outputs (modifications in operating capabilities) of organizational change through dynamic capabilities are depicted in Figure 4.2.

We now use this integrative view of how dynamic capabilities act in explaining when dynamic capabilities are useful for organizations. As Helfat and co-authors (2007) point out, the utility of dynamic capabilities can be evaluated at two levels. First, what types of organizational changes are dynamic capabilities effective in bringing about (that is, their "technical fitness")? Second, how beneficial these organizational changes are given an organization's environment and strategy (that is, their "evolutionary fitness")? We first examine the technical fitness of dynamic capabilities in implementing the various types of organizational change described above.

Effectiveness of Dynamic Capabilities

In the earlier section, we discussed that organizational change can vary in terms of discontinuity and permanence, depending on the extent to which existing resources are reconfigured and these novel reconfigurations are retained within capabilities. Organizational changes involving greater resource reconfigurations are more discontinuous while organizational changes where resource configurations are retained into operating capabilities are relatively more permanent. We also argued that dynamic capabilities act by reconfiguring firm resources and distilling resultant changes into operating capabilities. Integrating these arguments, it follows that a dynamic capability will be most effective in implementing organizational changes that are relatively discontinuous *and* permanent, that is, require significant reconfiguration of resources and their retention in operating capabilities. The effectiveness of the dynamic capability will be manifested in a relatively seamless execution such that the end-point of the change is distinct from the starting point (and thereby discontinuous) and continues to stay that way in future (and thereby permanent).

For example, among the types of changes with varying permanence, dynamic capabilities would be best suited to execute experimental changes which involve a moderate level of permanence. Dynamic capabilities can continuously help identify critical experiments and distill valuable learning from such experiments into organizational capabilities. Therefore, developing a dynamic capability is most advantageous for a firm that seeks to use this capability for generating experimental changes (Augier & Teece, 2008).

Even though planned changes also require a high level of permanence, dynamic capabilities developed to enable such changes may not be as effective. Too much permanence, inherent in a completely planned approach to change, often results in greater inertia in responding to new information (Mintzberg & McHugh, 1985; Pearce et al., 1987) and precludes experimentation from occurring at lower levels. While the concerned dynamic capability may be used to set the plan in motion through introductions of new resources, it becomes less useful at later stages of implementation when identification of new opportunities is not encouraged. To make dynamic capabilities effective for planned changes, organizations must complement their top-down planning processes with the recognition and implementation of bottom-up experimental initiatives (Augier & Teece, 2008).

Dynamic capabilities are perhaps least suited for implementing improvisatory change. As discussed earlier, dynamic capabilities typically generate modifications to firms' operating capabilities as the output of the change they produce. When such permanence is not a desired outcome of improvisatory change, it is costly and even counter-productive to carry out such improvisation by employing dynamic capabilities. The routines that underlie a dynamic capability are formed by distilling and codifying learning to make them applicable to different situations (Schreyogg & Kliesch-Eberl, 2007; Zollo & Winter, 2002). Developing a dynamic capability requires costs of codification and replication that are unnecessary if the response is not repeated in future. Moreover, the codification involved in developing a dynamic capability may slow down the speed and magnitude of the improvisatory response required in such cases (Heimeriks et al., 2012). However, dynamic capabilities can become relatively more useful if there is an experimental mindset to improvisation, say, when a series of improvisations are carried out to determine if any of these should be replicated in the future into firm capabilities. Therefore, we propose:

Proposition 1a: *Among the different types of organizational change with varying levels of permanence, dynamic capabilities developed by a firm to enable experimental changes will be most effective, followed by dynamic capabilities for planned changes, and finally, for improvisatory changes.*

Proposition 1b: *Dynamic capabilities can be made more effective in implementing planned changes if such changes are complemented by bottom-up experimental initiatives, and by improvisatory changes if such changes are implemented with an experimental mindset.*

Next, we consider the types of change with varying discontinuity. Of these, dynamic capabilities are best-suited to implement related changes that are moderately discontinuous. Such changes build on a firm's existing resource base making it easy for dynamic capabilities to recognize new resources that need to be introduced and reconfiguring these new resources with the existing ones. Therefore, developing a dynamic capability for generating related changes will be most advantageous for a firm (Chen et al., 2012).

Even though radical changes also involve a high degree of discontinuity, dynamic capabilities developed for such changes may not be as effective. Dynamic capabilities work best through recombination of existing and new resources. However, existing resources and expertise are of limited utility in performing novel and unfamiliar tasks (Heimeriks et al., 2012). Dynamic capabilities can only be useful if there is a conscious effort to generate synergies with existing resources while implementing such changes.

Dynamic capabilities are particularly ill-suited for facilitating incremental changes where no significant resource reconfigurations are required. For incremental enhancements to operating capabilities in the same business domains, building on own expertise in the particular capability is most effective and there is no need to borrow from other activities or external sources (Lapre & Wassenhove, 2001). Therefore, it is costly to employ dynamic capabilities to generate such changes because these capabilities will not be utilized efficiently (Zollo & Winter, 2002). Moreover, using dynamic capabilities may automatically result in resource reconfigurations that destabilize the learning possible through repetitive activity. Dynamic capabilities can only be useful for such changes if there is a conscious effort to apply the learning from repeated activities into other domains which might increase the rate of learning in those domains. These arguments lead to the following propositions:

Proposition 2a: *Among the different types of organizational change with varying discontinuity, dynamic capabilities developed by a firm to enable related changes will be most effective, followed by dynamic capabilities for radical changes, and finally, for incremental changes.*

Proposition 2b: *Dynamic capabilities can be made more effective in implementing radical changes by facilitating transfers of related resources from the rest of the organization, and in implementing incremental changes by facilitating transfers of related resources to the rest of the organization.*

Adaptive Benefits of Dynamic Capabilities

We now examine some conditions under which firms' dynamic capabilities have high evolutionary fitness, that is, they cause organizational changes that are beneficial to the concerned organization. This question is distinct from the question of effectiveness or technical fitness of dynamic capabilities. For example, some changes generated through dynamic capabilities may not prove beneficial for a firm despite having been implemented effectively.

The extant literature suggests two broad benefits to a firm of possessing dynamic capabilities: effective adaptation of a firm to its environment, and innovation that impacts the firm's environment in ways that are favorable for the focal firm. A primary form of adaptation involves exploiting attractive opportunities by using dynamic capabilities to build required competencies (Doving & Gooderham, 2008; Lampel & Shamsie, 2003). For instance, Lampel and Shamsie (2003) find that Hollywood production companies having dynamic capabilities in mobilizing and transforming resources can respond effectively to changing public tastes and thereby make more commercially successful movies. Florida and Kenney (2000) suggest that dynamic capabilities allow Japanese companies to transfer organizational forms to foreign countries in an attempt to exploit local demand. Adaptation could also take on the form of responses to environmental threats arising from sources such as new technological developments, social and demographic shifts, and competitive actions. Dynamic capabilities can be instrumental in helping incumbent firms recognize these threats and reacting effectively to them (Teece, 2007). For example, Rosenbloom (2000) shows that the leadership at NCR had dynamic capabilities that helped the firm overcome its established culture and adapt to the new era of electronics. Helfat (1997) similarly finds that dynamic capabilities in R&D helped U.S. oil companies commercialize new synthetic technologies and respond to the oil crisis of the 1970s.

We have already discussed how dynamic capabilities are particularly well-suited for implementing experimental and related changes. Such changes are good adaptive responses to environments where turbulence is moderate, especially if such turbulence is "punctuated" with periods of stability (Benner & Tushman, 2003). To adapt to such environments, incumbent need to implement frequent changes with moderate permanence (as in experimental changes) and moderate discontinuity (as in related changes). Since dynamic capabilities are usually effective in implementing these types of changes, such capabilities are extremely beneficial for incumbent firms to adapt to environments of moderate and punctuated turbulence.

However, environments that are extremely turbulent change frequently and discontinuously. Every environmental change is distinct from the previous one. Such environments require incumbent firms to respond quickly in ways that are often unfamiliar. Firms cannot predict environmental changes in advance and therefore do not have the time to plan effective responses in detail. Frequent, highly discontinuous transformations (as in radical changes) of low permanence (such as, improvisatory changes) are likely to be the most beneficial adaptation responses. Since dynamic capabilities are usually not very effective in implementing such radical and improvisatory changes, as we argued earlier, such capabilities are less beneficial for firms in extremely turbulent environments.

On the other hand, a high degree of planned and incremental change is necessary for firms to adapt to stable environments where it is essential to build continuously on strengths and eliminate weaknesses. When stability is high, changes required are relatively permanent (as in planned changes) and continuous (as in incremental changes). Since dynamic capabilities are usually not very effective in implementing such planned and incremental changes, as we argued earlier, such capabilities have limited benefits for firms in extremely stable environments. Therefore, we propose:

> **Proposition 3:** *Dynamic capabilities will be extremely beneficial for firms to adapt to environments of moderate turbulence punctuated by periods of moderate stability, by helping implement experimental and related changes. They will be relatively less beneficial in extremely turbulent environments where radical and improvisatory changes are more necessary and even less beneficial in extremely stable environments where planned and incremental changes are more necessary.*

In addition to enabling effective adaptive responses, dynamic capabilities also help firms create innovations which do not originate from adaptive responses but from the strategic vision and internal expertise of the concerned firms. Such innovative initiatives contribute to the "external flexibility" of firms, that is, their ability to impact their environment in favorable ways instead of merely reacting to it (Appleyard et al., 2000; Volberda, 1996). For example, Benner and Tushman (2003) argue that organizations can use dynamic capabilities to generate technological discontinuities by balancing exploration and exploitation. By creating such discontinuities, these firms transition their industries from a state of equilibrium to a state of ferment. Pil and Cohen (2006) similarly argue that firms' experience with modular design principles create dynamic capabilities relating to innovation. These dynamic capabilities help weaken competitive forces in the long run. Therefore, firms can use dynamic capabilities to execute visionary goals and strongly impact their environments.

We have already discussed how dynamic capabilities may be less beneficial in adapting to highly turbulent and highly stable environments. However, in such environments, dynamic capabilities may still help in generating innovations that help change these environments to benefit the focal firm. For example, dynamic capabilities can be used reasonably effectively for a combination of radical and related changes (to ensure that some new resources are configured with existing firm resources) and for a combination of experimental and improvisatory changes (thereby ensuring that some of the new resource configurations are retained permanently). Such a portfolio of changes can be used to develop standards in highly turbulent industries where there are no dominant designs currently and competing standards are engaged in winner-take-all battles (Shapiro & Varian, 1999). If the firm can pioneer such a dominant design, it would help transition the industry to a more moderately turbulent environment in which other firms adopt and build on its standard (Anderson & Tushman, 1990). As an example, despite being a late mover, Microsoft has managed to create the standard for several software products that have greatly reduced the number of uncooperative rivals and incompatible products in these businesses.

Similarly, dynamic capabilities can also trigger innovation in highly stable industries through combinations of related and incremental changes (to ensure that existing firm resources are leveraged for new applications) and experimental and planned changes (to ensure ideas for new opportunities emerge from bottom-up). Such an innovation might trigger disruptive shocks in these industries that cause punctuated equilibrium and a new era of moderate turbulence to emerge through new entrants (Anderson & Tushman, 1990; Benner & Tushman, 2003). As an example, Amazon.com's dynamic capabilities have caused it to generate turbulence in several stable and oligopolistic retail industries through its online retailing model, and have reduced the barriers to entry for small players in these industries. Therefore, we propose:

> **Proposition 4:** *Dynamic capabilities will be beneficial for firms in highly turbulent environments by helping to transition these environments to moderately turbulent ones. They will do so by enabling the creation of new standards through combinations of radical and related changes, and improvisatory and experimental changes.*

> **Proposition 5:** *Dynamic capabilities will be beneficial for firms in highly stable environments by helping to transition these environments to moderately*

stable ones. They will do so by creating disruptive shocks that punctuate the equilibrium in these environments through combinations of incremental and related changes, and planned and experimental changes.

Coevolution of Dynamic Capabilities

Finally, we advance our theoretical framework by discussing how dynamic capabilities' impacts on firm environments results in coevolution of the capabilities themselves. Coevolution implies not only the emergence of new dynamic capabilities but also refinement in the routines of existing ones. Therefore, as a dynamic capability is used to effect a particular organizational change, the capability itself evolves through a process of learning where the some positive aspects of its current use may be retained and some negative aspects eliminated, so that the capability may be used more effectively in future (McKelvie & Davidsson, 2009; Newey & Zahra, 2009). The development and modification of dynamic capabilities follow the classic evolutionary cycle of variation-selection-retention in which variations are introduced into routines through firms' transformational experiences (Zollo & Winter, 2002; King & Tucci, 2002). Elements of how the firm dealt with these experiences are then retrospectively identified as beneficial or detrimental and accordingly retained or eliminated. The favorable elements may be tacitly retained as "simple rules" or codified into formal procedures (Eisenhardt & Martin, 2000) and either form a new dynamic capability or add onto existing capabilities.

Dynamic capabilities can evolve out of organizational changes that are relatively non-routine and discontinuous, as well as from changes that are continuous and incremental (King & Tucci, 2002). Organizational changes which are relatively discontinuous and novel inherently involve more improvisation. As organizations undertake a series of such discontinuous changes with high improvisatory content, managers often try to make sense of these seemingly random experiences *ex-post* (Weick, 1998). What emerges gradually is a definite "method to fire-fighting," resulting in evolution of a new dynamic capability, usually of an informal nature, or the refinement of existing formal dynamic capabilities (Winter, 2003). For example, Vermeulen and Barkema (2001) discover that non-routine experience in executing acquisitions enhances both a firm's dynamic capability of carrying out future acquisitions and its dynamic capability of executing green-field ventures.

On the other hand, organizational changes which are relatively incremental and related to core operations inherently involve more experiential learning. "Static" experience, through the continuance of normal operations, can also yield variations by increasing firms' abilities to experiment (George, 2005), and allowing it to learn from anomalies and errors

(Eisenhardt & Martin, 2000). As a firm realizes efficiencies in multiple operating capabilities by moving along the learning curve for each of them, it is likely to derive some higher-order learning about learning itself (Cohen & Levinthal, 1990). This higher-order learning is of a conceptual nature, concerning cause-effect relationships that can be generalized to other contexts, and distinct from mere operational learning of the immediate task (Garud, 1997; Lapre & Wassenhove, 2001). Such conceptual learning can be the genesis of a new dynamic capability of a relatively informal nature, which can be employed to achieve steeper learning curves for future activities undertaken in new domains. Alternatively, the conceptual learning may add new informal elements to existing formal dynamic capabilities.

Therefore, as organizations use their dynamic capabilities to implement a combination of improvisatory and experimental changes to bring about transitions of highly-turbulent environments to moderately-turbulent ones, they are likely to add "improvisation-based" elements to new and existing dynamic capabilities. Since such organizations would use dynamic capabilities to engage in a series of improvisations akin to experiments. Managers would retroactively recognize important elements of such an improvisation process and include them as elements of relevant dynamic capabilities.

Moreover, as organizations use their dynamic capabilities to implement a combination of related and incremental changes to bring about transitions of highly-stable environments to moderately stable ones, they are likely to add "experience-based" elements to new and existing dynamic capabilities. Managers would deliberately include the experiential learning derived by riding the learning curve as elements of relevant dynamic capabilities.

As an example of an improvisation-based element of a dynamic capability, consider a firm adept at quickly attending to idiosyncratic customer complaints by improvisation. Over time, this ability to form close customer relationships and learn about emerging needs and expectations becomes more routinized and evolves either into a new informal dynamic capability or as part of a formal dynamic capability such as alliancing. As an example of an experience-based dynamic element of a dynamic capability, consider a firm that learns to efficiently manage its inventory levels as it services an increasing number of customers. Its managers might make conscious efforts to generate conceptual learning regarding cause-effect relationships that made this increase in efficiency possible. This learning could evolve into a new dynamic capability that is then applied to new businesses the firm enters, or again added onto an existing formal dynamic capability such as alliancing. Hence, we propose:

> **Proposition 6:** *When dynamic capabilities help in transitioning highly-turbulent environments to moderately turbulent ones, the combination of improvisatory and experimental changes generated help in adding new im-*

provisation-based elements to existing dynamic capabilities or creating a new improvisation-based dynamic capability.

Proposition 7: *When dynamic capabilities help in transitioning highly-stable environments to moderately turbulent ones, the combination of related and experimental changes generated help in adding new experience-based elements to existing dynamic capabilities or creating a new experience-based dynamic capability.*

As dynamic capabilities evolve, they are likely to contain either more improvisation-based elements or more experience-based elements based on how relevant elements were developed from prior organizational changes. Building on our earlier arguments, we suggest that dynamic capabilities with more improvisation-based elements will be more effective in helping firms adapt to moderately and extremely turbulent environments than dynamic capabilities with more experience-based elements. As discussed, improvisation-based elements of dynamic capabilities evolve through the *ex-post* selection of generalizable elements from a series of related improvisations. These improvisations, in turn, are originally responses to idiosyncratic problems encountered by the firm. In more turbulent environments where problems tend to be dissimilar, a higher-routine developed out of addressing dissimilar problems is likely to be more suitable for addressing new problems. However, in less turbulent environments, a primarily improvisation-based dynamic capability may not have suitable elements to execute gradual and predictable change.

On the other hand, experience-based elements of dynamic capabilities evolve from routine experiences with operating capabilities. Dynamic capabilities with more such elements are likely to be more suited to bring about gradual and predictable change. Hence, these dynamic capabilities will be more suited to adapt to moderately and extremely stable environments. However, the learning distilled in primarily experience-based dynamic capabilities may not be as effective in effecting adaptations to more turbulent environments. Hence, we propose:

Proposition 8: *Dynamic capabilities with a greater proportion of improvisation-based elements are more beneficial in helping firms adapting to turbulent environments than dynamic capabilities with a greater proportion of experience-based elements.*

Proposition 9: *Dynamic capabilities with a greater proportion of experience-based elements are more beneficial in helping firms adapt to stable environments than dynamic capabilities with a greater proportion of improvisation-based elements.*

To summarize our arguments, we propose that dynamic capabilities can most directly and strongly benefit firms in moderately turbulent environments. However, dynamic capabilities may still be of considerable value in extremely turbulent environments, although in a more indirect manner. First, these capabilities can impact these environments by transitioning them to more moderate levels of turbulence, where they can be deployed more effectively. Second, these capabilities coevolve through their deployment in extremely turbulent environments which increases their effectiveness in such environments over time. Similarly, dynamic capabilities can most directly and strongly benefit firms in moderately stable environments. However, they can still be of value in extremely stable environments by helping to transition these environments to moderately stable ones and coevolving to become more effective in such environments over time.

DISCUSSION AND CONCLUSION

Dynamic capabilities are widely thought to benefit possessing firms by enabling organizational change (Helfat et al., 2007). Such change helps firms adapt better to their changing environments or impact their environments favorably through innovation. However, not much is known regarding the type of organizational changes that dynamic capabilities are more effective in enabling, and when these changes are beneficial for firms. Barring a few exceptions (Eisenhardt & Martin, 2000; Winter, 2003), the extant literature has not developed boundaries or contingencies for the utility of dynamic capabilities. As Priem and Butler (2001) observe, the relevance of a concept in the real world is enhanced by evaluating boundary conditions for the applicability of that concept. Therefore, to enhance the relevance of building dynamic capabilities for managers, greater understanding is required of conditions under which dynamic capabilities may or may not be useful to firms. Such exercises will reduce possible tautological assertions that dynamic capabilities are always used or effective in implementing all types of organizational changes.

To address this important gap in the dynamic capabilities literature, we conceptualized organizational change as involving various degrees of discontinuity and permanence based on the extent to which existing resources are reconfigured and the new resource configurations are retained. We developed distinctions in types of organizational changes based on the extent of discontinuity and permanence that these involve. We first evaluated how the effectiveness of dynamic capabilities is likely to vary in implementing these different types of organizational change. We then elaborated how firms' adaptation requirements and innovative initiatives play a role in determining when the use of dynamic capabilities is beneficial for them.

Subsequently, we argued that use of dynamic capabilities also impacts their own evolution and thereby their future effectiveness and value as agents of firm adaptation and innovation.

Our theoretical propositions can also be reorganized to develop a normative model that could be used to guide managers in the development and use of dynamic capabilities as well as generate interesting streams of future academic research. This model is depicted in Figure 4.3.

According to this model, firms should develop dynamic capabilities to facilitate experimental and related changes that help in adapting to environments of moderate turbulence and moderate stability. These dynamic capabilities are relatively less useful in adapting to extremely turbulent environments. However, by combining experimental, related changes with improvisatory and radical changes (which may not be driven by dynamic capabilities), dynamic capabilities help transition extremely turbulent environments to moderately turbulent environments. As a firm undertakes a series of improvisations as experiments, managers should continuously evaluate elements of these improvisations that worked well and could be routinized *ex-post* to contribute to the further evolution of dynamic capabilities. Similarly, dynamic capabilities are even less useful in adapting to extremely stable environments. However, in combination with planned and incremental changes (which may not be driven by dynamic capabilities), dynamic capabilities help transition extremely stable environments to moderately stable environments. As firms become efficient across multiple operating capabilities, managers must deliberately analyze cause-effect relationships that allowed greater efficiencies so that this higher-order learning could be absorbed to contribute to the further evolution of dynamic capabilities. Through these iterative processes, firms can make their dynamic capabilities reasonably effective even in extremely turbulent and extremely stable environments.

Our conceptual model also makes some contributions to the organizational change literature. We tie several streams of seemingly disparate research on organizational change into a unifying framework involving the dimensions of discontinuity and permanence. We hope these dimensions will be used in further research to categorize and theorize about organizational change initiatives. We cast the traditional open systems perspective (Bertalanffy, 1956) in a new light to unify different streams of dynamic capability research and to demonstrate how dynamic capabilities can be linked tightly to organizational change concepts. We try to delink the effectiveness of organizational change from the benefits of such change and argue that the link between effectiveness and advantages is heavily dependent on the nature of the particular firm's environment.

Our model provides several promising directions that future research could test empirically and build on theoretically. For example, research could test our arguments regarding the types of organizational changes for

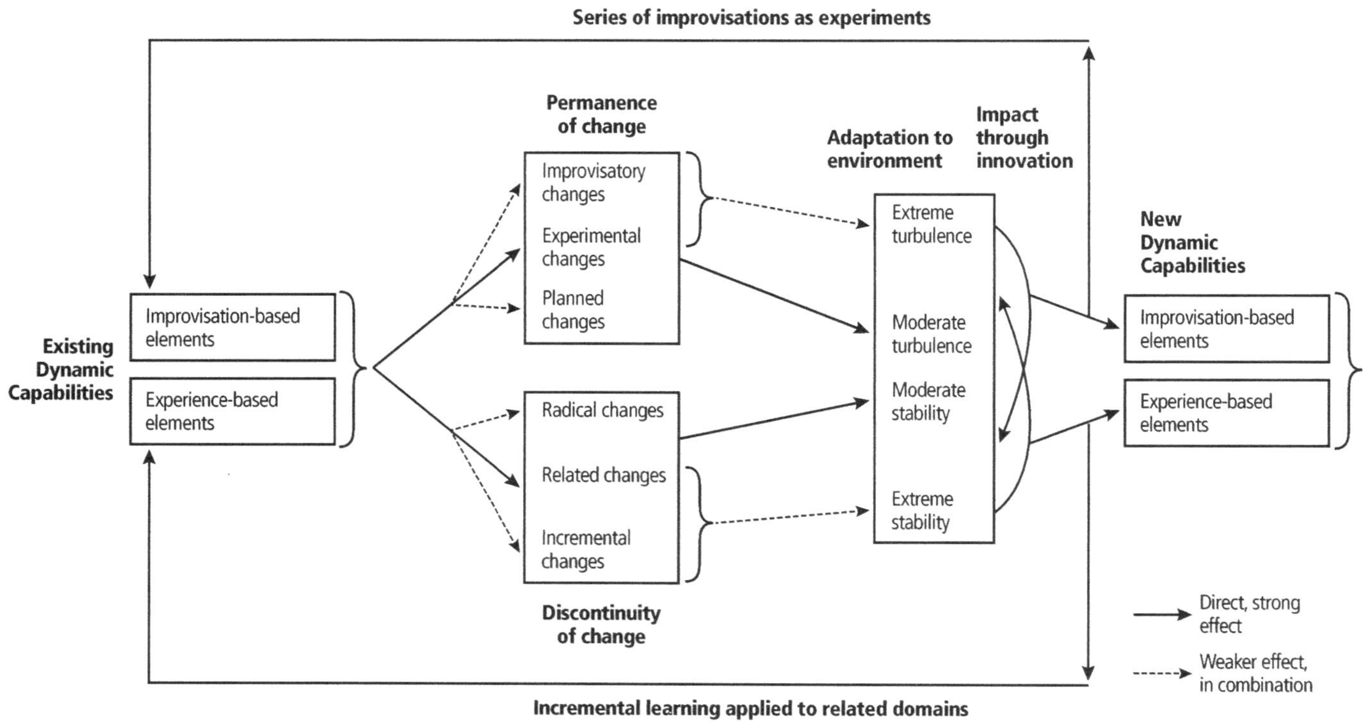

Figure 4.3 Model of dynamic capability utility and coevolution.

which dynamic capabilities are more effective, the environmental conditions for which they can be more effectively used to adapt, and the vital role of such capabilities in transforming firms' environments. Research could also develop other typologies of organizational change, examine when specific changes need to be carried out by firms, and if dynamic capabilities are effective in executing them.

Our review of the dynamic capabilities literature highlighted gaps in the understanding of when dynamic capabilities are effective and useful. By conceptualizing all organizational change as involving varying degrees of discontinuity and permanence, we evaluated when dynamic capabilities can help organizations change and thereby improve their performance. We hope that further exploration along these lines will remove some of the ambiguity in the dynamic capability construct and help clarify that these capabilities are commonly present in everyday strategic mechanisms that large and small firms employ (Barreto, 2010; Zahra et al., 2006). We believe that future studies of firms' dynamic capabilities will provide increasing evidence for why firms are different and develop normative recommendations for how firms can increase their competitive advantage vis-à-vis their rivals (Augier & Teece, 2008).

REFERENCES

Agarwal, R., & Helfat, C. E. (2009). Strategic renewal of organizations. *Organization Science, 20,* 281–293.

Ambrosini, V., & Bowman, C. (2009). What are dynamic capabilities and are they a useful construct in strategic management? *International Journal of Management Reviews, 11,* 29–49.

Amburgey, T. L., Kelly, D., & Barnett, W. P. (1993). Resetting the clock. The dynamics of organizational change and failure. *Administrative Science Quarterly, 38,* 51–73.

Anderson, P., & Tushman, M. L. (1990). Technological discontinuities and dominant designs: A cyclical model of technological change. *Administrative Science Quarterly, 35,* 604–633.

Amit, R. (1986). Cost leadership strategy and experience curves. *Strategic Management Journal, 7,* 281–292.

Amit, R., & Schoemaker, P. J. (1993). Strategic assets and organizational rent. *Strategic Management Journal, 14,* 33–46.

Appleyard, M. M., Hatch, N. W., & Mowery, D. C. (2000). Managing the development and transfer of process technologies in the semiconductor manufacturing industry. In G. Dosi, R. R. Nelson, & S. G. Winter (Eds.), *The nature and dynamics of organizational capabilities* (pp 183–210). New York, NY: Oxford University Press.

Argote, L., Beckman, S. L., & Epple, D. (1990). The persistence and transfer of learning in industrial settings. *Management Science, 36,* 140–155.

Augier, M., & Teece, D. J. (2008). Strategy as evolution with design: The foundations of dynamic capabilities and the role of managers in the economic system. *Organization Studies, 29,* 1187–1208.

Baker, T., Miner, A. S., & Eesley, D. T. (2003). Improvising firms: Bricolage, account giving and improvisational competencies in the founding process. *Research Policy, 32,* 255–276.

Barney, J. B. (1991). Firm resources and sustained competitive advantage. *Journal of Management, 17,* 99–120.

Barreto, I. (2010). Dynamic capabilities: A review of past research and an agenda for the future. *Journal of Management, 36,* 256–280.

Beck, N., Bruderl, J., & Woywode, M. (2008). Momentum or deceleration? Theoretical and methodological reflections on the analysis of organizational change. *Academy of Management Journal, 51,* 413–435.

Beck, N., & Kieser, A. (2003). The complexity of rule systems, experience, and organizational learning. *Organization Studies, 24,* 793–814.

Benner, M. J., & Tushman, M. L. (2003). Exploitation, exploration, and process management: The productivity dilemma revisited. *Academy of Management Review, 28,* 238–256.

Bertalanffy, L. v. (1956). General system theory. *General System Yearbook, 7,* 1–20.

Bigley, G. A., & Wiersema, M. F. (2002). New CEOs and corporate strategic refocusing: How the experience as heir apparent influences the use of power. *Administrative Science Quarterly, 47,* 707–727.

Boulding, K. E. (1956). General systems theory: The skeleton of science. *Management Science, 2,* 197–208.

Carroll, G. R., Dobrev, S. D., & Swaminathan, A. (2002). Organizational processes of resource partitioning. *Research in Organizational Behavior, 24,* 1–40.

Chen, P. L., Williams, C., & Agarwal, R. (2012). Growing pains: Pre-entry experience and the challenge of transition to incumbency. *Strategic Management Journal, 33,* 252–276.

Cohen, W. M., & Levinthal, D. A. (1990). Absorptive capacity: A new perspective on learning and innovation. *Administrative Science Quarterly, 35,* 569–596.

Cunha, M. P. E., Cunha, J. V. D., & Kamoche, K. (1999). Organizational improvisation: What, when, how and why. *International Journal of Management Reviews, 1,* 299–341.

Danneels, E. (2008). The organizational antecedents of second-order competences. *Strategic Management Journal, 29,* 519–543.

Dosi, G., Nelson, R. R., & Winter, S. G. (2000). Introduction: The nature and dynamics of organizational capabilities. In G. Dosi, R. R. Nelson, & S. G. Winter (Eds.), *The nature and dynamics of organizational capabilities* (pp. 1–24). New York, NY: Oxford University Press.

Doving, E., & Gooderham, P. N. (2008). Dynamic capabilities as antecedents of the scope of related diversification: The case of small firm accountancy practices. *Strategic Management Journal, 29,* 841–857.

Easterby-Smith, M., Lyles, M. A., & Peteraf, M. A. (2009). Dynamic capabilities: Current debates and future directions. *British Journal of Management, 20,* S1–S8.

Eisenhardt, K. M., & Martin, J. A. (2000). Dynamic capabilities: What are they? *Strategic Management Journal, 21,* 1105–1121.

Farjoun, M. (1994). Beyond industry boundaries: Human expertise, diversification, and resource-related industry groups. *Organization Science, 5,* 185–205.

Fehr, E., & Tyran, J. R. (2005). Individual irrationality and aggregate outcomes. *Journal of Economic Perspectives, 19,* 43–66.

Fladmoe-Lindquist, K. (1996). International franchising: Capabilities and development. *Journal of Business Venturing, 11,* 419–438.

Florida, R., & Kenney, M. (2000). Transfer and replication of organizational capabilities: Japanese transplant organizations in the U.S. In G. Dosi, R. R. Nelson, & S. G. Winter (Eds.), *The nature and dynamics of organizational capabilities* (pp. 281–310). New York, NY: Oxford University Press.

Galunic, D. C., & Eisenhardt, K. M. (2001). Architectural innovation and modular corporate forms. *Academy of Management Journal, 44,* 1229–1249.

Garud, R. (1997). On the distinction between know-how, know-what and know-why. In A. S. Huff & J. P. Walsh (Eds.), *Advances in strategic management* (pp. 81–101). Greenwich, CT: JAI Press.

George, G. (2005). Learning to be capable: Patenting and licensing at the Wisconsin Alumni Research Foundation 1925–2002. *Industrial and Corporate Change, 14,* 119–151.

Guth, W. D., & Ginsberg, A. (1990). Guest editors' introduction: Corporate entrepreneurship. *Strategic Management Journal, 11,* 5–15.

Heimeriks, K. H., Schijven, M., & Gates, S. (2012). Manifestations of higher order routines: The underlying mechanisms of deliberate learning in the context of post-acquisition integration. *Academy of Management Journal, 55,* 703–726.

Helfat, C. E. (1997). Know-how and asset complementarity and dynamic capability accumulation: The case of R&D. *Strategic Management Journal, 18,* 339–360.

Helfat, C. E., & Lieberman, M. B. (2002). The birth of capabilities: Market entry and the importance of pre-history. *Industrial and Corporate Change, 11,* 725–760.

Helfat, C. E., Finkelstein, S., Mitchell, W., Peteraf, M. A., Singh, H., Teece, D. J., & Winter, S. G. (2007). *Dynamic capabilities: Understanding strategic change in organizations.* Hoboken, NJ: Blackwell Publishing.

Helfat, C. E., & Peteraf, M. A. (2003). The dynamic resource-based view: Capability lifecycles. *Strategic Management Journal, 24,* 997–1010.

Henderson, R. M., & Clark, K. B. (1990). Architectural innovation: The reconfiguration of existing product technologies and the failure of established firms. *Administrative Science Quarterly, 35,* 9–30.

Henderson, R., & Cockburn, I. (1994). Measuring competence? Exploring firm effects in pharmaceutical research. *Strategic Management Journal, 15,* 63–84.

Kale, P., & Singh, H. (2007). Building firm capabilities through learning: The role of the alliance learning process in alliance capability and firm-level alliance success. *Strategic Management Journal, 28,* 981–1000.

Karim, S., & Mitchell, W. (2000). Path-dependent and path-breaking change: Reconfiguring business resources following acquisitions in the US medical sector, 1978–1985. *Strategic Management Journal, 21,* 1061–1081.

King, A. A., & Tucci, C. L. (2002). Incumbent entry into new market niches: The role of experience and managerial choice in the creation of dynamic capabilities. *Management Science, 48,* 171–186.

Lampel, J., & Shamsie, J. (2003). Capabilities in motion: New organizational forms and the reshaping of the Hollywood movie industry. *Journal of Management Studies, 40,* 2189–2210.

Lapre, M. A., & Wassenhove, L. N. V. (2001). Creating and transferring knowledge for productivity improvement in factories. *Management Science, 47,* 1311–1325.

Makadok, R. (2001). Towards a synthesis of the resource-based and dynamic capability views of rent creation. *Strategic Management Journal, 22,* 387–401.

March, J. G. (2006). Rationality, foolishness, and adaptive intelligence. *Strategic Management Journal, 27,* 201–214.

McKelvie, A., & Davidsson, P. (2009). From resource base to dynamic capabilities: An investigation of new firms. *British Journal of Management, 20,* S63–S80.

Miner, A. S., Bassoff, P., & Moorman, C. (2001). Organizational improvisation and learning: A field study. *Administrative Science Quarterly, 46,* 304–337.

Mintzberg, H., & McHugh, A. (1985). Strategy formation in an adhocracy. *Administrative Science Quarterly, 30,* 160–174.

Moliterno, T. P., & Wiersema, M. F. (2007). Firm performance, rent appropriation, and the strategic resource divestment capability. *Strategic Management Journal, 28,* 1065–1087.

Montgomery, C. A. (1982). The measurement of firm diversification: Some empirical evidence. *Academy of Management Journal, 25,* 299–316.

Newey, L. R., & Zahra, S. A. (2009). The evolving firm: How dynamic and operating capabilities interact to enable entrepreneurship. *British Journal of Management, 20,* S81–S100.

Pil, F. K., & Cohen, S. K. (2006). Modularity: implications for imitation, innovation, and sustained advantage. *Academy of Management Review, 31,* 995–1011.

Pisano, G. P. (2000). In search of dynamic capabilities: The origins of R&D competence in biopharmaceuticals. In G. Dosi, R. R. Nelson, & S. G. Winter (Eds.), *The nature and dynamics of organizational capabilities* (pp. 129–154). New York, NY: Oxford University Press.

Pearce, J. A., Freeman, E. B., & Robinson, R. B. (1987). The tenuous link between formal strategic planning and financial performance. *Academy of Management Review, 12,* 658–676.

Porter, M. E. (1996). What is strategy? *Harvard Business Review, 74(6),* 61–78.

Powell, T. C., Lovallo, D., & Fox, C. R. (2011). Behavioral strategy. *Strategic Management Journal, 32,* 1369–1386.

Prahalad, C., & Bettis, R. (1986). The dominant logic: A new linkage between diversity and performance. *Strategic Management Journal, 7,* 485–501.

Priem, R. L., & Butler, J. E. (2001). Is the resource-based "view" a useful perspective for strategic management research? *Academy of Management Review, 26,* 22–40.

Rindova, V., & Kotha, S. (2001). Continuous morphing: Competing through dynamic capabilities, form and function. *Academy of Management Journal, 44,* 1263–1280.

Rosenbloom, R. S. (2000). Leadership, capabilities and technological change: The transformation of NCR in the electronic era. *Strategic Management Journal, 21,* 1083–1103.

Scott, W. R. (1987). *Organizations: Rational, natural and open systems.* Englewood Cliffs, NJ: Prentice-Hall.

Schreyogg, G., & Kliesch-Eberl, M. (2007). How dynamic can organizational capabilities be? Towards a dual-process model of capability dynamization. *Strategic Management Journal, 28,* 913–933.

Shapiro C., & Varian, H. R. (1999). The art of standard wars. *California Management Review, 41*(2), 8–32.

Teece, D. J. (2007). Explicating dynamic capabilities: The nature and microfoundations of (sustainable) enterprise performance. *Strategic Management Journal, 28,* 1319–1350.

Teece, D. J., Pisano, G., & Shuen, A. (1997). Dynamic capabilities and strategic management. *Strategic Management Journal, 18,* 509–533.

Thaler, R. H., & Sunstein, C. R. (2008). *Nudge: Improving decisions about health, wealth, and happiness.* New Haven, CT: Yale University Press.

Vermeulen, F., & Barkema, H. (2001). Learning through acquisitions. *Academy of Management Journal, 44,* 457–476.

Volberda, H. W. (1996). Toward the flexible form: How to remain vital in hypercompetitive environments. *Organization Science, 7,* 359–374.

Weick, K. E. (1998). Improvisation as a mindset for organizational analysis. *Organization Science, 9,* 543–555.

Winter, S. G. (2003). Understanding dynamic capabilities. *Strategic Management Journal, 4,* 991–995.

Zahra, S. A., & George, G. (2002). Absorptive capacity: A review, reconceptualization and extension. *Academy of Management Review, 27,* 185–203.

Zahra, S. A., Sapienza, H. J., & Davidsson, P. (2006). Entrepreneurship and dynamic capabilities: A review, model and research agenda. *Journal of Management Studies, 43,* 917–955.

Zollo, M., & Winter, S. G. (2002). Deliberate learning and the evolution of dynamic capabilities. *Organization Science, 13,* 339–351.

Zott, C. (2003). Dynamic capabilities and the emergence of intra-industry differential firm performance: Insights from a simulation study. *Strategic Management Journal, 24,* 97–125.

CHAPTER 5

THE CHALLENGE OF DEVELOPING NEW META-MANAGEMENT PRACTICES OF FIRMS IN META-ORGANIZATIONS

Rick M. A. Hollen
Frans A. J. Van Den Bosch
Henk W. Volberda

ABSTRACT

Competitive and institutional pressures challenge established firms to create new ways to improve resource productivity, innovation, and sustainability. One of these ways is through inter-firm collaboration, which requires firms to manage resulting (inter)dependencies beyond firm-level boundaries so as to achieve system-level goals. Being conceptualized by Gulati, Puranam & Tushman (2012) as meta-organizations, collectives of multiple legally autonomous firms are found within and across a wide range of industries and geographies. Existing literature has emphasized the importance of developing new management practices (i.e., management innovation) to better align organizational design with changing environmental conditions in pursuing a firm's strategic goals. In a similar vein, new management practices at the level of the meta-organization are needed to enable its constituent firms to achieve

Behavioral Strategy: Emerging Perspectives, pages 105–127

their system-level goal over time. However, it remains largely unanswered how these firms can contribute to the development of such meta-management practices. We address this research gap by developing propositions based on a literature review. The propositions emphasize the enabling role of changes in the four core activities of management—direction, motivation, coordination and decision-making—in the meta-organizational context. We provide illustrative examples from the Port of Rotterdam. We discuss implications for the literature on meta-organizations and management innovation as well as for practice and suggest directions for future research.

INTRODUCTION

Established firms are continually triggered by competitive and institutional pressures to improve their resource productivity, innovation, and sustainability. As the ability to do so within their organizational boundaries might be limited, these firms often choose for collaboration up, down or outside the production chain (Gulati & Kletter, 2005). For instance, inter-firm collaboration can improve resource productivity and sustainability by converting firm's waste effluents such as residual chemical compounds into useful input streams for each other's production process (Doménech & Davies, 2011; Esty & Porter, 1998). Externalization of certain activities may enable established firms to be more responsive to shifting environmental demands and to tap into outside knowledge sources (Gulati, Puranam, & Tushman, 2012a). By integrating dispersed knowledge and capacity to innovate within an interorganizational setting, firms can also enable more complex innovation (Dougherty & Dunne, 2011; Newell, Goussevskaia, Swan, Bresnen, & Obembe, 2008). The international competitiveness of established firms is therefore largely influenced by their embeddedness in interorganizational networks (Dyer & Singh, 1998; Gulati, 2007; Ireland, Hitt, & Vaidyanath, 2002).

Scholars in the strategy field have extensively examined how to manage interorganizational relationships from a firm's perspective in a way that strengthens the firm's competitiveness and minimizes coordination and transaction costs (e.g., Dyer, 1997; Gulati & Singh, 1998). Some have emphasized the importance of not only improving the focal firm's competitive position but also that of other firms in its network (Dyer & Singh, 1998; Madhok & Tallman 1998; Ring & Van De Ven, 1994). Although these strains of literature have produced valuable insights, they pertain particularly to dyadic relations instead of collectives of multiple interrelated firms and their interrelationships. It is this latter level of analysis that is addressed in the emerging literature on *meta-organizations* (Ahrne & Brunsson, 2005, 2008; Gulati et al., 2012a; König, Schulte, & Enders, 2012). Conceptualized as collectives of multiple legally autonomous entities—such as firms—that are "characterized by a system-level goal" (Gulati et al., 2012, p. 573), meta-organizations represent a strategically interesting but underexplored unit of analysis. As exemplified in Exhibit 5.1, system-level goals challenge established firms to strategize beyond their firm-level boundaries in order to remain competitive in the long term.

Existing firm-level literature has emphasized the importance of developing new management practices, that is, *management innovation,* to better align organizational design with changing environmental conditions in pursuing a firm's goals (Birkinshaw, Hamel, & Mol, 2008; Damanpour & Aravind, 2012). By showing that management innovation may also take place in the interorganizational context, Hollen, Van Den Bosch & Volberda (2013)

EXHIBIT 5.1
Illustrative Example of a Meta-Organization Within the Port of Rotterdam: System-Level Goal and Associated Managerial Challenges

Being one of the world's largest port-industrial complexes, the Port of Rotterdam hosts a large number of refineries (including some of the largest refineries in Europe), chemical and power generating firms, cargo terminals, transport companies and other businesses. Altogether, the port area and its urban surroundings, including the city center of Rotterdam, is responsible for more than fifteen percent of carbon emissions in the Netherlands. In 2007, the port's employers' association Deltalinqs and the Port of Rotterdam Authority, in collaboration with the municipality of Rotterdam and regional environmental protection agency DCMR, initiated the Rotterdam Climate Initiative (RCI). The RCI developed into a Rotterdam-based network that includes firms, knowledge institutions and other organizations as well as citizens that collaborate to achieve the RCI's goals. Its main goal is to drastically reduce carbon emissions by fifty percent (34 Mton) in 2025 compared to 1990 levels. This represents a system-level goal, and Deltalinqs can be seen as a meta-organization whose constituent members—more than 700 registered logistical and industrial firms and associations—need to collectively contribute to this goal to ensure that the Port of Rotterdam becomes more sustainable. This is strategically important for the firms involved, as they are required to reduce their environmental footprint so as to maintain their license to operate and grow, to lease land from the Port of Rotterdam Authority, and to ensure that the port remains attractive for future employees and investors. In order to enable large reductions in carbon emissions, these firms need to strategize beyond their firm-level boundaries. They are challenged, for instance, to jointly develop and implement sustainable measures, to support each other's sustainability initiatives, and to enhance utilization of each other's by-products and waste.

Sources: Documents of Deltalinqs and the Port of Rotterdam Authority; Van Den Bosch, Hollen, Volberda, & Baaij (2011)

took the observation of Birkinshaw and Mol (2006, p. 82) that management innovation seems to emerge "on the fringes of the organization rather than in the core" a step further. Yet, management innovation at the level of the meta-organization has remained mostly unexplored. Hitherto, the literature on meta-organizations has been primarily focused on conceptualizing meta-organizations, clarifying the antecedents of the emergence of meta-organizations, meta-organization design choices regarding key structural elements such as its boundaries and hierarchical differentiation, and on the related inertia and strategic behavior of meta-organizations in reaction to environmental change (see Table 5.1).

It remains largely unanswered how the development of new management practices on a meta-organizational level—for which we coin the term *meta-management practices*—can increase the meta-organization's ability to achieve its system-level goal over time. Meta-management practices are related to the concept of meta-governance practices as used in a recent article on meta-organizations by Vifell & Thedvall (2012). Vifell & Thedvall (2012, p. 51) conceptualize these practices as "governance through bureaucratization" with which "meta-organizations are able to exercise authority over their members by effectively forcing them to comply with certain established processes," which is a way of coordinating activities (Birkinshaw & Goddard, 2009). New (meta-)management practices, however, not only imply new management practices in terms of new ways of coordination, but also new ways of setting objectives, motivating efforts, and decision-making regarding resource allocation (Birkinshaw & Goddard, 2009; Birkinshaw, 2010; Hollen et al., 2013; Van Den Bosch, 2012).

In this chapter, we aim to contribute to narrowing this research gap by developing propositions based on a literature review. In the literature review, we first elaborate on the concept of meta-organization and—drawing on the study by Gulati et al. (2012a) on meta-organization design—its

TABLE 5.1 Literature on Meta-Organizations: Research Topics

Research topic	Illustrative studies
• Conceptualization of meta-organizations	Ahrne & Brunsson (2005, 2008); Gulati, Puranam & Tushman (2012a)
• Antecedents of the emergence of meta-organizations	Gulati, Puranam & Tushman (2012a)
• Meta-organization design choices	Ahrne, Brunsson & Hallström (2007); Gulati, Puranam & Tushman (2012a); Vifell & Thedvall (2012)
• Meta-organizational inertia/ renewal behavior	Ahrne & Brunsson (2005, 2008); König, Schulte & Enders (2012)
• Development of meta-management practices	This chapter

conceptual attributes, and then elaborate on the literature on management innovation and its conceptualization. Next, we develop a series of propositions that suggest how firms can improve the system-level goal of their respective meta-organization by contributing to the development of four core management activities (cf. Birkinshaw & Goddard, 2009; Birkinshaw, 2010) on a meta-organizational level. We provide illustrative examples from the Port of Rotterdam. Finally, we discuss implications for the literature on meta-organizations and management innovation as well as for practice and suggest several directions for future research.

LITERATURE REVIEW

Meta-Organizations

Although not entirely new, the concept of a meta-organization has been used increasingly in the strategy and organizational theory literature in the last decade. As Reveley and Ville (2010, p. 839) pointed out, "the recency of the meta-organizations category [...] means that the attendant conceptual apparatus is underdeveloped." Table 5.2 provides illustrative examples of definitions of meta-organizations in the literature in the last decade.

Table 5.2 shows that whereas there has been general consensus among scholars that meta-organizations consist of members that are not interconnected by virtue of employment contracts, ideas concerning the type(s) of these members vary considerably. For instance, Ahrne & Brunsson (2008) define meta-organizations as organizations whose members may be states, firms or associations, and Gulati et al. (2012a, p. 573) as comprising "networks of firms or individuals not bound by authority based on employment relationships." König et al. (2012, p. 1327, italics added), however, define meta-organizations as "associations whose members are organizations, *rather than* individuals." In this chapter, we reconcile these views by focusing on meta-organizations whose constituent members are firms. Furthermore, whereas Ahrne & Brunsson (2008) state that the constituent members have considerable autonomy, Gulati et al. (2012a) suggest that these are completely legally autonomous. Next, our main focus is on the recent conceptual research and contributions by Gulati et al. (2012a).

Conceptual Attributes of Meta-Organizations

Gulati et al. (2012a) used the concept of a meta-organization to conceptually capture a wide variety of interorganizational network arrangements comprising multiple legally independent entities (such as firms) which (1) are

TABLE 5.2 Illustrative Examples of Definitions of Meta-Organizations in the Literature

Study	Definition of meta-organization	Examples
Ahrne & Brunsson (2005)	"organizations-of-organizations that have assumed the form of associations" (p. 431)	United Nations, FIFA, European Union
Shekhar (2006)	"the combination of multiple organizations working towards common business objectives" (p. 477)	Extended virtual organizations
Ahrne & Brunsson (2008)	"organizations [whose members] are other organizations" (p. 2); "the members of meta-organizations may be states, firms, or associations" (p. 3)	International Chamber of Commerce, World Trade Organization
Reveley &Ville (2010)	"organizations whose constituent members are other organizations" (p. 837)	Industry associations
König, Schulte, & Enders (2012)	"associations whose members are organizations, rather than individuals" (p. 1327)	Industry associations
Gulati, Puranam, & Tushman (2012)	"a meta-organization [is] defined as an organization whose agents are themselves legally autonomous and not linked through employment relationships" (p. 573); "meta-organizations comprise networks of firms or individuals not bound by authority based on employment relationships, but characterized by a system-level goal" (p. 573)	OEM-supplier networks, franchising networks, developer/open-source software communities, technical standards committees

interlinked by a system-level goal; and (2) lack an overarching formal authority structure based on employment contracts. Table 5.3 provides a structured overview of these and other conceptual attributes of meta-organizations as described by Gulati et al. (2012a) on which we will elaborate next.

A *system-level goal*—which corresponds to the goals of the meta-organization's architects (Gulati et al., 2012a)—requires firms involved to not just focus on managing their firm-level interactions with the external environment so as to enhance their own competitiveness, but also on contributing to the relations with one another in such a way that they can properly respond to environmental demands as if they were a single entity. In this vein, König et al. (2012, p. 1327) posited that meta-organizations "aim to install a higher level of order to the interaction of actors within a field and to the interaction between the field and the environment." Having a system-level goal does not mean that firms necessarily share this goal (Gulati et al., 2012a), but collectively achieving this goal will improve their joint competitive position. It can hence be stated that a focus on a system-level

TABLE 5.3 Overview of Conceptual Attributes of Meta-Organizations

• Goal:	meta-organizations are bound by a system-level goal.
• Structure:	meta-organizations comprise multiple legally independent organizational entities (members).
• Membership:	meta-organizations' membership is largely determined by approval and policing procedures, the specification of membership criteria, membership duration and membership exclusivity.
• Governance:	meta-organizational activities are governed by formalized control—except for employment contracts—and governance mechanisms associated with informal authority and bargaining power; the level of hierarchy in place can be high (hierarchical differentiation) or low (self-regulation).

Source: Adapted from Gulati, Puranam, & Tushman (2012a).

goal contributes to interorganizational competitive advantage (cf. Dyer & Singh, 1998).

The notion of reciprocity—which was initially elaborated by Gouldner (1960) and a few years later by Thompson (1967) in connection to interdependence—is an important one here. For instance, König et al. (2012, p. 1335) pointed out that a meta-organization's constituent firms share knowledge with each other "only when they are sure to receive some sort of an equivalent benefit." Moreover, the existence of a system-level goal implies that firms in meta-organizations are reciprocally interdependent in achieving this goal. As Gulati et al. (2012a, p. 573, italics added) point out, "meta-organizations resemble biological superorganisms, a multitude of individual organisms that coexist, collaborate, and coevolve via a complex set of *symbiotic and reciprocal relationships* which together form a larger organism (Tautz & Heilmann, 2008)." Reciprocal interdependence implies interactive transactions in which each firm or unit is "posing contingency for the other" (Thompson, 1967, p. 55). Reciprocal interdependence requires the highest form of interorganizational interaction and is considered the most difficult to coordinate for management (Newell et al., 2008; Thompson, 1967).

Das and Teng (2002a) pointed out that the meaning of reciprocity between more than two organizations could become less clear. For example, does each of the organizations reciprocate with all the others or are other reciprocal relationships possible? Taking a social exchange perspective, Das and Teng (2002a, p. 449) employs the construct "generalized reciprocity," defined as "a group-based exchange relationship in which members expect quid pro quo exchanges within the group but not necessarily with any specific member. Reciprocity becomes a generalized norm that all members are supposed to follow (Gouldner, 1960)."

As mentioned above, another defining feature of meta-organizations besides a system-level goal is "the absence of formal authority arising from an employment relationship between constituent entities" (Gulati et al., 2012a, p. 573). Gulati et al. (2012a) mention several ways in which firms in meta-organizations can substitute for the use of formal employment contracts in exercising control over other constituent firms. These include bargaining power—which "stems from the possession of unique resources [...] or investments in knowledge advantages" (p. 574) and the ensuing asymmetric dependence—as well as informal mechanisms based on such things as expertise, reputation, and gatekeeping privileges. They also indicate, however, that "it will be valuable to learn about other sources of authority in meta-organizations" (p. 581). In general, established firms can use several behavior and output control mechanisms (Das & Teng, 1998; Ouchi, 1977) other than employment contracts to exercise control over each other's activities (Vifell & Thedvall, 2012) and, by doing so, reduce the risks associated with interdependence. Examples are pre-established plans, standard operating procedures, dispute resolution procedures and non-market pricing systems (Gulati & Singh, 1998). A high level of formalization can be particularly important for those firms that are faced with high levels of asset specificity, transaction frequency and uncertainty (Poppo & Zenger, 2002).

Related to the use of these governance mechanisms is the degree of stratification: the level of hierarchical authority in meta-organizations. As Gulati et al. (2012a, p. 578) point out, "a high degree of stratification gives rise to, and enables the exercise of, status- or role-based authority structure," whereas a low degree of stratification is associated with "heterarchical [rather than hierarchical] coordination arrangements." A high degree of stratification can help reducing the complexity of coordination between a meta-organization's constituent firms and can serve as a mechanism to motivate these firms to contribute to the envisioned system-level goal (Gulati et al., 2012a). Highly stratified meta-organizations, however, are also at risk of increased bureaucracy that may reduce the meta-organization's responsiveness to achieve this goal. Furthermore, a high degree of stratification discourages the adoption of "peer-based approaches to coordination" and associated "broad participation in vital design/supervisory tasks" (Gulati et al., 2012a, p. 578), which may complicate the consensus-building necessary to achieve the system-level goal; hence, as stated by Gulati et al. (2012a, p. 579), stratification choices "have significant impacts on both motivation and coordination within meta-organizations." Most meta-organizations have a low level of hierarchy (Ahrne & Brunsson, 2008; König et al., 2012).

Whereas the system-level goal (goal attribute) and interrelatedness of multiple legally independent organizational entities (structure attribute) are inherent to all meta-organizations, the level of stratification (governance attribute) represents a dimension of meta-organizational design which can, hence, differ from one meta-organization to another. A second dimension of meta-organizational design considered by Gulati et al.

(2012a) is the degree to which the boundaries of a meta-organization are open for new entities to become part of it (i.e., boundary permeability). This dimension, which determines meta-organization membership (membership attribute), is predominantly determined by approval and policing procedures, the specification of membership criteria, membership duration and membership exclusivity (Gulati et al., 2012a). Approval and policing procedures vary in particular with the extent to which membership of the meta-organization is self-selective or subject to the approval by one or several—or all—existing members. Membership criteria are mainly related to the resources of potential member firms and the redundancy of these resources within the meta-organization. Finally, membership duration is influenced by exit barriers such as contracts that specify a minimum engagement period, while membership exclusivity is determined by the degree to which contributions of a meta-organization's constituent firms are made exclusively to this meta-organization. Hence, as stated by Gulati et al. (2012a, p. 577), boundary choices "fundamentally alter the behavioral dynamics within a meta-organization, as well as the range of feasible governance arrangement."

Management Innovation: Change in Core Management Activities

Collaboration can be a complex and difficult endeavor that needs to be managed properly to reap its potential benefits (Dyer, 2000; Gulati, Wohlgezogen, & Zhelyazkov, 2012b; Newell et al., 2008). In so doing, executives make choices regarding management activities associated with setting objectives, motivating efforts, coordinating activities and decision-making regarding resource allocation. Combined, these strategic managerial choices reflect firms' management model (Birkinshaw & Goddard, 2009; Hamel, 2007; Van Den Bosch, 2012). Previous firm-level literature has emphasized the importance of developing new management activities (i.e., management innovation) in order to enhance a firm's sustainable competitive advantage (Birkinshaw, 2010; Damanpour & Aravind, 2012; Hamel, 2006, 2007; Mol & Birkinshaw, 2009; Volberda, Van Den Bosch, & Heij, 2013). Birkinshaw, Hamel and Mol (2008, p. 829) defined management innovation as "the generation and implementation of a management practice, process, structure, or technique that is new to the state of the art and is intended to further organizational goals." They pointed out, however, that management innovation can equally be perceived as new to the organization rather than new to the state of the art. Also, Birkinshaw et al. (2008, p. 828) use the term "management practices" to cover the entire range of management practices, processes, structure and techniques. Hence, management innovation could be concisely described as the development (including generation and implementation) of new management practices.

Although the often-referenced definition of management innovation by Birkinshaw, Hamel, and Mol (2008) might be conceptually appealing, the distinctions among practices, processes, structures and techniques are, as they point out themselves, not conceptually nor empirically clean, and "there are important similarities *across* the different forms of management innovation" (p. 828). In examining how meta-organizations' constituent firms can contribute to the development of meta-management practices to enable system-level goals, we therefore choose an alternative way to conceptualize management innovation. This alternative conceptualization—which is based on studies by Birkinshaw and Goddard (2009) and Birkinshaw (2010)—discerns four conceptually separate, context-neutral sets of management activities (i.e., practices) which were already mentioned earlier: (1) setting objectives; (2) motivating efforts; (3) coordinating activities; and (4) decision-making regarding resource allocation. Management innovation implies an adaptation of the existing management model by changes in these four generic types of management activities and their interrelations (Hollen et al., 2013; Van Den Bosch, 2012); see also Table 5.4.

Previous literature has mainly examined what are the processes through which new management practices come about within an intra-organizational context (Birkinshaw et al., 2008; Damanpour & Aravind, 2012; Hamel, 2006; Mol & Birkinshaw, 2009). Taking an inter-organizational rather than an intra-organizational perspective, Hollen et al. (2013) and Meuer (2014) showed how the development of new management practices of a firm can also be enabled by and come about in an interorganizational context. In this chapter, we go one step further (see Table 5.5) by introducing a meta-organizational perspective of management innovation. In so doing, we examine the role of contributing to the development of new management practices on a meta-organizational level (i.e., meta-management practices). These practices can be seen as the product of the joint efforts of the meta-organization's constituent firms, implying a meta-organizational perspective.

TABLE 5.4 Conceptualizations of Management Innovation

- Definition of management innovation by Birkinshaw, Hamel & Mol (2008: 829): *"the generation and implementation of a management practice, process, structure, or technique that is new to the state of the art and is intended to further organizational goals."*
- Alternative conceptualization (used in this chapter) of management innovation: *adaptation of the existing management model by developing new management activities in terms of:*
  - *setting objectives* (associated with short-term or long-term direction);
  - *motivating efforts* (associated with extrinsic or intrinsic motivation);
  - *coordinating activities* (associated with formal or informal coordination);
  - *decision making* (associated with hierarchical or decentralized decision-making).

TABLE 5.5 Perspectives on the Management Innovation Process

Perspectives	Illustrative studies
Intra-organizational	Birkinshaw, Hamel & Mol (2008); Damanpour & Aravind (2012); Hamel (2006); Mol & Birkinshaw (2009); Vaccaro, Jansen, Van Den Bosch & Volberda (2012)
Inter-organizational	Hollen, Van Den Bosch & Volberda (2013); Meuer (2014)
Meta-organizational	Gap in the literature, addressed in this chapter

PROPOSITION DEVELOPMENT

Studies on meta-organizations differ from the mainstream literature on alliances and other forms of interorganizational relationships in that they explicitly treat a cluster of legally autonomous entities as an organization and acknowledge that such a meta-organization, like any other organization, "embodies key structural elements that can be designed" (Gulati et al., 2012a, p. 582). The key structural elements are associated with the management model that is in place, and the underlying design choices imply choices regarding the core management activities of management, that is, activities associated with setting objectives (i.e., providing direction), motivating employees, coordinating activities and decision-making (cf. Birkinshaw, 2010). In order for a meta-organization and constituent firms to achieve an existing system-level goal in a complex dynamic environment (or, for instance, to pursue new system-level goals), the meta-organization's management model may need to change over time. This is especially needed when the meta-organization is faced with non-paradigmatic environmental change (König et al., 2012). As elaborated next, we argue that this requires the development of meta-management practices, that is, new management practices on a meta-organizational level, with regard to respectively direction, motivation, coordination and decision-making.

System-level goals are often relatively long-term, broad goals. These goals might not have been formulated very specifically as future conditions in which they should be attained are largely unknown. Hence, it is needed to also introduce system-level *objectives* that support attainment of these goals. Because objectives that clarify and refine system-level goals are usually more specific and measurable than these goals themselves, they can be more easily used for comparison and monitoring purposes within the meta-organization. The visibility of these objectives can be increased through published action plans and standards (Vifell & Thedvall, 2012). In this way, alignment of these objectives within the meta-organization can be facilitated, which in turn enables a more collective, comparable and controllable effort to achieve the system-level goal. New objectives need to be set and evaluated to change behavior of the constituent firms towards the desired direction (Gruber & Niles, 1974).

By setting and aligning new objectives, a meta-organization may legitimize the engagement in long-term projects needed to enable its system-level goal. Its constituent firms might be interested only in investing in projects with a limited payback time, while the system-level goal might need investments in projects with a longer payback time. By setting the objective that there should be a certain amount of longer-payback investments in order to achieve the system-level goal, these investments can be partly legitimized among the constituent firms. Managers also need to set objectives that motivate the constituent firms to acquire new knowledge and experience from outside the meta-organization to prevent meta-organizational inertia (König et al., 2012). Additionally, new objectives serve to direct the terms of the meta-organizational agreement, which is needed to secure the cooperation of all constituent firms in making an effort to enable the system-level goal. These arguments lead to the following proposition:

> **Proposition 1:** *The ability of a meta-organization to achieve its system-level goal is likely to increase if the constituent firms contribute to develop meta-management practices that improve alignment of their objectives related to this goal.*

As pointed out by Gulati et al. (2012a, p. 581), an "important question about the internal organization of meta-organizations is how particular linkages can be incentivized." New motivation schemes and incentives are needed that stimulate inter-firm collaboration within the meta-organization and the overall pursuit of the system-level goal. The motivation of the constituent firms can be based on extrinsic and intrinsic values. The firms involved need to be motivated to optimally contribute to the system-level goal. This may require both behavioral and output control mechanisms (Das & Teng, 1998; Dekker, 2004; Ouchi, 1977). The firms also need to be motivated to cooperate by increasing their involvement in achieving the set objectives (e.g., Leufkens & Noorderhaven, 2011). Incentives should therefore be synchronized with the newly set objectives as discussed above. One way to attain enhanced intrinsic motivation of the firms is by giving special importance to the extent of firm-level contribution to the system-level goal. If firms' efforts and accomplishments are highly valued by all other firms in the meta-organization—which may include their industrial customers—they will be more motivated. The employees involved should also be motivated to learn how to properly collaborate with each other across organizational boundaries inasmuch as this is valuable for their firm's competitive advantage. The meta-organization's constituent firms should be stimulated to exchange operational knowledge. Gulati et al. (2012, p. 581) state that "privileged access to information or involvement in important decisions may serve as an intrinsic motivator for high priority relations in the collective." The larger the network of constituent firms, the more the meta-organizational context becomes a potentially rich knowledge base area in terms of both market and technology knowledge. The better the constituent firms can be motivated to communicate with and learn from each other, the more knowledge can be collectively generated, which may increase the meta-organization's ability to achieve its system-level goal. These arguments suggest the following proposition:

> **Proposition 2:** *The ability of a meta-organization to achieve its system-level goal is likely to increase if the constituent firms contribute to develop meta-management practices that enhance intrinsic and extrinsic motivation to support each other in achieving this goal.*

König et al. (2012, p. 1327) pointed out that meta-organizations "encourage the networking and knowledge sharing between members, and are engaged in the collaborative build-up of knowledge and trust." Indeed, this increases the ability of a meta-organization to achieve its system-level goal as the associated mutual adjustment facilitates collaborative efforts to do so. Open interfirm communication and knowledge sharing, which is largely based on trust (Das & Teng, 1998), is associated with a relational approach to managing interorganizational relations (Dyer & Singh, 1998; Ireland et al., 2002; Macneil, 1974; Ring & Van De Ven, 1994). This approach reflects the idea that firms need to collaborate as their competitiveness depends on "reaching positive-sum solutions to inter-firm coordination problems" (Uzzi, 1997, p. 51), which is related to a focus on interorganizational competitive advantage (Dyer & Singh, 1998). As mentioned before, such a focus represents a system-level goal.

Interfirm relationships within the meta-organization have to be effectively coordinated, particularly in the case of a high degree of interdependence in achieving the system-level goal. Firm-level activities need to be aligned with each other and with this goal. Malets (2010, p. 1741) emphasized that "in order to survive, meta-organizations have to creatively manage differences and similarities between members [...] and continuously balance their own identities with the identities of their members." Coordination might be focused on exploiting experiences and/or resources of each other (Liebeskind, Oliver, Zucker, & Brewer, 1996) and on the joint production of new experiences by engaging in collective explorative undertakings (Holmqvist, 2004; Santamaria & Surroca, 2011). Interrelated activities within the meta-organization need to be coordinated in such a way that the meta-organizational context provides incentives for both exploratory and exploitative activities in pursuing the system-level goal. This may require one or more entrepreneurial and ambidextrous meta-organizational staff members who will bear responsibility for all interorganizational activities that are associated with enabling the system-level goal. Relevant knowledge and experience of constituent firms regarding the achievement of goals comparable to the system-level goal needs to be integrated in order to realize the meta-organizational innovation's potential. Exchanging complex and tacit know-how within the meta-organization may require managers or technicians of the firms to visit each other. When objectives related to the system's level goal have been achieved, proceedings need to be monitored to see whether further changes are warranted. Coordination is also related to the means by which managers of the constituent firms value, assimilate and utilize new knowledge (Cohen & Levinthal, 1990) as acquired in the meta-organizational context. Besides coordinating communication and knowledge flows within its boundaries, meta-organizations also coordinate interaction of their constituent firms with external actors which, as pointed out by König et al. (2012, p. 1336), "can provide crucial information on the future of a field and on appropriate adaptation strategies, and act as catalysts for overcoming inertia." The above arguments give rise to the following proposition:

> **Proposition 3:** *The ability of a meta-organization to achieve its system-level goal is likely to increase if the constituent firms contribute to develop meta-management practices that improve coordination by mutual adjustment based on communication and knowledge sharing related to this goal.*

Exhibit 5.2 provides an empirical context in which proposition 3 can be investigated.

EXHIBIT 5.2
Illustrative Example of the Development of Meta-Management Practices

Situated in the Port of Rotterdam, Plant One is a test facility—unique in Western Europe—enabling sustainable process technology. The test facility is an independent limited-liability organization that has been initiated by a consortium of various Dutch organizations, including the Port of Rotterdam Authority, and governmental agencies. It can be considered as a meta-organization that is open to all firms aiming to develop technologies that contribute to the system-level goal of more sustainable process technologies. It facilitates the development phase of promising chemical process technologies by enabling these to be tested on production scale and further developed for industrial applications. The facility offers equipped office space, a machine park and various industrial utilities, and intermediates the storage and handling of chemicals. Under the test facility's umbrella environmental permit, it can ensure that the legally autonomous firms in the facility receive required permits for their pilots within weeks instead of months. The test facility's staff consists of a managing director, an operations manager and a health, safety and environment manager which provide support, including maintenance and technical support, licensing and safety advice, and boundary spanning efforts to attract clients for the firm's process technologies. Communication and knowledge exchanges take place between firms within the test-facility, which is facilitated by informal meetings and informal talks between employees from the firms during their daily activities. As the number of firms within Plant One increased, these practices have been largely developed over time and most likely contribute positively to the system-level goal.

Sources: Documents of Plant One; Van Den Bosch, Hollen, Volberda, & Baaij (2011).

The development of meta-management practices as mentioned above needs to be accompanied by putting in place new meta-management activities associated with decision-making about allocating resources, including human resources regarding meta-organizational projects. Resource allocation and commitment within the meta-organization is largely dependent on the constituent firms which, as pointed out by König et al. (2012, p. 1325), "typically have access to more resources than the meta-organization itself." The managers of these constituent firms are required to find and allocate discretionary time for effectively managing this endeavor (Gruber & Niles, 1974). New or adapted decision-making activities are required that take the interaction with other organizations within the meta-organization into account, for example by highlighting interorganizational decision-making (Tuite, Chisholm, & Radnor, 2009). Decision-making procedures on meta-organizational level should be clearly defined so as to prevent protracted decision-making that causes inertia in response to non-paradigmatic environmental change (König et al., 2012). In order to promote interorganizational knowledge sharing (e.g., Soekijad & Andriessen, 2003) in collective explorative undertakings, decision-making in meta-organizations may need to be less hierarchically structured than would be the case within the constituent firms themselves. Gulati et al. (2012a, p. 574) point out that "decisions about who is collocated with whom are as important as decisions about who is grouped with whom in the organization's divisional structure." Based on these insights, we suggest the following proposition:

Proposition 4: *The ability of a meta-organization to achieve its system-level goal is likely to increase if the constituent firms contribute to develop meta-management practices that enhance interorganizational decision-making regarding resource allocation related to this goal.*

DISCUSSION AND CONCLUDING REMARKS

When established firms become more interdependent in reaching a certain goal, it is particularly the set of interrelated interorganizational relationships—in the form of a meta-organization—that needs to be examined, which goes beyond the viewpoints of the individual firms involved. Meta-organizations are an "increasingly important form of organizing" (Konig et al., 2012, p. 1325) that are continuously challenged to achieve system-level goals for the benefit of their constituent firms (Gulati et al., 2012a). In this chapter we examined how established firms can increase their meta-organization's ability to achieve this system-level goal by contributing to the development of new meta-management practices (i.e., management innovation on a meta-organization level). Drawing on a literature review in which we distinguished four conceptually separate, generic types of meta-management practices (i.e., setting objectives, motivating efforts, coordinating activities and decision-making) that make up a *meta-organization's management model*, we developed a set of propositions that suggest how contributing to adaptation of this management model can increase the ability to achieve the meta-organization's system-level goal.

We particularly emphasized the importance of developing meta-management practices that enhance (1) alignment of objectives of the meta-organization's constituent firms related to the system-level goal; (2) intrinsic and extrinsic motivation to support each other in achieving this goal; (3) coordination by mutual adjustment based on communication and knowledge sharing related to this goal; and (4) interorganizational decision-making regarding resource allocation related to this goal. The speed with which choices are made regarding adaptation of the meta-management model in these ways and the chosen or emerging sequence (i.e., first changing decision-making, followed by changing motivation) are likely to be different for each meta-organization. We suggest that these differences in meta-organization-specific development of changes in the meta-management model result in differences in ability to achieve system-level goals and, hence, in the constituent firms' interorganizational competitive advantage. The fact that the distinguished meta-management practices are context-neutral (Birkinshaw & Goddard, 2009; Birkinshaw, 2010; Van Den Bosch, 2012) makes them applicable to various types of meta-organizations.

Enhanced collaboration between a meta-organization's constituent firms so as to achieve a system-level goal—which contributes to interorganizational competitive advantage (cf. Dyer & Singh, 1998)—requires a *relational approach* to managing interorganizational relationships and the associated interdependencies (e.g., Dyer, 2000; Ireland et al., 2002; Macneil, 1974; Ring & Van De Ven, 1994). Indeed, a relational approach is associated with a certain level of interorganizational knowledge sharing, disclosure of proprietary information, mutual adjustment and joint problem solving. Most established firms, however, are used to a more transaction-oriented (rather than relation-oriented) approach to managing interdependence relationships in order to protect their competitive advantage (Hollen & Van Den Bosch, 2013). Being principally motivated by self-interest from a short-term perspective, activities consistent with a transaction-oriented approach are embedded in "atomistic" network ties that lack social embeddedness (Uzzi, 1997, p. 36). A transition from a mainly transaction-oriented approach to a mainly relation-oriented approach emphasizes in particular the importance of trust-building efforts (Das & Teng, 1998; Neumann & Bachmann, 2011; Ring & Van De Ven, 1994) and, related to this, the importance of the development of a joint performance indicator (Hollen & Van Den Bosch, 2013).

Contributions

This chapter contributes in two related ways to the literature (see also Table 5.6). First, we contribute to the emerging *literature on meta-organizations* by distinguishing four generic and context-neutral types of meta-management practices that collectively define a meta-organization's management model, and by subsequently examining how adapting this management model improves a meta-organization's ability to achieve the envisioned system-level goal. König et al. (2012) have shown how general characteristics of meta-organizations cause inertia to non-paradigmatic changes in the external environment—which require achieving *new* system-level goals—and how these inertial forces can be partially offset by changes in meta-managements' constitution and routines. In this chapter, we examined how to improve meta-organizations' ability to achieve *existing* system-level goals by leveraging interorganizational collaboration within the meta-organization through the development of new meta-management practices.

TABLE 5.6 Contributions to the Literature

- Contribution to the literature on meta-organizations (i) by distinguishing four generic and context-neutral types of meta-management practices that collectively define a meta-organization's management model, and (ii) by developing propositions on how adapting this management model improves a meta-organization's ability to achieve the envisioned system-level goal.
- Contribution to the management innovation literature by theorizing beyond a firm-level locus of management innovation: we examine how established firms develop new management practices at meta-organizational level in order to achieve system-level goals that cannot be achieved via management innovation at a firm level only.

Second, by examining the development of new management practices in a meta-organizational context, this chapter contributes to the *management innovation literature*, which is still focused primarily focused on an intra-firm level of analysis (Birkinshaw et al., 2008; Damanpour & Aravind, 2012; Hamel, 2006; Mol & Birkinshaw, 2009; Vaccaro et al., 2012). Specifically, we examined how established firms develop new activities associated with setting objectives, motivating efforts, coordinating activities and decision-making at the level of their meta-organization in order to achieve system-level goals that cannot be achieved via management innovation at a firm level only. Accordingly, we theorize beyond a firm-level locus of management innovation. The focus on the interorganizational context of meta-organizations enables a broader recognition of the role of interorganizational interaction and the associated change agents (cf. Birkinshaw et al., 2008) in shaping and influencing the management innovation process.

How are these contributions related to a Behavioral Approach to Strategy? This question is not easy to address because the definition and discussions about the delineation of such an approach with related approaches do not yet result in broadly accepted views. A recent Special Issue (December 2011) of the *Strategic Management Journal* illustrates two different views. The introductory article claims: "Behavioral strategy merges cognitive and social psychology with strategic management theory and practice" (Powell, Lovallo, & Fox, 2011, p. 1371). The concluding article in the same Special Issue bears the provocative title: "A behavioral approach to strategy—what's the alternative?" In that article, Levinthal (2011, p. 1517) argues that "the divide between economic and behavioral approaches [...] is a false divide as any but the most trivial problems require a behavioral act of representation prior to invoking a deductive, 'rational' approach. In this sense, all approaches are behavioral." As the constructs and theoretical perspectives used in this paper are clearly related to the behavior of human actors, we believe our findings contribute to a Behavioral Approach to Strategy in two ways; first, by focusing on meta-organizations as an interesting research context for such an approach, and second, by investigating management innovation in this context as an important behavioral lever to accomplish system-level goals of meta-organizations.

Limitations and Directions for Future Research

Several limitations of this chapter merit discussion and suggest directions for future research. Indeed, Gulati et al. (2012a, p. 582) state that "many areas of inquiry about meta-organizations remain fertile ground for further investigation." First, by emphasizing the active role of managers of the meta-organization's constituent firms in improving the meta-organization's ability to achieve the system-level goal, our propositions reflect a rational perspective on management innovation (cf. Birkinshaw et al., 2008). Hence, we have focused on the actions and choices of key individuals, (i.e., managers). Future research could also examine the role of institutional conditions and attitudes of major influencer groups (institutional perspective), suppliers of new ideas and their legitimacy (fashion perspective) and organizational culture (cultural perspective).

Second, in investigating the development of new meta-management practices, we have taken account of reciprocal interdependence among interconnected firms in achieving a system-level goal. In future research, it would be interesting to apply in a meta-organizational context the social exchange perspective proposed by Das and Teng (2002a, 2002b). Applying this perspective will contribute to an improved understanding of the role of generalized exchange processes and associated social control mechanisms. Another related issue would be to investigate the similarities and differences between alliance constellations (Das & Teng, 2002a; Gomes-Casseres, 1996) on the one hand and meta-organizations on the other hand.

Third, we have not looked into the effect of the size of the meta-organization (i.e., the number of constituent firms) on the development of meta-management practices. A larger number of interconnected firms will lead to more contingencies, requiring more network activities to be orchestrated through mutual adjustment, and a larger network also limits the potential development of informal management practices (Doménech & Davies, 2011). This will increase the complexity, difficulties and costs of coordination (Thompson, 1967). Future research could examine to what extent meta-organization size has an effect on the constituent firms' behavioral strategy (Powell et al., 2011) regarding the management of interorganizational relations within the meta-organization.

Fourth, future research is needed to empirically examine how the development of meta-management practices can increase the meta-organization's ability to achieve its system-level goals over time. In particular, longitudinal case studies are required to properly investigate and illustrate the process dimension associated with this development. The empirical research could include examining secondary data sources (such as internal documents and publicly available archival sources) from the meta-organization and its constituent firms as well as conducting a series of in-depth, semi-structured interviews with key players within the meta-organization. In so doing, it is especially important to get a clear picture of key events associated with the development of new meta-management practices over time and to find yardsticks for measuring progress in achieving the system-level goal.

Notwithstanding the discussed limitations, we would argue that the conceptualization and examination of management innovation on a meta-organizational level of analysis extend and advance the literature on both meta-organizations and management innovation, and that this chapter contributes to a better understanding of the role of contributing to new ways of setting objectives, motivating efforts, coordinating activities and decision-making in improving the ability of meta-organizations and their constituent firms to achieve strategically important system-level goals over time and, in turn, to foster interorganizational competitive advantage.

ACKNOWLEDGMENTS

The authors gratefully acknowledge the financial support of the Port of Rotterdam Authority in funding the PhD research of the first author. They are also grateful for the interviews and discussions held with (senior) managers of the Port of Rotterdam Authority and various other organizations and companies in the Port of Rotterdam.

REFERENCES

Ahrne, G., & Brunsson, N. (2005). Organizations and meta-organizations. *Scandinavian Journal of Management, 21*, 429–449.

Ahrne, G., & Brunsson, N. (2008). *Meta-Organizations.* Cheltenham, UK: Edward Elgar.

Ahrne, G., Brunsson, N., & Hallström, K. T. (2007). Organizing organizations. *Organization, 14*, 619–624.

Birkinshaw, J. (2010). *Reinventing management: Smarter choices for getting work done.* Chichester, UK: John Wiley & Sons.

Birkinshaw, J., & Goddard, J. (2009). What is your management model? *Sloan Management Review, 50*(2), 81–90.

Birkinshaw, J., Hamel, G., & Mol, M. J. (2008). Management innovation. *Academy of Management Review, 33*, 825–845.

Birkinshaw, J., & Mol, M. J. (2006). How management innovation happens. *Sloan Management Review, 47*(4), 81–88.

Cohen, W., & Levinthal, D. 1990. Absorptive capacity: A new perspective on learning and innovation. *Administrative Science Quarterly, 35*, 128–152.

Damanpour, F., & Aravind, D. (2012). Managerial innovation: Conceptions, processes, and antecedents. *Management and Organization Review, 8*, 423–454.

Das, T. K., & Teng, B. (1998). Between trust and control: Developing confidence in partner cooperation in alliances. *Academy of Management Review, 23*, 491–512.

Das, T. K., & Teng, B. (2002a). Alliance constellations: A social exchange perspective. *Academy of Management Review, 27*, 445–456.

Das, T. K., & Teng, B. (2002b). A social exchange theory of strategic alliances. In F. J. Contractor, & P. Lorange (Eds.), *Cooperative strategies and alliances* (pp. 439–460). Oxford, UK: Elsevier Science.

Dekker, H. C. (2004). Control of inter-organizational relationships: Evidence on appropriation concerns and coordination requirements. *Accounting, Organizations and Society, 29,* 27–49.

Doménech, T., & Davies, M. (2011). The role of embeddedness in industrial symbiosis networks: Phases in the evolution of industrial symbiosis networks. *Business Strategy and the Environment, 20,* 281–296.

Dougherty, D., & Dunne, D. D. (2011). Organizing ecologies of complex innovation. *Organization Science, 22,* 1214–1223.

Dyer, J. H. (1997). Effective interfirm collaboration: How firms minimize transaction costs and maximize transaction value. *Strategic Management Journal, 18,* 535–556.

Dyer, J. H. (2000). *Collaborative advantage: Winning through extended enterprise supplier networks.* New York, NY: Oxford University Press.

Dyer, J. H., & Singh, H. (1998). The relational view: Cooperative strategy and sources of interorganizational competitive advantage. *Academy of Management Review, 23,* 660–679.

Esty, D. C., & Porter, M. E. (1998). Industrial ecology and competitiveness: Strategic implications for the firm. *Journal of Industrial Ecology, 2*(1), 35–43.

Gomes-Casseres, B. (1996). *The alliance revolution: The new shape of business rivalry.* Cambridge, MA: Harvard University Press.

Gouldner, A. W. (1960). The norm of reciprocity: A preliminary statement. *American Sociological Review, 25,* 161–178.

Gruber, W. H., & Niles, J. S. (1974). How to innovate in management. *Organizational Dynamics, 3*(2), 31–47.

Gulati, R. (2007). *Managing network resources: Alliances, affiliations, and other relational assets.* New York, NY: Oxford University Press.

Gulati, R., & Kletter, D. (2005). Shrinking core, expanding periphery: The relational architecture of high-performing organizations. *California Management Review, 47*(3), 77–104.

Gulati, R., & Singh, H. (1998). The architecture of cooperation: Managing coordination costs and appropriation concerns in strategic alliances. *Administrative Science Quarterly, 43,* 781–814.

Gulati, R., Puranam, P., & Tushman, M. (2012a). Meta-organization design: Rethinking design in interorganizational and community contexts. *Strategic Management Journal, 33,* 571–586.

Gulati, R., Wohlgezogen, F., & Zhelyazkov, P. (2012b). The two facets of collaboration: Cooperation and coordination in strategic alliances. *Academy of Management Annals, 6,* 531–583.

Hamel, G. (2006). The why, what, and how of management innovation. *Harvard Business Review, 84*(2), 72–84.

Hamel, G. (2007). *The future of management.* Boston, MA: Harvard Business School Press.

Hollen, R. M. A., Van Den Bosch, F. A. J., & Volberda, H. W. (2013). The role of management innovation in enabling technological process innovation: An inter-organizational perspective. *European Management Review, 10*(1), 35–50.

Hollen, R. M. A., & Van Den Bosch, F. A. J. (2013). *Managing interorganizational interdependencies in industrial ecosystems.* Paper presented at the Academy of Management Annual Meeting, Lake Buena Vista, FL.

Holmqvist, M. (2004). Experiential learning processes of exploitation and exploration within and between organizations: An empirical study of product development. *Organization Science, 15,* 70–81.

Ireland, R. D., Hitt, M. A., & Vaidyanath, D. (2002). Alliance management as a source of competitive advantage. *Journal of Management, 28,* 413–446.

König, A., Schulte, M., & Enders, A. (2012). Inertia in response to non-paradigmatic change: The case of meta-organizations. *Research Policy, 41,* 1325–1343.

Leufkens, A. S., & Noorderhaven, N. G. (2011). Learning to collaborate in multi-organizational projects. *International Journal of Project Management, 29,* 432–441.

Levinthal, D. A. (2011). A behavioral approach to strategy—What's the alternative? *Strategic Management Journal, 32,* 1517–1523.

Liebeskind, J. P., Oliver, A. L., Zucker, L., & Brewer, M. (1996). Social networks, learning, and flexibility: Sourcing scientific knowledge in new biotechnology firms. *Organization Studies, 7,* 428–441.

Macneil, I. R. (1974). The many futures of contracts. *Southern California Law Review, 47,* 691–816.

Madhok, A., & Tallman, S. B. (1998). Resources, transactions and rents: Managing value through interfirm collaborative relationships. *Organization Science, 9,* 326–339.

Malets, O. (2010). Book review of Göran Ahrne and Nils Brunsson: *Meta-Organizations* (2008), Cheltenham, UK: Edward Elgar. *Organization Studies, 31,* 1740–1744.

Meuer, J. (2014). Archetypes of inter-firm relations in the implementation of management innovation: A set-theoretic study in China's biopharmaceutical industry. *Organization Studies, 35,* 121–145.

Mol, M. J., & Birkinshaw, J. (2009). The sources of management innovation: When firms introduce new management practices. *Journal of Business Research, 62,* 1269–1280.

Neumann, K., & Bachmann, R. (2011). The containment of opportunism in the post formation period of interorganizational relationships. In T. K. Das (Ed.), *Strategic alliances in a globalizing world* (pp. 159–184). Charlotte, NC: Information Age Publishing.

Newell, S., Goussevskaia, A., Swan, J., Bresnen, M., & Obembe, A. (2008). Interdependencies in complex project ecologies: The case of biomedical innovation. *Long Range Planning, 41*(1), 33–54.

Ouchi, W.G. (1977). The relationship between organizational structure and organizational control. *Administrative Science Quarterly, 22,* 95–113.

Poppo, L., & Zenger, T. (2002). Do formal contracts and relational governance function as substitutes or complements? *Strategic Management Journal, 23,* 707–725.

Powell, T. C., Lovallo, D., & Fox, C. R. (2011). Behavioral strategy. *Strategic Management Journal, 32,* 1369–1386.

Reveley, J., & Ville, S. (2010). Enhancing industry association theory: A comparative business history contribution. *Journal of Management Studies, 47,* 837–858.

Ring, P. S., & Van De Ven, A. H. (1994). Developmental processes of cooperative interorganizational relationships. *Academy of Management Review, 19,* 90–118.

Santamaria, L., & Surroca, J. (2011). Matching the goals and impacts of R&D collaboration. *European Management Review, 8*(2), 95–109.

Shekhar, S. (2006). Understanding the virtuality of virtual organizations. *Leadership & Organization Development Journal, 27*, 465–483.

Soekijad, M., & Andriessen, E. (2003). Conditions for knowledge sharing in competitive alliances. *European Management Journal, 21*, 578–587.

Tautz, J., & Heilmann, H. R. (2008). *The buzz about the bees: Biology of a superorganism.* Berlin, Germany: Springer.

Thompson, J. D. (1967) [2003]. *Organizations in action: Social science bases of administrative theory.* New Brunswick, NJ: Transaction Publishers.

Tuite, M. F., Chisholm, R. K., & Radnor, M. (2009). *Inter-organizational decision making.* Chicago, IL: Aldine Publishing.

Uzzi, B. (1997). Social structure and competition in interfirm networks: The paradox of embeddedness. *Administrative Science Quarterly, 42*, 35–67.

Vaccaro, I. G., Jansen, J. J. P., Van Den Bosch, F. A. J., & Volberda, H. W. (2012). Management innovation and leadership: The moderating role of organizational size. *Journal of Management Studies, 49*, 28–51.

Van Den Bosch, F. A. J. (2012). *On the necessity and scientific challenges of conducting research into strategic value creating management models.* Rotterdam, Netherlands: Erasmus University Rotterdam, Erasmus Research Institute of Management (ERIM).

Van Den Bosch, F. A. J., Hollen, R. M. A., Volberda, H. W., & Baaij, M. G. (2011). *The strategic value of the Port of Rotterdam for the international competitiveness of the Netherlands: A first exploration.* Rotterdam, Netherlands: INSCOPE.

Vifell, Å. C., & Thedvall, R. (2012). Organizing for social sustainability: Governance through bureaucratization in meta-organizations. *Sustainability: Science, Practice & Policy, 8*(1), 50–58.

Volberda, H. W., Van Den Bosch, F. A. J., & Heij, C. V. (2013). Management innovation: Management as fertile ground for innovation. *European Management Review, 10*(1), 1–15.

CHAPTER 6

STRATEGIC RISK BEHAVIOR AND ITS TEMPORALITIES

T. K. Das
Bing-Sheng Teng

ABSTRACT

What are the determinants of strategic risk behavior? Are they the dispositional characteristics of decision makers or the situational constraints? Or both? The empirical evidence is on all sides. We believe the issue has not been satisfactorily resolved so far because of the continued neglect of the fundamental role of time in risk behavior. Given that risk is embedded in time, we need to recognize two critical aspects of the temporal dimension. The first is concerned with risk horizons, as in short-range and long-range risk horizons. The second temporal aspect relates to individual future orientations of the top managers, as in near-future and distant-future orientations. We propose in this chapter a temporal framework of strategic risk behavior in which the two temporalities are integrated with risk propensity and perceived decision context. We then develop, based on this temporal framework, the contingent answers for the relative roles of dispositional characteristics and situational constraints in determining strategic risk behavior.

Behavioral Strategy: Emerging Perspectives, pages 129–153

INTRODUCTION

Over four decades ago Kogan and Wallach (1967) articulated the fundamental question about the determinants of risk behavior in terms of the relative roles of the dispositional characteristics of decision makers and the situational constraints:

> Having gained an overview of the kinds of relationships that dispositions toward risk or conservatism exhibit with other kinds of differences among individuals, as well as with information on the kinds of situational characteristics that can be expected to influence the riskiness of a person's decisions, it is necessary to perform some kind of psychological weighing of these two classes of determinants. *How important are individual consistencies relative to situational constraints when it comes to predicting someone's inclination for risk or conservatism?* (pp. 207–208; emphasis added)

The issue remains unresolved. In recent years, however, risk and risk taking have assumed increasing significance in the study of strategic decision making. Strategic risk behavior constitutes an essential perspective in analyzing strategic behavior. Broadly defined, strategic risk taking refers to "corporate strategic moves that cause returns to vary, that involve venturing into the unknown, and that may result in corporate ruin" (Baird & Thomas, 1985, p. 231). Considering that risk is a problematic aspect in the management of business organizations, it is important to understand the reasons that lead strategists to engage in risky decision making behavior. In this chapter we attempt to at least partially answer the Kogan-Wallach question by developing a contingency framework of strategic risk behavior based on the decision maker's risk propensity and two significant, but thus far neglected, aspects of the temporal dimension.

We propose a temporal contingency framework that seeks to reconcile some of the conflicting theories about the determinants of risk behavior. Extensive research on risk taking carried out by psychologists over the years has resulted in two competing paradigms concerning the attributes of risk taking behavior—one suggested by the personality psychologists who focus on individual differences in risk taking behavior, and the other by the experimental psychologists who deal with risk taking in such terms as subjective expected utility (Lopes, 1987).

The view of the personality psychologists focuses on individual differences in risk taking, so that it ascribes risk behavior mostly to the general traits and dispositional tendencies of decision makers. Scholars have observed that individuals are fairly consistent in their attitudes toward risk—some people seem more comfortable with risk taking than others (Bromiley & Curley, 1992). Based on such a stable individual attribute, researchers differentiate decision makers in terms of their risk propensity—namely, as being either risk averters or risk seekers. Some researchers also believe that a dispositional risk propensity can help explain, to a large extent, the risk behavior of individuals.

In contrast, the experimental psychologists challenge the consistency of such dispositional traits, and argue that situational factors have a greater influence on risk taking behavior (Kahneman & Tversky, 1979; Slovic, 1972). Unlike other psychological attributes, the risk propensity of decision makers seems to lack constancy across decision situations (MacCrimmon & Wehrung, 1986; Schoemaker, 1990). Since this view attempts to understand Everyman's risk taking behavior, it regards the external stimulus as the more important. Many empirical studies suggest that situational factors such as outcome history and decision framing are salient in determining the riskiness of strategic decisions (Bowman, 1982). Hence, the view of the experimental psychologists—which treats risk taking as situation-contingent—seems to command substantial support.

Since both views have their virtues and considerable empirical support, efforts have been made to integrate them, mostly following an eclectic approach (e.g., Baird & Thomas, 1985; Sitkin & Pablo, 1992). These studies suggest that the dispositional risk propensity interacts with situational factors in determining risk taking behavior. In this chapter we present an alternative framework for reconciling the two views on the determinants of strategic risk behavior. The key to truly integrating both views, we believe, is to recognize that there is a temporal dimension in the risk taking construct (Strickland, Lewicki, & Katz, 1966). Time is critically relevant to risk taking, because risk and uncertainty are intimately related (Yates & Stone, 1992) and "uncertainty is embedded in time" (Lopes, 1987, p. 289). However, psychological theories of risk behavior rarely incorporate this temporal dimension as a core element. We propose a temporal framework that embraces both views of strategic risk behavior. In particular, risk horizons and the future orientations of top managers play key roles in this temporal contingency framework.

DETERMINANTS OF RISK BEHAVIOR: RISK PROPENSITY VERSUS DECISION CONTEXT

The field of strategic risk taking draws heavily on studies of individual risk behavior. The rationale is that, to a certain extent, the strategies of an organization reflect the dispositions of the top executives in terms of their subjective attributes, such as their background, beliefs, attitudes, and problem-solving styles (Das, 1986; Hambrick & Mason, 1984). Therefore, the risk taking behavior of top managers would have a significant impact on the riskiness of strategic choices (Baird & Thomas, 1985; Bowman, 1982).

Before examining strategic risk taking behavior—or strategic risk behavior for short—it would be helpful to clarify what we mean by risk. Risk appears to be one of the most commonly abused concepts in the social sciences and researchers often depart significantly in their constructs of risk (Yates & Stone, 1992). Economic and psychological sciences define risk as a condition in which decision makers know the possible consequences of the decisions as well as their associated probabilities (Arrow, 1971). In strategic management, it is seldom that all possible decision consequences and their probabilities are known. Thus, risk is often used as if it is the same as "uncertainty," or unpredictable consequences and/or probabilities (Baird & Thomas, 1985). In this sense, strategic management scholars refer to risk as variance in performance beyond the control of decision makers. In recent years, recognition has been growing in the strategy literature that managers conceive of risk only as "down-side" possibilities. That is, managers are more concerned with negative variations in performance, not performance variances as a whole (March & Shapira, 1987). For our purposes here, we define risk broadly as the unpredictability in decision outcomes. Thus, risk taking would be to consciously undertake tasks which are associated with uncertain consequences.

As we mentioned earlier, the major theories of risk taking are split into two competing paradigms—one focusing on individual dispositional differences and the other on emphasizing situational factors. In the remainder of this section, we briefly review the research on both views. We also note several approaches that have been proposed for integrating these two views of risk behavior.

Dispositional Characteristics

A large number of empirical studies have reported on individual differences in risk taking behavior (Alderfer & Bierman, 1970; Ghosh & Ray, 1992; Rowe, 1977). In his research with the "ring toss" game, McClelland (1961) found that children with high motivation to succeed tended to throw rings onto a peg from intermediate distances—that is, to take moderate risks. One study that directly examined the consistency of dispositional risk propensity was carried out by Schneider and Lopes (1986). They presented one risk-averse group and one risk-seeking group multiple lottery choices as a heterogeneous set of stimuli for risk taking. The results indicated that the risk-seeking group tended to consistently prefer riskier choices as compared with the risk-averse group. Furthermore, researchers have identified certain personal characteristics and attributes—such as gender, age, and locus of control—that are related to an individual's risk taking behavior (Miller, Kets de Vries, & Toulouse, 1982; Taylor & Dunnette, 1974; Vroom

& Pahl, 1971), supporting the idea that risk behavior is related to personal characteristics. Researchers have also used the term "risk propensity" to refer to a stable individual trait toward taking or avoiding risk (Fischhoff, Lichtenstein, Slovic, Derby, & Keeney, 1981; Rowe, 1977).

According to Sitkin and Weingart, risk propensity can be defined as "an individual's current tendency to take or avoid risks" (1995, p. 1575). They also note that even the critics of the dispositional approach to risk "have employed the traditional conception of risk propensity as a stable individual attribute" (p. 1575). Although their usage of the term differs somewhat from our definition, the belief underlying such usage is that some kind of stable within-person across-situation consistency does exist. Apparently, this definition links risk propensity causally with actual risky decision making. Although a risk seeking propensity does not automatically result in high-risk behavior, risk propensity is probably the single most important attribute that contributes to risk behavior (see Sitkin & Pablo, 1992). Previous studies have identified risk propensity as the causal antecedent of actual risk behavior (Sitkin & Weingart, 1995). Hence, we assume a linear causality between risk propensity and risk behavior—a risk seeking propensity leads to more risk taking or high-risk behavior.

Based on the belief that decision makers are distinct in their risk propensity—and consistently so—strategic management scholars have looked into the relationship between risk propensity of top managers and organizational outcomes (e.g., Taylor & Dunnette, 1974). This line of research may be subsumed under the so-called subjective view of strategic decision making (Das, 1986), or behavioral strategy making, in which the psychological and other characteristics of top managers are believed to be useful in explaining variations in strategic choices, including strategic risk taking (Das, 1986, 2004a, 2006; Das & Teng, 1997, 1999).

In contrast to the above belief, there is also some evidence that contradicts the consistency of dispositional risk propensity (Schoemaker, 1990; Slovic, 1962). Schoemaker (1990), for example, found low correlation of risk propensity within subjects across decision domains. Other researchers also report a low level of correlation among multiple risk measures (Kogan & Wallach, 1964; MacCrimmon & Wehrung, 1986). These results suggest that individual consistency in risk behavior across situations is open to some question.

Situational Characteristics

While the evidence for a robust dispositional risk propensity remains inconclusive, a large number of studies suggest that situational factors—such as problem framing and perceived context of the decision—have much to do with risky decisions (e.g., March & Shapira, 1987; Schoemaker, 1990).

Using four types of risk-taking measures, Slovic (1962, 1972) found low intercorrelations among the various measures of risk taking in different situations. He thus concluded that the results of his study "must be viewed more as support for the importance of situational factors than support for the notion of risk-taking propensity as a stable trait" (1972, p. 133).

A good example supporting the situation-contingent view is concerned with individuals' risk-averseness. On the one hand, it has been found that most people are risk averse in gain situations—that is, they prefer sure gains (say \$300) to risky options (say 80% chance of winning \$400) even though the expected value of risky options (80% × \$400 = \$320) is higher. On the other hand, decision makers also tend to be risk-seeking in loss situations—that is, they prefer risky options (say 80% chance of losing \$400) to sure loss (say \$300). Although some studies suggest an opposite preference—for example, Thaler and Johnson (1990)—in general, the pattern reflected in the above example has been fairly well supported (March, 1988; MacCrimmon & Wehrung, 1986; Tversky & Kahneman, 1991).

Over the years, psychologists have proposed various theories to account for such changes in risk behavior due to situational differences. One of the best known is Kahneman and Tversky's (1979) prospect theory, according to which decision makers evaluate the risky options through a subjective value system characterized by reference dependence and loss aversion. Essentially, individuals are believed to code outcomes relative to some reference point—such as the status quo—and then interpret the outcomes as either a loss or a gain. Prospect theory suggests that people can shift their reference points—or adaptive aspirations (March, 1988)—so that their risk behavior may change accordingly. In addition, since people are loss-averse, they weigh losses and disadvantages more heavily than gains and advantages. Empirical studies show that losses are weighted about twice as much as gains (Tversky & Kahneman, 1992). Therefore, people tend to be risk-averse in gain situations to avoid possible loss, and they become risk-seeking in loss situations in order to recover the loss.

The same phenomenon has been identified in strategic risk taking. Managers report that they take fewer risks when their companies are performing well (MacCrimmon & Wehrung, 1986; March & Shapira, 1987; Shapira, 1995). With few exceptions, the literature largely confirms a negative correlation between risk and performance—that is, troubled firms tend to take more risk, which leads to even worse performance (Bowman, 1982; Bromiley, 1991).

Against this background, Bateman and Zeithaml (1989a, 1989b) identified "perceived current context" as one of the key dimensions of the psychological context of strategic decisions. In line with prospect theory, the essence of the perceived decision context is that decision makers adjust their risk taking behavior by assessing their current situation with regard to their aspiration level. When the decision context is perceived as positive, decision makers tend to be risk averse. Nevertheless, the very same person could become a risk seeker if he or she perceives the decision context as negative (i.e., being lower than the aspiration level or reference point). In a recent study, Hodgkinson, Bown, Maule, Glaister, and Pearman (1999) confirmed that strategic decision making is strongly affected by the positive or negative framing of decision scenarios.

Integrative Approaches

It would seem that the two approaches discussed above are at odds as to the sources of risk behavior—while the personality psychologists' view is intended to understand how people are different, the experimental psychologists' view probes into the risk behavior of people as if they were basically all alike. Extending this controversy beyond risk behavior, Davis-Blake and Pfeffer (1989) suggest that dispositional effects in organizational research are "just a mirage" (p. 385). However, in defending the dispositional approach, House, Shane, and Herold (1996) reviewed the literature and concluded that "the evidence for the predictive validity of dispositions is too strong to dismiss" (p. 204). In fact, most theorists today would agree that behavior is jointly determined by both dispositions and situations.

Given this background, it is easy to see that the core dispute in the area of risk behavior has remained the same for decades—"How important are individual consistencies relative to situational constraints when it comes to predicting someone's inclination for risk or conservatism?" (Kogan & Wallach, 1967, p. 208). Thus, integrative models constitute the third approach to understanding strategic risk behavior, mainly as an attempt to reconcile the positions of the other two approaches. As Bromiley and Curley (1992) conclude, the key would be to recognize "the joint influence of situation and personality characteristics" (p. 125).

One such integrative model was proposed by Baird and Thomas (1985), who provided an exclusive list of factors—including both personal and strategic problem variables—that possibly affect strategic risk behavior. Whereas personal variables include a decision maker's self-confidence, knowledge, biases, heuristics, and preferences, strategic problem variables include framing, variance, probabilities, outcomes, and reversibility and controllability. In addition, Baird and Thomas (1985) discussed the impact of environmental, industry, and organizational variables on strategic risk behavior. By comparison, Sitkin and Pablo's (1992) model is more specific and holds that risk behavior is mostly determined by risk propensity. Risk perception regarding positive versus negative decision context only helps "to explain variation in individual risk behavior within the bounds generally defined by risk propensity" (Sitkin & Pablo, 1992, p. 29). Nevertheless, risk propensity itself is believed to vary on the basis of outcomes of previous risk behavior—failure promotes decision makers to alter their risk propensity.

Lopes (1987) proposes a two-factor theory that "uses both a dispositional factor and a situational factor to explain risky choice" (p. 275). To her, the dispositional factor describes an individual's general trait regarding either risk averting (i.e., achieving security) or risk seeking (i.e., exploiting potential). The situational factor refers to a decision maker's response to immediate needs. Lopes suggests that the relative preference among risky options is the product of the dispositional factor and the situational factor—the higher the value, the more preferable the choice. Since people are supposed to move toward the choice that has more value to them, the two-factor theory has been called a motivational theory.

In sum, all existing models which attempt to reconcile the two views of risk taking are integrative—that is, they seek to describe the *joint effect* of dispositional and situational factors on any single risky decision.

It is our belief that a more effective integration should adopt a contingent approach—namely, consider the effects of the dispositional and situational factors in conjunction with the temporal dimension of decisions. The temporal element is critical in understanding risk behavior because it "gives risk both savor and sting" (Lopes, 1987, p. 289). Pope (1983) noted that risk theorists have failed to appreciate the "fundamental import of time for uncertainty" (p. 137). Risk decisions can be differentiated as involving future consequences that are either immediate or delayed (Stevenson, 1986). Although time has been increasingly incorporated in more recent studies on risk (Loewenstein, 1988; Stevenson, 1992; Wu & Gonzalez, 1999), the temporal dimension is remarkably missing in the attempts to integrate dispositional and situational factors.

In this chapter we propose to include the temporal characteristics of decisions to examine the above dispute about strategic risk behavior, and thereby develop a richer framework for further research and understanding. More specifically, we propose that the time horizon of decisions has significant saliency for both the factors. We suggest that either the dispositional or the situational factor may dominate an individual's thinking and behavior, given the specific temporalities of decisions. Hence, one of the two factors may not be temporally salient in particular kinds of decisions.

TIME IN STRATEGIC RISK BEHAVIOR

As indicated earlier, we propose to develop an alternative contingent model of strategic risk behavior by incorporating in it the dimension of time. The role of time in organization and management has been attracting increasing interdisciplinary interest in recent years (Bluedorn & Denhardt, 1988; Das, 1990, 1993; Das & Teng 1997; Thoms & Greenberger, 1995). Every managerial decision involves a time horizon. Time serves as an important variable for differentiating strategic decisions—their duration, periodicity, and pace. Strategies that focus on time and the future (Das, 2004b) are the subject of a number of research investigations and practitioner-oriented publications. The perception of the future time dimension was found to be particularly salient in strategic planning (Das, 1986). Strategic planning is concerned with future events, and the effects of strategic decisions unfold in the flow of time. Indeed, time has been called "the hidden dimension of strategic planning" (Das, 1991). Furthermore, studies have identified the time perspective as a determinant of strategic decision making processes (Das, 1987).

On the topic of strategic risk behavior, the time perspective is especially relevant. One key aspect of risk taking is discounting in time. In other words, individuals' risk behavior differs as it relates to immediate results and postponed results (Nisan & Minkowich, 1973; Shelley, 1994). Researchers hypothesize that risks are more easily accepted if "intended benefits are obtained at a shorter term" and/or "undesired consequences have delayed... effects" (Vlek & Stallen, 1980, p. 291). The theory that explains this phenomenon is the discounted utility model, which suggests that decision makers discount the expected effects of their decisions in relation to their temporal distance from the present. Thus, more distant gains/losses will have lesser significance to the decision maker. It has been found, however, that individuals' discount rates are inconsistent across decision scenarios (Kirby, 1997; Prelec & Loewenstein, 1991). For example, decision makers discount future gains more than future losses, and the discount rates decline with time and size of reward (Loewenstein & Thaler, 1989).

Other than the anomalies in the discounted utility model, researchers have also examined the effects of timing, decision numbers, and decision patterns on risk taking. Strickland, Lewicki, and Katz (1966) found that subjects showed greater restraint in risk taking in after-the-event gambling as compared to normal before-the-event gambling. Lopes (1996) and others explored different risk behaviors in one single game versus repeated games. Read, Loewenstein, and Kalyanaraman (1999) compared the difference between simultaneous choices (making several decisions at a time) and sequential choices (making one decision at a time). They reported that simultaneous decisions tend to be more risk seeking and more diversified, and to also give more weight to delayed consequences. Although time and temporality are increasingly being recognized as important in studying risk, it appears that they have not been employed to help address the issue concerning dispositional versus situational influences in risk taking.

TEMPORALITY ONE: RISK HORIZONS

In this chapter we apply the idea of temporality to one key concept in risk—individuals' risk propensity, or their current tendency to take or avoid risks. For the sake of clarity we will use the terms *risk seeking* (for risk taking) and *risk averting* (for risk avoiding), as the term "risk taking" often connotes the generic process in the literature.

We suggest that individual risk propensity can manifest itself with different saliencies in decisions involving different time horizons. We examine this question by dichotomizing this horizon—which we call *risk horizon*—into short-range and long-range. Clearly, of course, one could also consider medium-range. To many theorists, strategic risk taking is closely related to strategic planning (Drucker, 1972; Miller, Kets de Vries, & Toulouse, 1982), because both risks taking and planning have their foundation in futurity. Hence, time, strategic risk taking, and strategic planning are dynamically interrelated. Short-range risk behavior (high or low) refers to seeking or averting risk in short planning horizons, while long-range risk behavior (high or low) is seeking or averting risk in longer planning horizons.

These two types of risk behavior are distinct because strategic risk taking may fall into either short or long planning horizons—and strategists' risky decisions for these two horizons are not necessarily the same. For example, many people take little risk with their financial security in retirement occurring in the long run—and hence they start investing early in their lives rather than just buying lottery tickets later. However, the same people may be very aggressive in their short term investment activities. Thus, for the long run, they would have a low-risk behavior, while for the short run relatively high-risk. In fact, studies show that outcomes occurring at various points in time trigger different risk taking behaviors (Mowen & Mowen, 1991; Nisan & Minkowich, 1973).

An experiment by Lopes and Casey (1994) provides some indirect support for our differentiation between short-range and long-range risk behavior. In their experiment, the subjects were assigned to one of the two strategic positions—the defensive and the offensive. The subjects were then asked to play games that had immediate outcomes, in both winning and losing situations. They found that an individual's risk behavior ("risk preference" in the terminology of these researchers) was responsive to their decision situations (i.e., winning or losing), but not to their strategic positions (i.e., defensive or offensive). Indeed, our differentiation would predict that people's short-range risk behavior would not be influenced by their strategic positions (which are, by definition, long-range).

Basically, we are suggesting that decision makers do show a consistent pattern of risk behavior, but only under two specific conditions. First, in close-to-neutral contexts that do not involve significant previous gain/loss, decision makers tend to exhibit their dispositional preference toward risk seeking. As originally observed by Mischel (1968), dispositional effects are most noticeable in weak situations—that is, where stimulus conditions are either weak or ambiguous. On the other hand, when stimulus conditions are strong, the effects of dispositions are unlikely to surface, as situational factors would tend to dominate. Given this, it is understandable that some studies did not reveal consistent dispositional risk propensity across different decision contexts (e.g., Schoemaker, 1990). Second, when individuals make decisions involving long planning horizons, they are relatively free from the impact of situational factors—so that their individual dispositional differences can play a more prominent role. Adopting Mischel's (1968) idea, long-range decisions may represent weak situations, in that the consequences of actions are more ambiguous. On the contrary, because short-range decisions are usually more predictable in terms of their routes and results, they tend to represent strong conditions—namely, those in which the decision makers are influenced heavily by situational factors. In this sense, those who plan for short time horizons will be more likely to contend with knowledge of prior outcomes, and their willingness to take risk will thus be dominated by the perceived decision context.

Short-Range Risk Behavior

The concept of short-range risk behavior is based on the situation-contingent view of risk taking, such as prospect theory. As we noted earlier, previous studies consistently reported that individuals in losing situations become greater risk seekers. Similarly, firms with performance below desired levels also tend to take more risks. The reason might be that people are loss averse—that is, they "value" loss more than gain, so that an expected loss justifies increased risk taking (Kahneman & Lovallo, 1993). It must be stressed, however, that it is the *perceived* decision context that is directly responsible for risk taking (Bateman & Zeithaml, 1989a, 1989b). According to prospect theory, decision makers transform—by interpretation—an objective gain/loss into a subjective gain/loss. A subjectively chosen reference point, or adaptive aspiration, is used to perceive the decision context. As a result, the definition of positive or negative decision context is always a relative appreciation, leaving a lot of room for decision makers' own aspirations.

This subjectivity helps explain why some people are emboldened by their initial wins, instead of turning conservative. It is possible that their wins have not reached their aspiration levels. For example, despite recent gains in a stock, an investor may continue to take risk by holding on to the stock, if her aspiration level has not been reached. The same situation may well be perceived as a winning one, if she never expected the stock price to go up in the first place. To her, the more likely behavior would be risk averse—in other words, selling the stock.

In case the performance is below the aspiration level, the motivation for risk taking appears to be pertinent only to short term decisions. Lopes states that "the situational factor describes people's responses to *immediate* needs and opportunities" (1987, p. 275; emphasis added). Taking the time dimension into account, Mowen and Mowen (1991) propose that only "when decision outcomes occur in the present, decision makers tend to act in a risk-taking way if the decision is framed from a loss position" (p. 57). Apparently, only risk taking within a short time horizon enables decision makers to quickly recover from their loss position. Thaler and Johnson (1990) consider such motivation as based on "break-even effects"—that is, "in the presence of prior losses, outcomes that offer a chance to break even are especially attractive" (p. 643).

An example of a strategic decision with primarily immediate consequences would be whether or not an airline should initiate an aggressive marketing campaign. We maintain that this decision would be significantly influenced by the recent market gains or losses of the airline (decision context). A negative condition featured by recent market losses would likely prompt the firm to be aggressive in its advertising efforts (Lee, 1994). In contrast, a strategic decision with primarily distant consequences would be whether or not a firm should invest heavily in basic research that would eventually transform the technological standards of the industry. We suggest that this decision would be less constrained by current competitive conditions. Thus, following Mowen and Mowen's (1991) view, we suggest that a perceived negative decision context stimulates more willingness to take chances in the short run—which translates to a short-range high-risk behavior. (The interplay of these two factors—risk propensity and decision context—is shown in Figure 6.1.) This suggestion should not be construed as a mere restatement of prospect theory—rather, we apply prospect theory to its proper boundary condition, namely, the short planning horizon. Indeed, it is evident that almost all experimental evidence regarding prospect theory was gathered in decision situations with very short planning horizons, usually for immediate outcomes.

Integrating prospect theory and the temporal dimension, Thaler, Tversky, Kahneman, and Schwartz (1997) noted the effect of "myopic loss aversion," or a tendency to avoid short-term losses at the expense of much greater long-term gains. It was found that myopic loss aversion results from "the combination of short horizons and strong distaste for losses" (Thaler et al., 1997, p. 648), and observed that it can be eliminated by having less frequent feedback (i.e., in our terms, long-range horizon). This finding supports our contention here.

As compared to decision context, dispositional factors will play a less important role in short-range risk behavior. As Mischel (1968) noted,

Risk Propensity		Decision Context: Positive	Decision Context: Negative
	Risk Averter	(a) Short-Range Low-Risk Behavior (b) Long-Range Low-Risk Behavior Cell A	(c) Short-Range High-Risk Behavior (d) Long-Range Low-Risk Behavior Cell B
	Risk Seeker	(e) Short-Range Low-Risk Behavior (f) Long-Range High-Risk Behavior Cell C	(g) Short-Range High-Risk Behavior (h) Long-Range High-Risk Behavior Cell D

Figure 6.1 Strategic risk behaviors based on risk propensity, decision context, and risk horizon.

dispositional differences will be significant only when the impact of stimulus conditions is weak. That is, when the decision context is held constant, decision makers who are risk seekers will take more short-range risk than risk averters. However, this difference is unlikely to be consistent when decision contexts are heterogeneous. In sum, we maintain that although both situational and dispositional factors are relevant, their relative importance varies with the planning horizon. In short-range risk horizons, the more significant one is the situational factor. Therefore:

> **Proposition 1:** *Decision makers will exhibit high-risk behavior in short-range risk horizons, if the decision context is perceived as a loss position (negative context).*

> **Proposition 2:** *Decision makers will exhibit low-risk behavior in short-range risk horizons, if the decision context is perceived as a gain position (positive context).*

Hence, in summary, we have two distinct contingent relationships. If the risk horizon is short-range, decision makers (both risk averters and risk seekers) will exhibit high-risk behavior if the decision context is perceived as a loss position (negative context), and low-risk behavior if the decision context is perceived as a gain position (positive context). These risk behaviors are indicated in Figure 6.1 as, respectively, (c) and (g) for a negative decision context, and (a) and (e) for a positive decision context. At this stage of our exposition, it would appear that the decision context is salient when the risk horizon is short-range. Hence, our partial response to the original Kogan-Wallach question is that the "situational constraints" are more important than "individual consistencies" or dispositional characteristics when we have short-range risk horizons.

Long-Range Risk Behavior

In contrast with decisions in short planning horizons, strategic decisions that involve long-term outcomes are less relevant to strategists' motivation to recover current loss or to retain current gain. That is, current situations have much less influence on long-range strategic risk taking compared to short-range risk taking. The reason is that long-range decisions have potential payoffs in the distant future and will be heavily discounted (Kirby, 1997; Loewenstein & Thaler, 1989; Stevenson, 1992). In other words, because a long term decision has limited impact on the current decision context, the influence of the current decision context on this decision tends to be limited as well. As we reasoned earlier, the opportunity to alter or maintain the current situation is exactly why the decision context influences risk propensity for the short run. Although it may be argued that even long-term performance is somewhat influenced by current performance, the effect would not be as great as it would be for short-range decisions. Because decision makers are relatively free from the "pressure" of the current decision situation, their handling of longer term strategic risks can be expected to exhibit more of their dispositional risk propensity. Clearly, this dispositional attribute should be evident in its fullest potential when the decision context, or the domain of current situations, does not come into play. When the strategists are risk seekers, their preferred strategy in long planning horizons is likely to be riskier than that preferred by risk averters.

Indeed, the very idea of individual differences in risk propensity suggests that, at least in certain decision contexts, risk seekers tend to take more risks than risk averters. Mischel (1968) suggests that such decision contexts are weak situations as they have no strong or obvious contextual stimuli. Because of the limited impact on the current situation, long term decisions represent such a weak situation (i.e., they are relatively neutral to current decision stimuli). Thus, dispositional factors will be more salient in long-range decisions. For example, while drinking and driving on a particular occasion entails short-range risk, taking up smoking involves long-range risk. While the former is more affected by the specific circumstance of the occasion (situational factors), the latter is less subject to immediate decision contexts (and more influenced by one's own risk propensity). Thus, perceiving long-term risk to health, a risk-averter is less likely to smoke than a risk-seeker. Consequently, the dispositional attribute would tend to be more salient in long-range strategies. Thus:

> **Proposition 3:** *Decision makers who are risk averters will exhibit low-risk behavior in long-range risk horizons.*

> **Proposition 4:** *Decision makers who are risk seekers will exhibit high-risk behavior in long-range risk horizons.*

Hence, in summary, we have two further distinct contingent relationships. If the risk horizon is long-range, then irrespective of how the decision context is perceived (positive and negative), decision makers who are risk averters will exhibit low-risk behavior, whereas decision makers who are risk seekers will exhibit high-risk behavior. These risk behaviors are indicated in Figure 6.1 as, respectively, (b) and (d) for risk averters, and (f) and (h) for risk seekers. At this stage of our exposition, then, it would appear that the individual disposition (i.e., risk propensity) is salient when the risk horizon is long-range. Hence, our additional partial response to the core issue is that "individual consistencies" or dispositional characteristics are more important than "situational constraints" when we have long-range risk horizons.

TEMPORALITY TWO: INDIVIDUAL FUTURE ORIENTATIONS

The above framework is not, however, quite complete. From an upper echelon perspective, we have not explored the psychological attribute that is decidedly relevant to risk horizons—namely, strategists' personal cognition of future time, or individual future orientation (Das, 1986). Scholars suggest that the temporal orientations of decision makers have important consequences for the effective performance of organizational tasks. Studies show that not all planning horizons are appropriate for any particular organization—rather, there needs to be a fit between strategists' future orientations and the organizational planning horizons (Das, 1986, 1987). Hence, the inclusion of the strategists' future orientations should help remedy the above deficiency, enabling us to identify the appropriate planning horizons in strategic risk taking.

In the strategic management literature, the concept of "individual future orientation" was first proposed and empirically studied with a large sample of senior business executives by Das (1986). Unlike the clock-and-calendar-time conception, individual future orientation refers to "the psychological conceptions of the future" (Das, 1991, p. 51). The construct of future time perspective has been well established in the psychology literature (Cottle, 1976; Fraisse, 1963; Kastenbaum, 1961; Klineberg, 1968). This psychological characteristic helps form one's vision of possible futures, ranging from a near future to a distant future. Hence, decision makers can be categorized as having either a near-future orientation or a distant-future orientation. In strategic decision making, "it is the strategy making executives, through their perspective on the future time dimension, who eventually help constitute the specific temporal horizon of the organization" (Das, 1991, p. 51). Executives with a distant-future orientation were found to prefer longer planning horizons, while executives with a near-future orientation preferred shorter planning horizons for the same activities in the same organization. If executives with a near-future orientation are forced to plan in a time horizon longer than their comfortable range, these plans would receive no managerial input of value, because these executives are incapable of conceiving such a distant future.

The critical distinction between future orientation and planning horizon should be obvious but is oftentimes unwittingly ignored. Future orientation relates to an individual's internal attribute concerning the conception of the flow of time in the future—that is, in the future time segment. Thus, some individuals may grasp only a relatively short span of the future time segment, compared to other individuals who are capable of "seeing" a more expansive terrain of the future time segment. Planning horizon, on the other hand, is what that individual considers as the length of time appropriate for engaging in certain activities (e.g., strategic planning) by an entity (such as an organization). (We use the terms "*near*-future" and "*distant*-future" to designate the polar values of the individual future orientation dimension, to clearly distinguish them from the conventional terms "*short*-range" and "*long*-range" for the planning horizon.) And, as alluded to in the preceding paragraph, the empirical findings are that indeed individuals differ both in their future orientations and in their preferences for appropriate planning horizons and, also, that the two are correlated in statistically significant ways (Das, 1986, 1987). Thus, in discussing risk propensity along varying risk horizons, it is important to examine the manner in which decision makers' orientations to the future affect their risk behavior.

INTEGRATING RISK PROPENSITY WITH TWO TEMPORALITIES

In this section we integrate risk propensity with the two temporalities (risk horizon and future orientation) just elaborated to develop a temporal contingency framework of strategic risk behavior. The argument we make is that for those strategists who have a near-future orientation, long-range risk behavior is unlikely to come into play. The reason is that such decision makers are simply incapable of perceiving risks residing in a distant future. These strategists would of course show their dispositional risk propensity in contexts with no known previous outcomes. But their long-range risk behavior would not be very meaningful as they cannot seriously measure risk taking in extended planning horizons.

We may mention here the notion of "intrapersonal empathy gap" (Loewenstein, 1996; Read & van Leeuwen, 1998), or one's inability to imagine what it will be like in a state different from one's current state. According to this notion, decisions regarding a future state (e.g., whether to have breakfast a week later) will be heavily influenced by the current condition (e.g., whether one is currently hungry). By our reasoning, a person who cannot "place" herself in future states has a near-future orientation. Such a person will bestow disproportionate weight to the current and short-term position in terms of gains and losses. Thus, people with a near-future orientation will tend to apply high discount rates, which makes decision making more impulsive and myopic (Bazerman, Tenbrunsel, & Wade-Benzoni, 1998; Loewenstein & Thaler, 1989).

A near-future orientation also suggests a lack of "mental accounting" ability, as decisions and outcomes are framed in narrow terms and short-term choices are preferred (Thaler et al., 1997). Research shows that individuals differ in terms of their natural tendency and ability to engage in thought, or "need for cognition" (Cacioppo & Petty, 1982; Cacioppo, Petty, Feinstein, & Jarvis, 1996). Smith and Levin (1996) found that people with low need for cognition are more influenced by framing biases (or situational factors). Apparently, individuals who reason less would be more easily manipulated by the framing of a situation. Framing is important because the same situation may be described as either a gain or a loss position. We argue that a low need for cognition would be associated with a near-future orientation because thinking about long-term developments requires a relatively more pronounced ability to reason how things may unfold in the future. This association suggests that the framing of a situation (gain or loss) may well have similarly strong influences on people with a near-future orientation. Conversely, strategists with a distant-future orientation would be more likely to take long-range risk based on their risk propensity.

Ordinarily, they would not feel adequately engaged in the making of strategic decisions that have relatively short planning horizons. Thus:

> **Proposition 5a:** *Decision makers with a near-future orientation will exhibit short-range low-risk behavior, if the decision context is perceived as a gain position (positive context).*

> **Proposition 5b:** *Decision makers with a near-future orientation will exhibit short-range high-risk behavior, if the decision context is perceived as a loss position (negative context).*

> **Proposition 6a:** *Decision makers who are risk averters will exhibit long-range low-risk behavior, if they have a distant-future orientation.*

> **Proposition 6b:** *Decision makers who are risk seekers will exhibit long-range high-risk behavior, if they have a distant-future orientation.*

Hence, in summary, we have two distinct sets of contingent relationships. First, decision makers—both risk averters and risk seekers—with a near-future orientation will exhibit short-range low-risk behavior if the decision context is perceived as a gain position, and short-range high-risk behavior if the decision context is perceived as a loss position. These are indicated in Table 6.1 as, respectively, (a) and (e) for a positive decision context, and (c) and (g) for a negative decision context. It would thus appear that the decision context is salient when the individual has a near-future orientation. Hence, our further response to the core question is that the "situational constraints" are more important than "individual consistencies" or dispositional characteristics when we have near-future oriented decision makers.

And second, for decision makers with a distant-future orientation—irrespective of how the decision context is perceived (positive or negative)—those who are risk averters will exhibit long-range low-risk behavior, whereas those who are risk seekers will exhibit long-range high-risk behavior. These risk behaviors are indicated in Table 6.1 as, respectively, (b) and (d) for risk averters, and (f) and (h) for risk seekers. At this stage of our exposition, then, it would appear that individual dispositions (or risk propensities) are salient when the decision makers have distant-future orientations. Hence, our additional response to the core question is that "individual consistencies" or dispositional characteristics are more important than "situational constraints" when we have distant-future oriented decision makers.

The implication here is that it is critical to achieve a fit between the characteristics of top executives, including their risk propensities and future orientations, and the strategic orientation of a firm. Lewin and Stephens (1994) discussed the importance of matching organization-design variables, including strategy, control, and information processing, with individual characteristics

TABLE 6.1 Strategic Risk Behaviors Based on Risk Propensity, Decision Context, Risk Horizon, and Future Orientation

Risk Propensity and Decision Context	Future Orientation	
	Near-Future Orientation	Distant-Future Orientation
Risk Averter & **Positive Context** [Cell A of Figure 6.1]	(A) Short-Range Low-Risk Behavior	(B) Long-Range Low-Risk Behavior
Risk Averter & **Negative Context** [Cell B of Figure 6.1]	(C) Short-Range High-Risk Behavior	(D) Long-Range Low-Risk Behavior
Risk Seeker & **Positive Context** [Cell C of Figure 6.1]	(E) Short-Range Low-Risk Behavior	(F) Long-Range High-Risk Behavior
Risk Seeker & **Negative Context** [Cell D of Figure 6.1]	(G) Short-Range High-Risk Behavior	(H) Long-Range High-Risk Behavior

of top managers (see also Finkelstein and Hambrick, 1996). The fit, in our framework, can be achieved through a careful selection of top management teams and developing appropriate planning horizons.

On the one hand, when the strategic orientation of a firm is toward long-range planning and risk taking, executives with a distant-future orientation and high risk propensity would be more effective. For example, Wiersema and Bantel (1992) found that personal traits of the top management team members affect a firm's willingness to take risk and, thus, the degree of corporate change. In this case, because corporate change entails risk seeking and long-range planning, both distant-future orientation and high risk propensity would be valuable. Wally and Baum (1994) reported that top managers' tolerance for risk influences the pace of decision making in firms. Since a fast decision-making pace suggests risk seeking and short-range planning, the fit will be with top managers of a high risk propensity and a near-future orientation. On the other hand, planning horizons may be modified to fit the characteristics of top managers. Decision support techniques such as scenarios and linear models may be helpful here.

CONCLUDING REMARKS

One of the most intriguing questions that remain unanswered today in the area of risk behavior is concerned with the relative roles of dispositional and situational factors. It has been so for several decades, but particularly since Kahneman and Tversky (1979) complicated matters by introducing a situational dimension in risk taking with their prospect theory. An integration of the two sets of factors is clearly needed, but a satisfactory solution is yet to emerge.

In suggesting an alternative approach by introducing the time dimension—we have perhaps further complicated the subject. In as much as risk is intrinsically embedded in time, the temporal dimension would seem to provide a meaningful way of clarifying and integrating various influences emanating from dispositional and situational characteristics. It appears to us that the temporal contingency framework of strategic risk behavior proposed here should place us in a stronger position than before to respond to Kogan and Wallach's (1967) basic question mentioned at the outset of this chapter—"How important are individual consistencies relative to situational constraints when it comes to predicting someone's inclination for risk or conservatism?" (p. 208).

Thus, the contribution of our proposed temporal contingency framework is to integrate two competing lines of research on the determinants of strategic risk behavior by incorporating an important but largely ignored factor—the time dimension. The temporal dimension plays two distinct roles in the framework. In regard to the first role, the framework introduces the key concept of short-range and long-range risk horizons. This facilitates, we believe, a reconciliation of the competing influences of dispositional and situational factors. Previous research which seemed contradictory can now be reinterpreted contingently along temporal lines to yield a cogent picture. Both dispositional and situational factors exert their influences on strategic risk behavior—but through different channels and with different saliencies. This first aspect of the temporal dimension is instrumental in providing us with a fairly clear divide—the short-range side is dominated by situational factors (perceived decision context), while the long-range side is influenced more by the dispositional risk propensity.

The second role of the temporal dimension incorporated in our framework is individual future orientations of the decision makers. The framework thus enriches our understanding of the significant role of strategic actors in terms of their personal attributes. Being temporally related to risk horizons, individual future orientations constitute a key predictor in our framework of strategic risk behavior.

Indeed, since two of the three basic elements in the framework are psychological attributes, it would seem that a more comprehensive approach to exploring the subjective side of strategy making (Das, 1986) may well be justified by including other psychological factors that are potentially related to the perception of positive or negative decision contexts. A range of psychological variables are likely to be important in this respect, including (but by no means restricted to) the following: locus of control, tolerance of ambiguity, trust in people, need for cognition, and propensity to act. At the very least, the various propositions developed in the chapter should help in the empirical testing of the different contingent relationships in the temporal framework.

In sum, the temporal framework of strategic risk taking behavior proposed in this chapter enables us to respond—both conceptually and empirically—to the insightful question of Kogan and Wallach (1967). We believe that we can now begin to answer the question about the relative importance of dispositional versus situational determinants in strategic risk behavior by incorporating the two temporalities introduced here. The answer is fairly categorical, and takes a contingent form—it depends on whether we are dealing with short-range or long-range risk horizons, and whether, also, the decision makers have near-future or distant-future orientations. The typology of strategic risk behaviors developed here, together with the accompanying propositions, should facilitate the empirical testing of the different contingent relationships identified within the temporal framework.

ACKNOWLEDGMENT

This chapter, save some minor changes, was earlier published as Das, T. K., & Teng, B. (2001). Strategic risk behavior and its temporalities: Between risk propensity and decision context. *Journal of Management Studies, 38*, 515–534.

REFERENCES

Alderfer, C. P., & Bierman, H. (1970). Choices with risk: Beyond the mean and variance. *Journal of Business, 43*, 341–353.

Arrow, K. J. (1971). *Essays in the theory of risk-bearing*. Chicago, IL: Markham.

Baird, I. S., & Thomas, H. (1985). Toward a contingency model of strategic risk taking. *Academy of Management Review, 10*, 230–243.

Bateman, T. S., & Zeithaml, C. P. (1989a). The psychological context of strategic decisions: A model and convergent experimental findings. *Strategic Management Journal, 10*, 59–74.

Bateman, T. S., & Zeithaml, C. P. (1989b). The psychological context of strategic decisions: A test of relevance to practitioners. *Strategic Management Journal, 10*, 587–592.

Bazerman, M. H., Tenbrunsel, A. E., & Wade-Benzoni, K. (1998). Negotiating with yourself and losing: Making decisions with competing internal preferences. *Academy of Management Review, 23*, 225–241.

Bluedorn, A. C., & Denhardt, R. (1988). Time and organizations. *Journal of Management, 14*, 299–320.

Bowman, E. H. (1982). Risk seeking by troubled firms. *Sloan Management Review, 23*(4), 33–42.

Bromiley, P. (1991). Testing a causal model of corporate risk taking and performance. *Academy of Management Journal, 34*, 37–59.

Bromiley, P., & Curley, S. P. (1992). Individual differences in risk taking. In J. F. Yates (Ed.), *Risk-taking behavior* (pp. 87–132). Chichester, UK: Wiley.

Cacioppo, J. T., & Petty, R. E. (1982). The need for cognition. *Journal of Personality and Social Psychology, 42*, 116–131.

Cacioppo, J. T., Petty, R. E., Feinstein, J. A., & Jarvis, W. B. G. (1996). Dispositional differences in cognitive motivation: The life and times of individuals varying in need for cognition. *Psychology Bulletin, 119*, 197–253.

Cottle, T. J. (1976). *Perceiving time: A psychological investigation with men and women.* New York, NY: Wiley.

Das, T. K. (1986). *The subjective side of strategy making: Future orientations and perceptions of executives.* New York, NY: Praeger.

Das, T. K. (1987). Strategic planning and individual temporal orientation. *Strategic Management Journal, 8*, 203–209.

Das, T. K. (1990). *The time dimension: An interdisciplinary guide.* New York, NY: Praeger.

Das, T. K. (1991). Time: The hidden dimension in strategic planning. *Long Range Planning, 24*(3), 49–57.

Das, T. K. (1993). Time in management and organizational studies. *Time & Society, 2*, 267–274.

Das, T. K. (2004a). Time-span and risk of partner opportunism in strategic alliances. *Journal of Managerial Psychology, 19*, 744–759.

Das, T. K. (2004b). Strategy and time: Really recognizing the future. In H. Tsoukas & J. Shepherd (Eds.), *Managing the future: Foresight in the knowledge economy* (pp. 58–74). Oxford, UK: Blackwell.

Das, T. K. (2006). Strategic alliance temporalities and partner opportunism. *British Journal of Management, 17*, 1–21.

Das, T. K., & Teng, B. (1997). Time and entrepreneurial risk behavior. *Entrepreneurship Theory and Practice, 22*(2), 69–88.

Das, T. K., & Teng, B. (1999). Cognitive biases and strategic decision processes: An integrative perspective. *Journal of Management Studies, 36*, 757–778.

Das, T. K., & Teng, B. (2001). Strategic risk behavior and its temporalities: Between risk propensity and decision context. *Journal of Management Studies, 38*, 515–534.

Davis-Blake, A., & Pfeffer, J. (1989). Just a mirage: The search for dispositional effects in organizational research. *Academy of Management Review, 14*, 385–400.

Drucker, P. F. (1972). Long-range planning means risk-taking. In D. W. Ewing (Ed.), *Long-range planning for management* (pp. 3–19), (3rd ed.). New York, NY: Harper & Row.

Finkelstein, S., & Hambrick, D. C. (1996). *Strategic leadership: Top executives and their effects on organizations.* Minneapolis/St. Paul, MN: West Publishing.

Fischhoff, B. Lichtenstein, S., Slovic, P., Derby, S. L., & Keeney, R. L. 1981. *Acceptable risk.* Cambridge, UK: Cambridge University Press.

Fraisse, P. (1963). *The psychology of time.* New York, NY: Harper.

Ghosh, D., & Ray, M. R. (1992). Risk attitude, ambiguity intolerance and decision making: An exploratory investigation. *Decision Science, 23*, 431–444.

Hambrick, D. C., & Mason, P. A. (1984). Upper echelons: The organization as a reflection of its top managers. *Academy of Management Review, 9*, 193–206.

Hodgkinson, G. P., Bown, N. J., Maule, A. J., Glaister, K. W., & Pearman, A. D. (1999). Breaking the frame: An analysis of strategic cognition and decision making under uncertainty. *Strategic Management Journal, 20*, 977–985.

House, R. J., Shane, S. A., & Herold, D. M. (1996). Rumors of the death of dispositional research are vastly exaggerated. *Academy of Management Review, 21*, 202–224.

Kahneman, D., & Lovallo, D. (1993). Timid choices and bold forecasts: A cognitive perspective on risk taking. *Management Science, 39*, 17–31.

Kahneman, D., & Tversky, A. (1979). Prospect theory: An analysis of decisions under risk. *Econometrica, 47*, 262–291.

Kastenbaum, R. (1961). The dimensions of future time perspective: An experimental analysis. *Journal of General Psychology, 65*, 203–218.

Kirby, K. N. (1997). Bidding on the future: Evidence against normative discounting of delayed rewards. *Journal of Experimental Psychology: General, 126*(1), 54–70.

Klineberg, S. L. (1968). Future time perspective and the preference for delayed reward. *Journal of Personality and Social Psychology, 8*, 253–257.

Kogan, N., & Wallach, M. A. (1964). *Risk taking: A study in cognition and personality.* New York, NY: Holt, Rinehart and Winston.

Kogan, N., & Wallach, M. A. (1967). Risk taking as a function of the situation, the person, and the group. In G. Mandler & P. Mussen, P. (Eds.), *New directions in psychology III.* New York, NY: Holt, Rinehart and Winston.

Lee, D. Y. (1994). The impact of firms' risk-taking attitudes on advertising budgets. *Journal of Business Research, 31*, 247–256.

Lewin, A. Y., & Stephens, C. U. (1994). CEO attitudes as determinants of organization design: An integrated model. *Organization Studies, 15*, 183–212.

Loewenstein, G. F. (1988). Frames of mind in intertemporal choice. *Management Science, 34*, 200–214.

Loewenstein, G. (1996). Out of control: Visceral influences on behavior. *Organizational Behavior and Human Decision Processes, 65*, 272–292.

Loewenstein, G., & Thaler, R. H. (1989). Anomalies: Intertemporal choice. *Journal of Economic Perspectives, 3*(4), 181–193.

Lopes, L. L. (1987). Between hope and fear: The psychology of risk. *Advances in Experimental Social Psychology, 20*, 255–295.

Lopes, L. L. (1996). When time is of the essence: Averaging, aspiration, and the short run. *Organizational Behavior and Human Decision Processes, 65*, 179–189.

Lopes, L. L., & Casey, J. T. (1994). Tactical and strategic responsiveness in a competitive risk-taking game. *Acta Psychologica, 85*, 39–60.

MacCrimmon, K. R., & Wehrung, D. A. (1986). *Taking risks: The management of uncertainty.* New York, NY: Free Press.

March, J. G. (1988). Variable risk preferences and adaptive aspirations. *Journal of Economic Behavior and Organization, 9*, 5–24.

March, J. G., & Shapira, Z. (1987). Managerial perspectives on risk and risk taking. *Management Science, 33*, 1404–1418.

McClelland, D. C. (1961). *The achieving society.* Princeton, NJ: Van Nostrand.

Miller, D., Kets De Vries, M. F. R., & Toulouse, J.-M. (1982). Top executive locus of control and its relationship to strategy-making, structure, and environment. *Academy of Management Journal, 25,* 237–253.

Mischel, W. (1968). *Personality and assessment.* New York, NY: Wiley.

Mowen, J. C., & Mowen, M. M. (1991). Time and outcome valuation: Implications for marketing decision making. *Journal of Marketing, 55*(4), 54–62.

Nisan, M., & Minkowich, A. (1973). The effect of expected temporal distance on risk taking. *Journal of Personality and Social Psychology, 25,* 375–380.

Pope, R. (1983). The pre-outcome period and the utility of gambling. In B. P. Stigum & F. Wenstop (Eds.), *Foundations of utility and risk theory with applications* (pp. 137–177). Dordrecht, Netherlands: Reidel.

Prelec, D., & Loewenstein, G. (1991). Decision making over time and under uncertainty: A common approach. *Management Science, 37,* 770–786.

Read, D., Loewenstein, G., & Kalyanaraman, S. (1999). Mixing virtue and vice: Combining the immediacy effect and the diversification heuristic. *Journal of Behavioral Decision Making, 12,* 257–273.

Read, D., & van Leeuwen, B. (1998). Predicting hunger: The effects of appetite and delay on choice. *Organizational Behavior and Human Decision Processes, 76,* 189–205.

Rowe, W. D. (1977). *An anatomy of risk.* New York, NY: Wiley.

Schneider, S. L., & Lopes, L. L. (1986). Reflection in preferences under risk: Who and when may suggest why. *Journal of Experimental Psychology: Human Perception and Performance, 12,* 535–548.

Schoemaker, P. J. H. (1990). Are risk-attitudes related across domains and response modes? *Management Science, 36,* 1451–1463.

Shapira, Z. (1995). *Risk taking: A managerial perspective.* New York, NY: Russell Sage Foundation.

Shelley, M. K. (1994). Gain/loss asymmetry in risky intertemporal choice. *Organizational Behavior and Human Decision Processes, 59,* 124–159.

Sitkin, S. B., & Pablo, A. L. (1992). Reconceptualizing the determinants of risk behavior. *Academy of Management Review, 17,* 9–38.

Sitkin, S. B., & Weingart, L. R. (1995). Determinants of risky decision-making behavior: A test of the mediating role of risk perceptions and propensity. *Academy of Management Journal, 38,* 1573–1592.

Slovic, P. (1962). Convergent validation of risk-taking measures. *Journal of Abnormal and Social Psychology, 65,* 68–71.

Slovic, P. (1972). Information processing, situation specificity, and the generality of risk-taking behavior. *Journal of Applied Psychology, 22,* 128–134.

Smith, S. M., & Levin, I. P. (1996). Need for cognition and choice framing effects. *Journal of Behavioral Decision Making, 9,* 283–290.

Stevenson, M. K. (1986). A discounting model for decisions with delayed positive or negative outcomes. *Journal of Experimental Psychology: General, 115*(2), 131–154.

Stevenson, M. K. (1992). The impact of temporal context and risk on the judged value of future outcomes. *Organizational Behavior and Human Decision Processes, 52,* 455–491.

Strickland, L., Lewicki, R. J., & Katz, A. M. (1966). Temporal orientation and perceived control as determinants of risk taking. *Journal of Experimental Social Psychology, 2*, 143–151.

Taylor, R. N., & Dunnette, M. D. (1974). Influence of dogmatism, risk-taking propensity, and intelligence on decision-making strategies for a sample of industrial managers. *Journal of Applied Psychology, 59*, 420–423.

Thaler, R. H., & Johnson, E. J. (1990). Gambling with the house money and trying to break even: The effects of prior outcomes on risky choice. *Management Science, 36*, 643–660.

Thaler, R. H., Tversky, A., Kahneman, D., & Schwartz, A. (1997). The effect of myopia and loss aversion on risk taking: An experimental test. *Quarterly Journal of Economics, 112*, 647–661.

Thoms, P., & Greenberger, D. B. (1995). The relationship between leadership and time orientation. *Journal of Management Inquiry, 4*, 272–292.

Tversky, A., & Kahneman, D. (1991). Loss aversion in riskless choice: A reference-dependent model. *Quarterly Journal of Economics, 106*, 1039–1061.

Tversky, A., & Kahneman, D. (1992). Advances in prospect theory: Cumulative representation of uncertainty. *Journal of Risk and Uncertainty, 5*, 297–323.

Vlek, C., & Stallen, P. J. (1980). Rational and personal aspects of risk. *Acta Psychologica, 45*, 273–300.

Vroom, V. H., & Pahl, B. (1971). Relationship between age and risk taking. *Journal of Applied Psychology, 55*, 399–405.

Wally, S., & Baum, J. R. (1994). Personal and structural determinants of the pace of strategic decision making. *Academy of Management Journal, 37*, 932–956.

Wiersema, M. F., & Bantel, K. A. (1992). Top management team demography and corporate strategic change. *Academy of Management Journal, 35*, 91–121.

Wu, G., & Gonzalez, R. (1999). Nonlinear decision weights in choice under uncertainty. *Management Science, 45*, 74–85.

Yates, J. F., & Stone, E. R. (1992). The risk construct. In J. F. Yates (Ed.), *Risk-taking behavior* (pp. 1–25). Chichester, UK: Wiley.

CHAPTER 7

AGENTIC ORGANIZATIONS IN INSTITUTIONAL ENVIRONMENTS

Jiulin Teng

ABSTRACT

This chapter illustrates that institutions come into being and evolve to coordinate costs and to incentivize economic activities. Conversely, transaction cost, agency cost, and even production cost provide explanations as to why organizations deviate from the prescriptions of institutions. Two crucial views help us understand the mechanisms: Organizations exhibit characteristics of their members, which include the agentic characteristics of self-interest and bounded rationality. Meanwhile, in most cases institutions related to organizations serve as nexuses for a set of contracting relationships among organizations. These contracts can be explicit as in the case of formal institutions or implicit as in the case of informal institutions. The two views enable us to integrate a range of propositions from institutional and organizational theories and to answer a set of questions, including those of institutional change from the bottom up.

Behavioral Strategy: Emerging Perspectives, pages 155–175

INSTITUTIONAL THEORY

Institutions are the humanly devised constraints that coordinate social, economic, and political interactions (North, 1991) and are closely related to the prospects of survival for organizations (Meyer & Rowan, 1977). While they have long been central to social science, approaches to understand them differ: Selznick's *Leadership in administration* (1957) is a source of old institutionalism in organization theory that made sense of earlier works (Selznick 1949, 1952). In the words of Selznick, the focus of old institutionalism is on two key ideas: "*character*" and "*competence*"; further, character is formed "over time and in the course of responding to external threats" to improve competence (Selznick, 1957). Whereas old institutionalism contends that competence is the motive that drives organizations to take on the special character of institutionalization and that the transformation from unstable, loosely organized, or narrowly technical activities to stable, orderly, and socially-integrated patterns ensures smooth future adoption of unforeseeable competences (Selznick, 1996), new institutionalism emphasizes two other closely-knit key points (North, 1991): that the institutional framework, the consequent organizational structure, and institutional change are related, and that institutional change is path dependent. Precisely because of these two points, institutions can replicate and develop themselves regardless of concerns for competences as certain institutional elements become rationalized and as modern organization and exchange become more complex. As DiMaggio and Powell (1983) so aptly put it, "the engine of rationalization and bureaucratization has moved from the competitive marketplace to the state and the professions."

According to researchers of new institutionalism, the adaptation to socially rationalized institutional rules is in tension with internal coordination and control, two elements deemed crucial for competitive efficiency, but endows organizations with legitimacy which rewards them for possessing it (Meyer & Rowan, 1977). By this logic, internal coordination and control become means to conformity to institution. In the same vein, they define the unit of analysis of institutional field, which leads disparate organizations to become more similar as they change, a process called "isomorphism" (DiMaggio & Powell, 1983). Following this line of reasoning, two forces drive isomorphism: competitive and institutional. The former emphasizes that certain practices are adopted for competence reasons; the latter emphasizes institutional forces that at times disregard competences in favor of legitimacy. Empirical studies have provided corroborating evidences. For instance, in their examination of the diffusion of organizational change Tolbert and Zucker (1983) confirm that institutionalized changes spread vertically and fast and observe that changes without state endorsement (not legitimized) spread slowly and horizontal until the changes are rationalized over time (legitimized). This empirical example illustrates not only the two types of isomorphism but also the two steps of institutionalization, with the coming of age of the organizational field as the turning point. In another example, Kogut, Walker, and Anand (2002) observe that the path dependence nature of institutions differentiating the five countries examined, rather than the immediate technical and market conveniences that associate them, provides the strongest explanation to the pattern of diversification across industries.

As new elements are constantly introduced, some scholars believe it is premature to declare the death of old institutionalism. Greenwood and Hinings (1996), for instance, demonstrate a model of organizational change that acknowledges the ever-evolving loop of context-organization-change-context in an attempt to bring the two schools together. Their important observation that both market context and institutional context are in the feedback loop with organizations enriches the interpretation of institutionalism and reconciles with organization theories (economic theories of the firm in the scope of this chapter) that examines cost in view of bounded rationality. It is noteworthy that under bounded rationality, which explains rational choice bounded by such cognitive limitations as knowledge, cognitive capacity, and time frame (Simon, 1955), agents may not be strictly maximizers (Simon, 1957). As a result, at the organizational level firms may not be strictly maximizing.

Still, perhaps the profoundest finding of new institutionalism is the decoupling of the elements of structure from activities and from each other in institutionalized organizations (Meyer & Rowan, 1977). This belief leads to a rich reservoir of empirical studies of the relationship between conformity to institutions and organizational performance / survival (see Zucker, 1987). We therefore can summarize the relevant findings of institutional theories as the following:

> **Proposition 1:** *Institutionalization brings competence and legitimacy that contribute to organizational performance and survival.*

> **Proposition 2:** *Environment, organizational structure, and organizational change constitute a loop.*

> **Proposition 3:** *Organizational and institutional changes are path dependent.*

A NEW LOOK AT INSTITUTIONAL THEORY

Institutional theories, however, do not provide all the explanations to organizational performance and survival (for example Heugens & Lander,

2009). A simple example suffices to illustrate why: According to organizational theory, both pecuniary and non-pecuniary benefits contribute to organizational performance and survival; therefore, the utility function of performance is dependent on profit and non-pecuniary benefits (simplified as legitimacy). Due to the ordinal nature of utility functions, it is reasonable to write this function as the sum of two functions:

$$u(\textit{profit, legitimacy}) = v(\textit{profit}) + w(\textit{legitimacy}) =$$
$$v(\textit{product, cost}) + w(\textit{legitimacy}) \text{ (assuming the production of private good)}$$

Let P represent product, C represent cost, and L represent legitimacy, and let α be the weight; we get:

$$u = P - C + \alpha L \tag{7.1}$$

If institutionalization brings changes in utility such that $u_1 = P(1+\beta) - C(1+\gamma) + \alpha L(1+\varepsilon)$, the incremental utility would be:

$$\Delta u = \beta P - \gamma C + \alpha\varepsilon L \tag{7.2}$$

Since α and ε are both unknown parameters, we can simplify them as α.

$$\Delta u = \beta P - \gamma C + \alpha L \tag{7.3}$$

Institutional theories suggest that $\alpha L > 0$.

If we further simplify the example and assume that product is a function of cost such that $P = kC (k \geq 1)$. We can solve the linear inequality of $\Delta u > 0 : \Delta u = (\beta k - \gamma)C + \alpha L > 0$

$$\begin{cases} L > \dfrac{\gamma - \beta k}{\alpha} C (L > 0) \\ L < \dfrac{\gamma - \beta k}{\alpha} C (L < 0) \end{cases} \tag{7.4}$$

Figure 7.1 illustrates the incentive to conform with regard to the discrimination line

$$L = \frac{\gamma - \beta k}{\alpha} C$$

in one scenario, scenario I. Here, $\gamma - \beta k > 0$, representing the cases when (*a*) institutionalization adds to costs, (*b*) it reduces production or cannot boost production enough to offset cost increases, or (*c*) a combination of both. *A*

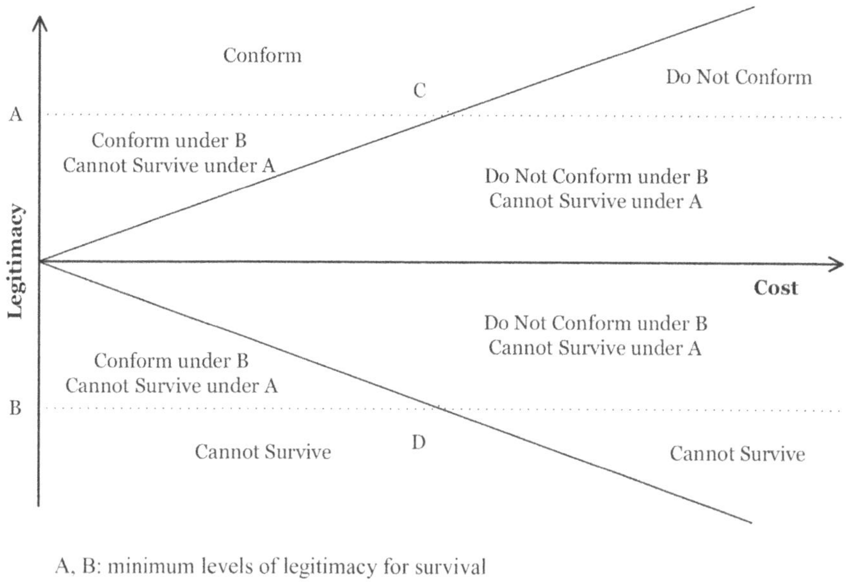

Figure 7.1 The incentive to conform.

and *B* represent different levels of minimum legitimacy required for organizational survival. *A* is positive, whereas *B* is negative. We can think of *A* as the minimum reputation for a hospital while *B* as the maximum tolerance of law before severe repercussions for a chemical plant. A viable organization would choose to conform to institutions when its cost-legitimacy set falls above the discrimination line in the first quadrant when its initial legitimacy is positive and below the discrimination line in the fourth quadrant when its initial legitimacy is negative, and has little incentive to conform otherwise. In scenario II, $\gamma - \beta k < 0$, representing the cases when (*d*) institutionalization reduces costs ($\gamma < 0$), (*e*) it boosts production significantly, or (*f*) a combination of both. $\Delta u > 0$ is always true (i.e., the cost-legitimacy set falls above the discrimination line in the fourth quadrant when L is positive and below than the discrimination line in the first quadrant when L is negative). In all scenarios, a viable organization is one that possesses at least the minimum legitimacy (i.e., its cost-legitimacy set falls above *A* or *B*.

The most intriguing finding is perhaps the following: In scenario I under the minimum legitimacy of *A*, a viable organization that is small in size (cost smaller than *C*) has to conform to institutions; however, a similarly viable organization that is large in size (cost larger than *C*) need not conform. In fact, a large organization only has incentive to conform fully to institutions when its initial legitimacy is very high and that the legitimacy can increase as a result of institutionalization ($\alpha > 0$). In the same scenario under the minimum legitimacy of *B*, the similar holds true. Organizations that are large (cost larger than *D*, *C* need not equal *D*) observe more situations in which non-conforming behaviors may be more rewarding than smaller organizations do. In fact, these results have an intuitive meaning: if the incremental pecuniary benefit outweighs the incremental non-pecuniary benefit conformity becomes less important, and vice versa. One real-world example may be the investment banking industry vis-à-vis financial regulations. Financial regulations are likely to add to costs and unlikely to boost revenue, a combination that makes the industry resemble scenario I. Even assuming a positive minimum legitimacy requirement, it is not difficult to understand why large investment banks do not always have to conform fully to institutions.

Despite its weakness hitherto outlined, institutions do provide the general framework for economic, social, and political interactions. Throughout human history, as North (1991) observes, institutions have developed to facilitate trade and to incentivize production; due to the path dependent nature of institutions, some regions has developed free markets, while others have less developed institutions. Further developments of this line of thought include perhaps one of the most hotly debated topics, legal origins theory (for example La Porta, Lopez-de-Silanes, & Shleifer, 2008), as well as the mechanisms underpinning this path dependence nature (David, 1994). Regardless of the validity of the former or of the success of the latter, scholars generally agree, as North (1991) put it, "together with the standard constraints of economics institutions define the choice set and therefore determine transaction and production costs and hence the profitability and feasibility of engaging in economic activity."

Underlying this argument in fact is the belief that market is a type of institutions, providing a set of rules for interactions taking place in it. This recognition has two advantages: First, it resonates with the view that "market context" and "institutional context" together contribute to the structuring of organizations and are at the same time together fed back by organizational changes. More important, it confronts the dissonant view that institutions are myths and that institutionalized organizations, which possess legitimacy and viability, also actively behave in ways normative theories suggest would undermine performance and viability (e.g., avoidance of inspection and effective evaluation; Meyer & Rowan, 1977). In fact, most institutions are like markets in the sense that the agents participating in economic, social, and political interactions do not and, due to bounded rationality, cannot fully understand all the constraints that constitute institutions which set the rules. Since most contemporary economists would not suggest organizations to be led by the nose by markets and provide positivist descriptions as well as normative prescriptions of why firms emerge (Coase, 1937), what defines the boundary of the firm (Williamson, 1991), and how organizations are structured internally (Alchian & Demsetz, 1972), etc. with market taken into account, it is conceivable institutions can be further understood. We therefore can summarize the relevant arguments into the following:

> **Proposition 4:** *Institutional theories do not provide all explanations to organizational performance and survival.*
>
> **Proposition 5:** *The incentive to conform to institutions is contingent on the scale of production and on the effects of institutionalization on costs and products.*
>
> **Proposition 6:** *Institutions provide the framework for economic activity.*
>
> **Proposition 7:** *Market is a type of institution.*

NEW INSTITUTIONAL ECONOMICS

Finding its foundation on Coase's works on transaction cost (the cost incurred in making an economic exchange; Coase, 1937) and property rights (that determine the ownership and usage of a resource; Coase, 1960), new institutional economics (NIE) embraces two important propositions: that institutions matter, and that the determinants of institutions are susceptible to analysis by the tools of economic theory (Matthews, 1986). The second of these, which the current chapter falls in line with, distinguishes NIE from the "old" institutional economics that is critical of mainstream economics (Williamson, 2000). What differentiates NIE from mainstream economics, meanwhile, is perhaps the level of social analysis it operates in (L1: social theory; L2: property rights; L3: transaction cost; L4: mainstream economics/agency theory; Williamson, 2000). As Williamson observes, the higher level imposes constraints on the level immediately below while at the same time is fed back by the lower level; whereas NIE focuses on L2 and L3, mainstream economics focuses on L4. When it comes to transaction cost economics (TCE), which is one of the most important aspects of NIE, in particular, Williamson (1996) points out several other differences between mainstream economics and TCE such as the behavioral assumption of bounded rationality, transaction as the unit of analysis, and incomplete contracts. Related to this view are the two orders of economizing (Williamson, 1991): first-order economizing refers to getting the rules of the game right and is often considered operating on the institutional environment, while second-order economizing refers to getting the governance structures right and answers a series of questions regarding the boundary of the firm (market or internalize) and the choice of organization (market, firm, or hybrid).

The prime issue of first-order economizing is property rights. The Coase theorem observes that the problem of externalities and property rights should be treated as a reciprocal problem; therefore, if transaction cost does not exist, free bargaining will result in the same efficient resource allocation regardless of liability assignment (though wealth distribution would be affected; Coase, 1960). In reality, however, transaction cost is conceivably high. Demsetz (1967) provides the necessary condition to make costs and benefits externalities—that the cost of internalization must exceed the gains from this transaction—and argues that the primary function of property rights is that of guiding incentives to achieve a greater internalization of externalities. Here, we can think of liabilities as "negative properties" that help to incentivize the internalization of negative externalities.

One example of positive externality is user interface design: It is costly for a firm to bring together a complete set of design elements that increase efficiency and decrease complexity; however, it is usually easy, and therefore not costly, for a competitor to "me too" because the implementation of these design elements is easy and can be materialized in numerous ways. Without proper copyright protection, it is conceivable that the gains of investing in such designs could not always exceed the cost, because whereas the cost is borne by one firm the gains are shared by its competitors. Still, the correct choice of first-order economizing (i.e., proper assignment of copyright protection, may not be sufficient to address all problems associated with externalities).

Let us consider the case when firm X makes investment C for a technology that would result in gain G, and that there are competitors ready to imitate. For simplicity, let us also assume that the gain would be equally shared by the firms, that is, each receives a gain of $G/(n+1)$, that the legal fees for each dispute is identical for the plaintiff and the defendant (L), and that the expected award for firm X from each dispute is identical (A). We therefore obtain the following conditions:

$$\frac{G}{n+1} - L - A < 0 \tag{7.5}$$

$$\frac{G}{n+1} + n(A-L) - C > 0 \tag{7.6}$$

If (7.5) is satisfied, the competitors would strictly avoid imitation. However, if (7.5) is not satisfied, firm X has incentive to invest in the technology if and only if (7.6) is satisfied. If (7.5) is not satisfied:

$$nA \le \frac{n}{n+1} G - nL \tag{7.7}$$

Introduce (7.7) to (7.6), we get a weaker condition:

$$G-2nL-C>0 \tag{7.8}$$

Therefore:

$$L<\frac{G-C}{2n} \tag{7.9}$$

Meanwhile, (5) can be written as:

$$L>\frac{B}{n+1}-A \tag{7.10}$$

Because we know $G \geq C$ (the condition that firm X would invest in the perfect institutional environment (i.e., proper property rights and perfect legal system), the decision whether to invest in a technology becomes a decision between the gains from that technology and the legal fees. This example illustrates the effects of transaction cost on the incentives to deviate from what institutions prescribe; that is, if transaction cost is large enough to satisfy (7.10) property rights infringement would not occur, but if transaction cost is small enough to satisfy (7.9) firm X would have incentive to invest in the technology and the competitors would have incentive to infringe.

Here, the superfluous assumption is that

$$\frac{G}{n+1}-A>\frac{G-C}{2n},$$

which need not be the case. By solving this inequality, we get:

$$A<\frac{(n-1)G+(n+1)C}{2n(n+1)} \tag{7.11}$$

This inequality shows that as the expected award from dispute increases to the point that the inequality no longer holds, the upper limit of legal fees such that competitors still have incentive to infringe would lower to:

$$L<\frac{G}{n+1}-A \tag{7.12}$$

This result suggests that, due to transaction cost, the total expected award (nA) need not exceed the gains lost ($nG/n+1$) to deter infringement.

On the side of second-order economizing, the prime issue is transaction cost. In fact, since all complex contracts are unavoidably incomplete (by reasons of bounded rationality) ex ante incentive alignment is insufficient an approach to understanding incentives and contracts; as a result, transaction cost economics prioritizes ex post contractual economizing (Williamson, 2000). Coase (1937) observes that the existence of transaction cost in the market renders certain activities less efficient when the market is used and more efficient when the activities are internalized, thereby necessitating the firm; meanwhile, overheads and other governance costs may grow disproportionally as the organization grows, thereby limiting the boundary of the firm. Williamson (1984) introduced the ideas of bounded rationality and opportunism to examine the dimensions of asset specificity, uncertainty, and frequency with regards to transaction cost. These together with later additions to transaction cost theory provide explanations to the choice of organizational structure. The ideas are that along each dimension different structural types observe different cost curves for reasons of bounded rationality and opportunism, and that the optimal organizational structure should demand the lowest governance cost with regards to the dimension.

In the previous example, if we acknowledge that in (7.5) A is the expected award perceived by the competitors, what stops competitor Y from infringing is not the amount prescribed by the legal system (say $\tilde{A}$) but a function of $\tilde{A}$ that takes into account the likelihood that the claim of the plaintiff would be upheld by the court (say p); that is, the expected award $A = \tilde{A}p$. Meanwhile, is a function of a range of factors that include at least the ease to provide evidence (e), where

$$f(e) = \frac{\partial p}{\partial e} > 0.$$

Since the rationality of competitors is bounded, $f(e)$ is different and unpredictable for each of them; therefore, different competitors may exhibit different degrees of opportunism, thereby making first-order economizing doubly difficult. This is especially the case when in reality the court may declare the defendant guilty mistakenly. If the punishment for infringement is too severe, the cost of mistrial would be so considerable that many economic activities cannot take place. This scenario can be represented as:

$$n\tilde{A}p' > G - C \tag{7.13}$$

Where n is the number of competitors and p' is the perceived likelihood of mistrial when firm Y makes an investment of C for a gain of G. If $\tilde{A}$ is so large that it satisfies (7.13), firm Y would not make the investment. In the next section we shall analyse the source of opportunism, but for now let us summarize the relevant propositions of NIE as follows:

> **Proposition 8:** *The determinants of institutions are susceptible to analysis by the tools of economic theory.*
>
> **Proposition 9:** *Property rights incentive the internalization of externalities.*
>
> **Proposition 10:** *Since all complex contracts are unavoidably incomplete, bounded rationality and opportunism add to transaction cost, the lowering of which explains the choice of organizational structure.*
>
> **Proposition 11:** *For reasons of mistrial, the legal prescription of property rights compensation, which has to be high enough to incentivize economic activity, cannot be so high that it dis-incentivizes economic activity.*

AGENCY THEORY

In its current shape, agency theory (also known as the economic theory of incentives) focuses on two problems: the agency problem, that is, conflict of interest exists but information of behaviour is not freely available, and the risk sharing problem, that is, difference in risk preferences exists (Holmstrom & Milgrom, 1991). As the name "economic theory of incentives" suggests, the cornerstone of this theory is the observation that agents are self-interested. That is, individuals would maximize their interest, though in a boundedly rational way (Jensen, 1994). A word of caution is that "interest" or utility is not solely pecuniary; however, many nonmonetary sources of interest can be monetized. Reviewing the work of Alchian and Demsetz (1972), Jensen and Meckling (1976) make the following insightful observations: (*i*) most organizations are simply legal fictions which serve as a nexus for a set of contracting relationships among individuals; (*ii*) the firm is characterized by the existence of divisible residual claims on assets and freely tradable cash flows; and (*iii*) by the logic of the preceding observations the firm is not an individual and should not be treated as one. Based on these observations, they are able to provide ex ante explanations of property rights within a firm with regard to the use of equity versus the use of debt (or residual claim versus fixed claim). Here, agency cost of the firm is the sum of (*a*) monitoring cost, (*b*) bonding cost (to cover the assurance that certain actions will not take place), and (*c*) residual loss (divergence from maximum); agency cost of the debt is the sum of (*d*) opportunity debt loss caused by the impact of debt on investment decisions of the firm, (*e*) the monitoring and bonding costs, and (*f*) the bankruptcy costs (Jensen & Meckling, 1976).

Whereas the positivist tradition of agency theory focuses on interest realignment via governance structure as a solution to the agency problem (Eisenhardt, 1989), the normative tradition of agency theory acknowledges that at the center of the agency problem is incomplete information. In the topic of formal contracts, the two aspects commonly examined are adverse selection, which is the ex ante risk as a result of asymmetric information, and moral hazard, which is the ex post risk of asymmetric information. Akerlof (1970) examines the former and observes that in a market characterized by quality differences and uncertainty, sellers have incentive to use faux quality cues to sell products of low quality in order to boost their margins; as a result, there tends to be a general reduction of average quality of goods in the market. Akerlof also suggests that many institutions, such as guarantees and brand-names, serve as attempts to mitigate the effects of quality uncertainty (Akerlof, 1970). Holmstrom (1979) examines the latter and observes that when payoff alone is observable the optimal contracts cannot reach optimum due to moral hazard, and that additional information sources can help improve contracts. In another study of more complex, multitask principal-agent problems, Holmstrom and Milgrom (1991) observes that when multiple tasks coexist incentive pay serves not only to allocate risks and to motivate hard work but also to direct the allocation of the agents' attention among various tasks, and that as a result incentive problems must be analyzed in totality. In the topic of authority, studies find their foundation on the "first legal modification" of property rights observed by Demsetz (1967); namely, a small management group become de facto owners and takes effective control of property. Aghion and Tirole (1997) derive from asymmetric information, that is, for the principal to be informed about a particular activity of the agent a cost would have to be incurred, the argument that real authority is determined by the structure of information, which in turn depends on the allocation of formal authority.

With these understandings, let us re-examine Williamson's analysis of governance choice, this time with regards to agency cost. In the presence of asymmetric information as well as the unavoidable adverse selection and moral hazard it entails, an entrepreneur/investor making the decision of governance structure, that is, how much market and how much hierarchy, can be certain of two things: First, the ex ante risk of adverse selection can be reduced to the greatest if and only if s/he can obtain the richest and most accurate information, and in fact the most perspicacious position to obtain such information is when the firm internalizes the activity. Second, without increasing the monitoring cost the ex post risk of moral hazard can be largely avoided if and only if the firm externalizes the activity and, thereby, transfers this risk to a different party. Let $f(0 \leq f \leq 1)$ denote the percentage

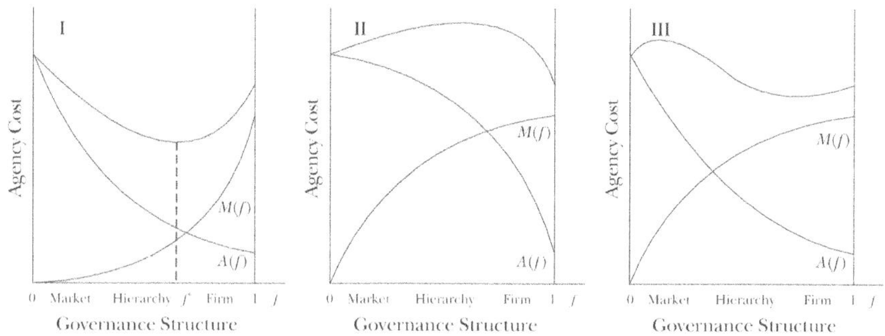

Figure 7.2 Agency cost and governance structure.
$A(f)$: the agency cost of adverse selection; $M(f)$: the agency cost of moral hazard

the firm internalizes the activities, and continuous functions $A(f)$ and $M(f)$ denote the agency cost of adverse selection and the agency cost of moral hazard respectively, we observe the following scenarios (see Figure 7.2).

As stated in the assumptions, $A'(f) < 0$ and $M'(f) > 0$. In scenario I, $A''(f) > 0$ and $M''(f) > 0$; there is always a value of $f^* (0 \le f^* \le 1)$ such that $A(f) + M(f)$ reaches minimum (please note that f^* need not be the point of intersection). In scenario II, $A''(f) < 0$ and $M''(f) < 0$; when $A(f) + M(f)$ reaches minimum $f^* \in \{0,1\}$. In scenario III, one of the functions is convex while the other is concave; we have less confidence about f^*, but for a real function in a closed range a minimum value always exists. The proof in scenario I can be written as follows:

Let $C(f) = A(f) + M(f)$, we get

$$C''(f) = A''(f) + M''(f) > 0 \tag{7.14}$$

Because $C''(f) > 0$, and because it is a continuous function, in the range of $0 \le f \le 1$, $C(f)$ has a local minimum.

Similarly, the proof in scenario II can be written as follows:

$$C''(f) = A''(f) + M''(f) < 0 \tag{7.15}$$

Because $C''(f) < 0$, and because it is a continuous function, in the range of $0 \le f \le 1$, $C(f)$ only has a local maximum; therefore, the minimum can only be found when f touches the range (i.e., $f^* \in \{0,1\}$).

In fact, in most cases the agency cost curves should be of the scenario I flavor. For adverse selection, as the firm externalizes the activities the deterioration of its access to information is likely to speed up, precisely when its need to obtain information is increasing. Further, other firms on the market may observe that this firm does not have the expertise in these activities and is less likely to be able to distinguish faux quality cues; therefore, in the presence of opportunism they would have higher incentive to use these faux cues. For moral hazard, as the firm internalizes the activities the increase of the difficulty to monitor the activities of a growing workforce is likely to be faster than linear

$$(\text{i.e., } \frac{\partial monitoring\_cost}{\partial workforce} > 1),$$

precisely when the cognitive capacity of the owner-manager becomes a constraint. On top of that, staffs in the firm may observe that it is harder for shirking to be monitored and that their personal payoff may be greater if they choose to shirk. These two reasons answer the question why modern firms are likely to use a combination of firm and market to coordinate activities.

An important point about $C(f)$ is that f^* can be seen as a function of agency cost. Let C^{-1} denote the inverse function of $C(f)$, A be the activity or a set of activities that have a characteristic cost function $D(A)$, we get:

$$f^* = C^{-1}(\min_A D(A)) \tag{7.16}$$

Here, an underlying argument emerges: in fact, agency cost and transaction cost are not always separable insofar as we acknowledge the assumptions of bounded rationality and self-interest. To push this argument one step further, we may observe that the sources of opportunism in the analysis of transaction cost are in fact (*a*) misaligned interest and (*b*) incomplete information—precisely the sources of the agency problem—in transactions. Therefore, the biggest difference between transaction cost and agency cost is not ex ante versus ex post or higher versus lower level of social analysis; this difference lies in the fact that transaction cost exists even without opportunism.

So far, we assumed that the cost functions are continuous in the entire range; this need not be the case. The existence of institutions, especially formal institutions such as tax codes and labor laws, may strongly influence the curvature and continuity of the optimal cost curve in Figure 7.3. Discussion of such issues, however, is not within the scope of this chapter. For agency theory, we can summarize the relevant propositions as the following:

Proposition 12: *Organizations are legal fictions which serve as a nexus for a set of contracting relationships among individuals.*

Proposition 13: *The agency problem can be considered as a problem of agency cost if we acknowledge that asymmetric information can be remedied by monitoring which comes at a price.*

Proposition 14: *The source of opportunism is the agency problem.*

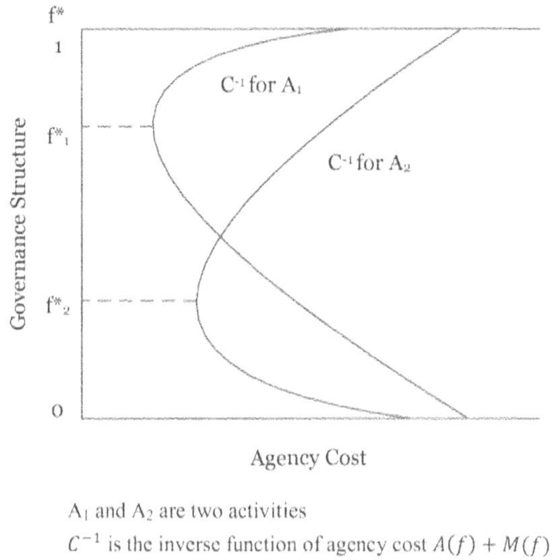

Figure 7.3 The choice of governance structure.

AGENTIC ORGANIZATIONS AND INSTITUTIONS

In the foregoing analyses, the underlying argument that has been on the tip of our tongues is that organizations exhibit characteristics of agents such as self-interest and bounded rationality. In fact, as Jensen and Meckling (1976) observe, organizations serve as nexuses for a set of contracting relationships among *individuals* (Proposition 12); therefore, the personalization of organizations (e.g., the treatment of organizations as "black boxes" or the choice of a complete different way of analyzing activities inside organizations than that of analyzing activities between organizations) risks missing some vital points. Organizations do not possess clear-cut boundaries such that all characteristics of their members are strictly contained; therefore, organizations reflect, at times, directly the qualities of their members and, more often, indirectly these qualities through the contracting relationship adapted to them. Whether our analysis focuses on organizations in the market or on individuals within organizations, the prime reason things get complicated is the agency problem. For the latter kind of analyses, few scholars would disagree that bounded rationality and self-interest pose constraints that makes it difficult, if not virtually impossible, to design organizations such that the total cost reaches minimum. For the former kind of analyses, the agentic characteristics of organizations bring opportunism to the market (Proposition 14) and thereby add to transaction costs.

Throughout the analyses, the central aspect repeatedly involved is cost; these costs include agency cost, transaction cost, and even production cost. As many scholars have observed (e.g., Akerlof, 1970; Coase, 1960; Demsetz, 1967; North, 1991), institutions come into being and evolve as a response to these costs. Further, institutions go beyond responding to costs and provide the framework that coordinates these costs and incentivizes economic activities to ensure that they can take place efficiently (Propositions 6 and 9). In fact, the converse also holds true: transaction cost, agency cost, and even production cost provide explanations to why organizations deviate from the prescriptions of institutions (Proposition 5); this happens when institutions cannot coordinate these costs efficiently. Unfortunately, the complexity of the totality of economic activities, exacerbated by the common problem of bounded rationality and self-interest, renders it extremely difficult for institutions to provide precision and generality at the same time. Further, since new elements are continually introduced into economic activities, institutions do not always adapt swiftly enough. A convenient example is the adaptation of measuring systems vis-à-vis the co-existence of the metric and the imperial systems.

Since institutions related to organizations primarily coordinate costs, we can indeed think of institutions as nexuses for a set of contracting relationships among organizations; the difference between formal and informal institutions is that the former involves formal contracts while the latter informal ones. This view explains why the determinants of institutions are susceptible to analysis by the tools of economic theory (Proposition 8; Matthews, 1986). More important, it releases the tension between different "levels of social analysis" (Williamson, 1991); namely, cost operates at L3 and L4, while institution operates at L1 and L2. The current view acknowledges that the levels of social analysis exist but suggests that their interactions are much more dynamic than Williamson observes. In fact, there is no shortage of stories where an economic incident involving individuals get magnified through modern media and shifts legal and, to some degree, informal institutions without going through all the feedback processes. Another advantage of the current view is that by seeing institutions as nexuses for contracts we can use contract as the unit of analysis, which is also the unit of analysis for a range of costs. One point worth mentioning is that most contracts among and within organizations serve as extensions to the contracts of institutions, which are, as all complex contracts, incomplete in nature.

With the preceding views, it is possible for us to integrate the remaining relevant propositions examined hitherto. Institutionalization ensures that organizations adopt a set of interfaces that are common among themselves, thereby lowering the cost of current and future competence introduction (production cost as well as transaction cost). Meanwhile, it ensures that organizations follow the rule of the game (formal and informal), thereby lowering the cost of mistrust (transaction cost as well as agency cost). Therefore, institutionalization brings competence and legitimacy that together contribute to organizational performance and survival (Proposition 1).

Because market provides a set of constraints that coordinate economic activities, it indeed is a type of institutions related to market transactions (Proposition 7). Together with other institutions related to organizations, the institution of market constitutes the context for organizational structure. It follows that as organizations evolve and bring in new elements the original institutions may no longer coordinate the costs well enough; in response to these new developments, institutions change. Involved in this process is an ever-evolving loop of context (institution), organization, and context (Proposition 2). This loop essentially explains why organizational and institutional changes are path dependent (Proposition 3).

We can also explain why institutional theories do not provide all explanations to organizational performance and survival (Proposition 4): Similar to how organizations reflect the characteristics of their members, institutions reflect, at times, directly the qualities of the organizations involved and, more often, indirectly these qualities through the contracting relationship adapted to them. However, just as organizations are not the sum of individuals, institutions are not the sum of organizations. Whereas the goal of institutions is to reflect the characteristics of the organizations and to lower the costs, thereby explaining organizational performance and survival, it is the costs that most directly determine organizational performance and survival.

As we reach lower levels of social analysis, the presence of institutions becomes less obvious. For Propositions 10 and 13, the direct causes of bounded rationality and self-interest are much more salient. Nonetheless, as explained in the foregoing sections, institutions can greatly influence the operation at these levels; meanwhile, as mentioned in the preceding paragraphs, this chapter argues that as economic activities evolve at the lower levels, institutions adapt. Proposition 11 illustrates an example how this may work. Now, let us finally summarize the arguments in this chapter into the following:

Argument 1: *Organizations exhibit characteristics of their members, which include the agentic characteristics of self-interest and bounded rationality.*

Argument 2: *Institutions come into being and evolve as a response to costs, including production cost, transaction cost, and agency cost. They aim to coordinate these costs and incentivize economic activity.*

Argument 3: *Conversely, costs provide explanations to why organizations deviate from the prescriptions of institutions.*

Argument 4: *Institutions related to organizations are nexuses for a set of contracting relationships among organizations. As the level of analysis goes down, new contracts are written as extensions to those of higher levels.*

CONCLUDING REMARKS

A few points are worth mentioning lest I should confuse the readers. First, "organizational theory" in this chapter refers to the economic theory of the firm, which differs from the traditional categorization of organizational theory. The reason is that the economic theory of the firm interacts with institutional theory more tightly. Secondly, the examples provided in this chapter are only for illustrative purposes and are overly simplified. They should neither be considered to have any normative meaning nor be regarded as descriptive tools; they serve more to demonstrate that the scenarios exist and are worth studying. Related to the second point is the note that the minimum legitimacy in the first example need not be a flat line; however, the model serves its purpose because only in the virtually impossible case when the minimum legitimacy coincides with the discrimination line can the observations in that example be completely nullified. Fourthly, this chapter does not suggest empirical studies at the organizational level may be futile; it only contends that theoretical explanations of the problems in an organization can almost always be found in the characteristics of its members.

At last, let us try imprudently to answer North's query ("What is it about informal constraints that gives them such a pervasive influence upon the long-run character of economies?" Williamson, 2000; citing North, 1991). First, informal institutions consist of large sets of implicit contracts. In order for informal institutions to evolve, large numbers of contracts have to be renegotiated. However, unlike the case with formal institutions, for which we have usually democratic legislatures that collect the feedbacks from economic activities through mass voting, modifications to informal institutions calls for underlying public consensuses that, without a formal structure, are hard to reach. As a result, informal constraints evolve slowly. Second, though we cannot always renegotiate the contracts of informal constraints, they do lay out the foundations for us to negotiate further contracts. Consequently, the formal constraints we develop are based on these informal constraints. It follows that the contracts we write indeed are all anchored indirectly on these informal constraints. Therefore, it is hardly surprising that they have a pervasive influence.

With these in mind, we can see that institutions matter, but not because they are myths. On the contrary, they come into being and evolve in response to very tangible costs. At their best, institutions coordinate costs and incentivize economic activities. However, due to the complexity of the totality of economic activities, institutions cannot provide all the explanations to organizational performance and survival. At times, organizations choose to deviate from the prescriptions of institutions because it is less costly for them to do so. By viewing organizations as reflecting the agentic qualities of their members and institutions as nexuses of contracting relationships among organizations, we observe that a range of propositions from institutional and organizational theories can be integrated and a set of questions can be answered.

One may ask: Would there be institutions if we are all completely honest? The answer is positive. In fact, we need institutions even under the assumption of absolute, unbounded rationality. Transaction costs and production costs would still exist and need be coordinated, and it is only when everything should come at absolutely no cost (if this should be imaginable, since even in the most primitive hunter-gatherer societies this condition cannot be satisfied) we could do without institutions.

ACKNOWLEDGMENTS

I thank my colleagues and the series editor who have given me valuable advice. An earlier version of this chapter was presented at the 2013 Annual Meeting of the Academy of Management in Lake Buena Vista, FL. I also owe my gratitude to the reviewers whose suggestions helped me improve my manuscript.

REFERENCES

Aghion, P., & Tirole, J. (1997). Formal and real authority in organizations. *Journal of Political Economy, 105*, 1–29.

Akerlof, G. A. (1970). The market for "lemons": Quality uncertainty and the market mechanism. *Quarterly Journal of Economics, 84*, 488–500.

Alchian, A. A., & Demsetz, H. (1972). Production, information costs, and economic organization. *American Economic Review, 62*, 777–795.

Coase, R. H. (1937). The nature of the firm. *Economica, 4*, 386–405.

Coase, R. H. (1960). The problem of social cost. *Journal of Law and Economics, 3*, 1–44.

David, P. A. (1994). Why are institutions the "carriers of history"? Path dependence and the evolution of conventions, organizations and institutions. *Structural Change and Economic Dynamics, 5*, 205–220.

Demsetz, H. (1967). Toward a theory of property rights. *American Economic Review, 57*, 347–359.

DiMaggio, P. J., & Powell, W. W. (1983). The iron cage revisited: Institutional isomorphism and collective rationality in organizational fields. *American Sociological Review, 48*, 147–160.

Eisenhardt, K. M. (1989). Agency theory: An assessment and review. *Academy of Management Review, 14*, 57–74.
Greenwood, R., & Hinings, C. R. (1996). Understanding radical organizational change: Bringing together the old and the new institutionalism. *Academy of Management Review, 21*, 1022–1054.
Heugens, P. P., & Lander, M. W. (2009). Structure! Agency! (and other quarrels): A meta-analysis of institutional theories of organization. *Academy of Management Journal, 52*, 61–85.
Holmstrom, B. (1979). Moral hazard and observability. *Bell Journal of Economics, 10*, 74–91.
Holmstrom, B., & Milgrom, P. (1991). Multitask principal-agent analyses: Incentive contracts, asset ownership, and job design. *Journal of Law, Economics, & Organization, 7*, 24–52.
Jensen, M. C. (1994). Self-interest, altruism, incentives, and agency theory. *Journal of Applied Corporate Finance, 7*, 40–45.
Jensen, M. C., & Meckling, W. H. (1976). Theory of the firm: Managerial behavior, agency costs, and ownership structure. *Journal of Financial Economics, 3*, 306–360.
Kogut, B., Walker, G., & Anand, J. (2002). Agency and institutions: National divergences in diversification behavior. *Organization Science, 13*, 162–178.
La Porta, R., Lopez-de-Silanes, F., & Shleifer, A. (2008). The economic consequences of legal origins. *Journal of Economic Literature, 46*, 285–332.
Matthews, R. C. (1986). The economics of institutions and the sources of growth. *The Economic Journal, 96*, 903–918.
Meyer, J. W., & Rowan, B. (1977). Institutionalized organizations: Formal structure as myth and ceremony. *American Journal of Sociology, 83*, 340–363.
North, D. C. (1991). Institutions. *Journal of Economic Perspectives, 5*, 97–112.
Selznick, P. (1949). *TVA and the grass roots: A study in the sociology of formal organization*. Berkeley: University of California Press.
Selznick, P. (1957). *Leadership in administration: A sociological interpretation*. Evanston and White Plains: Row, Peterson and Co.
Selznick, P. (1996). Institutionalism "old" and "new." *Administrative Science Quarterly, 41*, 270–277.
Simon, H. (1955). A behavioral model of rational choice. *Quarterly Journal of Economics, 69*, 99–118.
Simon, H. (1957). *Models of man: Social and rational*. Oxford: Wiley.
Tolbert, P. S., & Zucker, L. G. (1983). Institutional sources of change in the formal structure of organizations: The diffusion of civil service reform, 1880–1935. *Administrative Science Quarterly, 28*, 22–39.
Williamson, O. E. (1984). The economics of governance: Framework and implications. *Journal of Institutional and Theoretical Economics*, 195–223.
Williamson, O. E. (1991). Comparative economic organization: The analysis of discrete structural alternatives. *Administrative Science Quarterly, 36*, 269–296.
Williamson, O. E. (1996). *The mechanisms of governance*. Oxford: Oxford University Press.

Williamson, O. E. (2000). The new institutional economics: Taking stock, looking ahead. *Journal of Economic Literature, 38*, 595–613.

Zucker, L. G. (1987). Institutional theories of organization. *Annual Review of Sociology, 13*, 443–464.

CHAPTER 8

A BEHAVIORAL VIEW OF BUSINESS MODELING

Arash Najmaei

ABSTRACT

This chapter introduces the concept of business modeling defined as the managerial deliberate continuous involvement in the process of developing and adjusting a business model for their firm. This conceptualization (1) bridges the business model literature with the strategic leadership and managerial dynamic capabilities; and (2) pronounces the inseparable link between managerial agency and the business model of the firm as a unit of analysis in the micro-foundations of strategy and competitiveness. To develop this model, insights from the behavioral perspective have been used. This chapter posits that the business model of the firm follows an evolutionary path that is set and managed by executives. The current business model acts as a reference point for executives and shapes their aspiration and business modeling goals. These goals in conjunction with the performance of the firm, perceived capacities and subjective evaluation of proximate and distant opportunities govern executives business modeling in the form of minor adjustments or major changes (transformation, reinvention, even dismissal and adoption of a new business model) to the business model or the firm. Therefore, business modeling is a path-dependent activity and its trajectory is determined by

Behavioral Strategy: Emerging Perspectives, pages 177–203

the dynamic interactions between executives' perception of goal attainment discrepancies through historical and social comparisons attributed to the current business model and environmental demands.

INTRODUCTION

In principle, a business firm is a productive entity which competes with other firms in markets for obtaining resources and selling products. It uses different strategies to direct these affairs in a superior way leading to a competitive position (Rumelt, Schendel, & Teece, 1991). A competitive position is achieved when a firm's strategies enable it to both create superior market offerings and commercialize those offerings. The former refers to value creation and the latter in known as value capture (Bowman & Ambrosini, 2000). Therefore, executives of the firm as top managers who are at the helm of the firm have to deal simultaneously with value creating and capturing activities. Recent advancements in the strategy literature suggest that the business model of the firm defines the logic behind these activities. It helps executives understand and manage how value can be created and captured (Zott, Amit, & Massa, 2011).

More importantly, whenever a firm is established it adopts a business model which determines how it runs its business by defining (1) what value it offers; (2) how it produces this value offering; and (3) how it commercializes it in the marketplace (Teece, 2010). Therefore, a business model serves as a recipe that guides executives to lead their firms from opportunities to market profits. By succeeding in the market, this model becomes subject to imitation and obsolescence. Particularly as the business ecosystem evolves, technological disruptions challenge the established production and commercialization methods and new customers' preferences change the patterns of supply and demand. These forces erode the business model of the firm and reduce its competitive effectiveness (Gambardella & McGahan, 2010).

Running a business based on an ineffective business model results in the loss of competitive position and would eventually lead to an inability to co-evolve with the environment (Doz & Kosonen, 2010). So, executives have consistently to keep their business competitive by adjusting their business model (Katkalo, Pitelis, & Teece, 2010; Pitelis & Teece, 2009). This importance places the business model of the firm at the centre of the contemporary strategy research (Achtenhagen, Melin, & Naldi, 2013; Chatterjee, 2013; Demil, Lecocq, Ricart, & Zott, 2013; Desyllas & Sako, 2013; Najmaei, 2012; Sako, 2012; Sinfield, Calder, McConnell, & Colson, 2012; Spieth, Tidd, Matzler, Schneckenberg, & Vanhaverbeke, 2013). Research in this field is guided by two assumptions: First, the business model of the firm is a new unit of analysis different from strategy and the firm itself.

Thus, studying business models advances literature on both strategic and organizational views of the firm (Zott et al., 2011). Second, managing the business model of the firm has been argued to be a key, previously ignored task of executives central to their development of capabilities (Augier & Teece, 2009; Katkalo et al., 2010). Thus, analysis of this task not only gives us a sense of the firm in action but also enriches the understanding of the way executives lead their firm in changing environments (McGrath, 2010).

Despite this significance, the existing business models literature fails to provide a comprehensive explanation for the way executives and by implication their firm(s) adjusts the business model to keep abreast of environmental changes. Specifically, with few exceptions (Achtenhagen et al., 2013; Doz & Kosonen, 2010) the literature in business model is dominated with a static view leaving a gap in understanding how a business model changes. Therefore, a dynamic view proves to be the appropriate yet an underemphasized perspective.

Given the above, it is the intention of this essay to tackle this issue by developing an analytic framework that explains how executives manage their business model by making required adjustments to the current business model of their firm. Building on the existing literature it is shown that the task of business model management could take different forms ranging from minor improvements to the existing business model of the firm to a reinvention or transformation of the business model. In this study, this procedure will be broadly called the 'business modeling' of the firm. Since changes in the business model of the firm have direct impacts on value creation and value capture of the firm, insights from the behavioral view of the strategy (Gavetti, Greve, Levinthal, & Ocasio, 2012; Powell, Lovallo, & Fox, 2011) were used to inform our understanding of how these changes are initiated and enacted upon.

Behavioral view attempts to explain how executives initiate and manage necessary changes using assumptions derived from literature on cognition and psychology (Levinthal, 2011; Lovallo & Sibony, 2010; Powell et al., 2011). Although, the behavioral view has been informing organization science for decades (Bougon, Weick, & Binkhorst, 1977; Cyert & March, 1963; March & Simon, 1958; McKenney & Keen, 1974; Mintzberg, 1976; Simon, 1961), its use in business modeling of executives has not been discussed. Therefore, a behavioral view of business modeling, as proposed in this study, would focus on the psychological factors of executives, as the guardians of the firm's business model that determine how a business model comes to exist and goes through different changes.

The rationale behind this approach is that business modeling from selection (adoption), use (implementation), to adjustment (improvement or transformation/reinvention) is carried out by choices that executives make. This choice-making is explained by behavioral assumptions (i.e., assumptions that root in the psychology of executives).

By doing so, this study contributes to the strategy literature in two related ways. First, it extends the literature on behavioral strategy to the business model realm and shows how the behavioral assumptions contribute to a better understanding of business modeling behavior of executives as a key strategic task required for achieving sustained market success (Bock, Opsahl, George, & Gann, 2012; George & Bock, 2011; Pohle & Chapman, 2006). Second, in response to the concern raised by Zott et al. (2011) that the business model remains theoretically underdeveloped, this study enriches the business model literature and sheds new light on its evolution by proposing a theoretical discussion on the foundation of business model change. This framework opens the black-box of business modeling (Achtenhagen et al., 2013) and creates new avenues for research on dynamism of business models.

Given the above, this chapter is organized in four sections. The first section reviews the basic assumptions of the behavioral view derived from the existing literature on the behavioral theory of the firm, the behavioral resource-based theory and behavioral strategy in order to form a conceptual ground for a behavioral view of business modeling. The second section reviews the key aspects of the business model literature from an evolutionary perspective. It discusses different phases involved in the evolution of a business model (change or alternatively the life cycle of business model). Subsequently, the notion of business modeling will be conceptualized in this section. In the third section, a behavioral view of business modeling will be developed and a number of propositions will be made. Finally, in the last section implications of this study and a number of potential directions for future research will be presented.

BEHAVIORAL VIEW: ORIGIN AND POTENTIAL

Neoclassic economics assumes that conditions for all firms are the same. Specifically, firms in an industry (markets) enjoy perfect information and certainty about the environment and suffer no adaptability or control problems (Pierce, Boerner, & Teece, 2008). Particularly, in the so-called neo-classical view of the firm, managers/executives are fully rational and act according to the axioms of expected utility theory implying that they are equally equipped with required information and their decisions are based on a complete understanding of the consequence of each alternative option (Levinthal, 2011). Under this assumption, not only the internal mechanisms of the firm remain unexplored and the concept of the firm becomes simplistic and unrealistic but also the resultant literature fails to explain strategic behaviors of the firm and leaves no room for various activities of executives and their heterogeneous performance consequences (Cyert & Williams, 1993).

In an attempt to address this deficiency, Cyert and March (1963) developed a behavioral theory of the firm in which strategic behaviors of the firm and the role of executives in formulating and executing those behaviors are explained. According to this view, firms are heterogeneous adaptive entities. If they are to survive they have different choices to make that may include selection of goals, products and services to offer, and configuration of different policies underlying the position of the firm in the markets (Rumelt et al., 1991). Executives make these choices based on organizational goals, past performance of the firm and performance of other firms (Gavetti et al., 2012). Central to this process are several postulations and concepts which are of great value for this study. These can be summarized as follows.

First, unlike the neo-classical view, in the behavioral view managers/executives are intendedly rational but only limitedly so (Simon, 1957, 1961), meaning that their rationality is bounded. They have neither the complete information nor the capacity to perform an optimal rational analysis. Therefore, "bounded rationality puts limit upon the ability of managers to adapt optimally, or even satisfactorily, to complex environments" (Simon, 1991, p. 132). This assumption shapes the cognitive foundation of the behavioral view which challenges the unrealistic view of rational man in the neo-classical view.

An important consequence of bounded rationality is that executives do not maximize utility, they satisfice. It means that, "they choose the first alternative they expect to be satisfactory" (Gavetti et al., 2012). Put simply, Simon (1987) has elaborated the difference between optimizing and satisficing acts of managers as "'looking for the sharpest needle in the haystack' (optimizing) and 'looking for a needle sharp enough to sew with' (satisficing)" (p. 244). Therefore, according to the behavioral view, executives' behavior is satisficing not optimizing. What is satisfactory in this sense is determined by performance aspirations (Winter, 2000).

Performance aspirations also known as goals can be defined as desired performance levels in specific organizational outcomes (Shinkle, 2011). Due to bounded rationality and unknown factors in the environment executives set aspirations as guidance or a reference point for their activities and a desired performance level for their firm. An aspiration has a level that is the smallest outcome found by an executive to be satisfactory (Greve, 2008). This level is the borderline between success and failure (Greve, 1998b).

Aspirations are formed based on four factors: historical self-comparison, social-comparison, past experience (backward-looking), and expectations (forward-looking) (Shinkle, 2011). Historical self-comparison refers to the performance history of the firm. In particular executives use feedback of recent performance to form an aspiration level (Audia & Greve, 2006;

Greve, 1998b). Uncertainty and competitive forces also provoke executives to use performance of similar other firms to justify their aspiration level. To choose similar firms executives rely on closely related firms in their industry whose performance is relevant to their performance (Greve, 2008). This social-comparison helps executives evaluate their aspiration level and reduce uncertainty.

Although historical and social comparison has been argued to be the main determinants of aspiration level (Greve, 1998a, 1998b, 2008) behavioral view also suggests that past goals serve as additional reference points to set new aspiration levels. Executives navigate their attention towards past-goals and manage activities accordingly. If past-goals have been achieved, new goals are developed otherwise focus is redirected towards past-goals. This backward-looking approach is sometime coupled with expectations of the future. These expectations represent a forward-looking approach and refer to the forecast of what is likely to occur in the future (Lant & Shapira, 2008). They form a cognitive representation of the future of the business environment and serve as anticipatory logic which help executives interpret information, link past goals to future goals, and organize search activities for adjusting aspirations (Gavetti et al., 2012).Expectations are derived from observations of the internal organization and interpretation of the external environment (Gavetti et al., 2012).

Behavioral view of the firm assumes that firms are inherently heterogeneous. That is, firms vary in terms of resources, knowledge, division of labor, and operational procedures. Therefore, the internal organization of the firm is diverse. This diversity cause executives of relatively similar firms to search for different information in different ways and interpret the external environment differently (Gavetti et al., 2012; Shinkle, 2011).

These differences imply that firms vary in setting their aspirations and adjusting their aspirations according to their performance, performance of others and interpretation of the environment and meeting their aspirations by using their resources (Lant, 1992; March & Shapira, 1992). This causes heterogeneous abilities in organizational adaptive actions (Winter, 2000) and makes some firms better or worse suited than others to succeed in a given environment (Pierce et al., 2008).

Given the above, the key prediction of the behavioral view of strategy is that behavior of firms in pursuit of adaptation is guided by the discrepancy between aspiration and performance (Shinkle, 2011). That is, because executives have an element of control over the outcomes of their actions, they set goals and respond to goals-attainment feedback (Lant & Shapira, 2008). Therefore, firms are led in a way that enhances their degree of success in achieving aspirations (Lant, 1992). Put simply, when a firm's performance is below the aspiration level, executives would change strategies and adjust the current courses of action in order to increase performance.

Analogously, activities leading to performance above the aspiration level are reinforced (Gavetti et al., 2012). This prediction has been empirically tested and substantiated for different strategic activities such as innovation (Greve & Taylor, 2000), risky strategic change (Greve, 1998b), resource acquisition (Greve, 2011), product quality management (Rhee, 2009) and R&D intensity (Chen & Miller, 2007).

Although the behavioral view of the firm, as briefly explained above, is extremely influential in understanding the way executives lead their firms, its focus is not strategic. The primary goal of behavioral view of the firm was operational activities inside the firm not market performance and competitive behavior of the firm (Pierce et al., 2008).

Two extensions of the original behavioral view of the firm have been developed to address this deficiency. First is the behavioral view of strategy or behavioral strategy view (Lovallo & Sibony, 2010; Powell et al., 2011) and the second one is the behavioral resource-based view (Garbuio, King, & Lovallo, 2011; Pitelis, 2007).

First, the behavioral strategy is primarily concerned with the sources and persistence of superior performance of the firm and variations of this sustained performance (i.e., competitiveness and its sustainability) (Gavetti, Levinthal, & Ocasio, 2007). Therefore, the notion of firm heterogeneity in terms of resources, knowledge, skills and internal operational mechanisms, as initially proposed in the behavioral view of the firm, lies at the heart of this view (Pierce et al., 2008).

Building on the assumption of heterogeneity, behavioral view of strategy advocates the notion of a firm's strategic leadership (Hambrick, 1989; Hambrick & Mason, 1984) by focusing on "the people (i.e., executives, general managers, board of directors) who have overall responsibility for an organization—the characteristics of those people, what they do, and how they do it" (Hambrick, 1989, p. 6). This view is guided by two principles. First, issues in the business environments are either controllable (can be changed) or uncontrollable (cannot be changed) and managers require the wisdom and courage to discriminate between what is and is not controllable and navigate their attention towards those that can be changed (Gavetti & Levinthal, 2004). Second, their ability to turn controllable factors to their advantage is limited because managers have limited cognitive capacity and supportive firms' resources and capabilities may not be readily available for enacting required changes (Gavetti & Levinthal, 2004).

Strategy field uses this framework and offers a more specialized picture of how executives as strategic leaders develop, implement, and adjust different strategies (Ansoff, 1987; Fiegenbaum, Hart, & Schendel, 1996; Moussetis, 2011). It moves beyond simple goal-setting and attainment as described in the behavioral view of the firm by looking into deeper psychological foundation of findings opportunities, setting goals and deploying resources to exploit them in a more competitive fashion.

Particularly, the behavioral view of strategy mergers cognitive and social psychology with strategic management theory and practice in order to bring realistic assumptions about human cognition, emotions, and social behavior to the strategic behavior of the firm (Powell, Lovallo, & Fox, 2011). The importance of this view is manifested in the fact that behavioral components involved in executives' actions bound firms' abilities to create and capture value (Gavetti, 2012). Therefore, behavioral view of strategy has a potential to create a more complete picture of firms' success and failure by focusing on how executives identify and exploit sources of superior competitive performance and what role their cognitive and psychological attributes play in this regard.

As noted earlier, a branch of the behavioral strategy is the behavioral resource-based view (Garbuio et al., 2011; Pitelis, 2007). Research on this strand focuses on the cognitive and psychological factors involved in management of and formation of capabilities (Teece, 2007). It deals with issues such as how executives acquire, bundle or dispose different resources to develop and execute competitive strategies (Garbuio et al., 2011; Gavetti et al., 2012).

To sum up, the behavioral view of strategy and the behavioral resource-based view are based on the cognitive limitations and biases involved in a search for solutions and evaluation of alternatives. Behavioral theory of the firm suggests that limitations are unavoidable and ubiquitous.

Acknowledging these limitations, the present research extends this stream by introducing a behavioral view of business modeling. It particularly adds three points to the behavioral strategy. First, it argues that the business model of the firm plays a central role in enabling and constraining executives to find opportunities. Second, it shows that business models help executives manage their resources to exploit opportunities to generate superior competitive performance; and third, it explains how managers (and by extension their firms) vary in developing and managing business models and, establish the notion that this variation can be explained by insights from the behavioral perspective.

FROM BUSINESS MODEL TO BUSINESS MODELING

It has been argued that, "whenever a firm is established it either explicitly or implicitly employs a particular business model that describes the design or architecture of the value creation, delivery, and capture mechanisms it employs" (Teece, 2010, p. 172). This statement may explain what business models do but it does not explain why they do what they do.

To understand why business models do what they do let's begin with a fundamental intriguing issue: what is the difference between firms and markets? Or simply, why do firms exist at all? Literature offers two answers to this question based on which to expand our understanding of business models. First, as discussed in transaction costs economics, some transactions can be performed more effectively in firms that are in the markets leading to the emergence and growth of different firms (Williamson, 1981). Second, as argued by Penrose (1959), firms are a bundle of resources which are coordinated by an administrative organization that is not available in the markets. This administrative organization defines the boundary of the firm and distinguishes it from markets.

These two are not competing views; rather, they converge to the notion that executives (the administrative body) set directions for organizational activities to perform transactions necessary for the survival and growth of the firm (Pitelis, 2009). Setting these directions and managing transactions is impossible without a clear understanding of what the firm does and how it does it. As previously discussed, it is the business model of the firm that defines what the firm does and how it actually does it. Therefore, a business model, above all, is a recipe in the hand of executives explaining how to get from an idea (for forming a firm) to results (success in the marketplace) (Chesbrough, Minin, & Piccaluga, 2013).

Therefore, the business model of the firm links the administrative side to the transactional sides of the firm. Therefore, the business model is neither a business or venture idea nor a business opportunity or financial plan; rather it is a cognitive representation of the business in the mind of executives which is then translated into different activities that perform various transactions. Structure and governance of these activities shape the design of the business model (Amit & Zott, 2012; Zott & Amit, 2007, 2008, 2010). The design of the business model can be simple or sophisticated depending on the nature of the idea behind the business model and its requisite transactions.

The above reasoning implies that a business model has two representational roles. On the one hand, it represents the firm (e.g., IBM's business model, Dell's business model, etc.). This representational role denotes the specialization of the firm's business model. On the other hand, a business model can represent the recipe shared by a firm's specific industry. For example, a social network business model shared by Facebook, LinkedIn, MySpace, etc., low cost carrier (LCC) also known as no-frill business model of the airline industry shared by firms such as Air Asia, Ryanair, Southwest, etc.

This study focuses on the former and posits that the latter pertains to the business model of an industry not the firm which is used as a reference point by executives to adjust the business model of their firms. This issue will be further explained in the next section.

When a firm participates in market transactions it exposes its business model to competition. Executives of rival firms tend to decipher each other's' business models to adopt them causing effective designs to diffuse quickly or to develop new business models or adjust their current ones to outperform those of rivals. Further, unlike technological designs the design of business models cannot be patented (Dickinson, 2000) and new technological advancements shorten the life span of unprotected business models based on out-dated technologies. These various forces erode business models (Gambardella & McGahan, 2010) making them dysfunctional, ineffective or completely obsolete.

Ineffective, dysfunctional or obsolete business models becomes a wrong recipe inhibiting a firm's evolutionary fitness by preventing it from co-evolving with the environment (Doz & Kosonen, 2010).The business model of the firm lacks the property of self-improvement. It requires a managerial agency to function and stay functional. So, executives have consistently to keep their business on track by adjusting their business model (Chesbrough, 2010; Demil & Lecocq, 2010).This crucial task can be called "business modeling." Business modeling takes different forms ranging from minor improvements to the existing business model of the firm to a reinvention or transformation of the business model (Achtenhagen et al., 2013; Aspara, Lamberg, Laukia, & Tikkanen, 2011; Johnson, Christensen, & Kagermann, 2008).

Accordingly, business modeling refers to the set of administrative tasks pertaining to the management of the business model of the firm. Because business model is a firm-level construct embedded in the administrative structure of the firm, business modeling is assumed to be best explained from the behavioral view of strategy which is about behavior of executives who shape the administrative body of the firm.

Adopting the term "business modeling" shifts the attention from "business model" as a static entity to a dynamic view in which "business model" constantly evolves similar to a living entity. Further, business modeling denotes the centrality of managerial agency in the business model literature.

The rationale behind this approach is summarized as follows. Business modeling from selection (adoption), use (implementation), to adjustment (improvement or transformation/reinvention) of the business model is carried out through choices that executives make. These choices are explained by behavioral assumptions (i.e., assumptions rooted in the psychology of executives).

Having defined the outline of a behavioral view of business modeling, a summary of the key aspects of the three behavioral views explained in this section is illustrated in Table 8.1. In light of this comparison, it is reasonable to expect that a behavioral view of business modeling is closely associated with the other two behavioral views (firm and strategy). The next

TABLE 8.1 Comparing a Behavioral View of Business Modeling with Behavioral Views of the Firm and Strategy

	Behavioral Theory of the Firm	Behavioral Strategy/ Behavioral RBV	Behavioral View of Business Modeling
Unit of Analysis	Firm	Strategic leaders (executives)	Business model of the firm
Primary Intention	Opening the black box of firm	Understanding strategic choice making	Opening the black box of business model
Key Questions Addressed	How firms as social units perform daily activities, learn and adapt to the environment	How executives formulate strategies(make strategic choices)	How business models come to being and change
Underlying Principles	Bounded rationality Satisficing	Bounded rationality Satisficing	Bounded rationality Satisficing

section sheds more light on these associations by discussing some behavioral aspects of business modeling.

ARRIVING AT A BEHAVIORAL VIEW OF BUSINESS MODELING

As suggested earlier, once a firm is established it employs a business model which defines both value creating and capturing activities. Thus, adjusting this business model influences the entire enterprise and is a risky change initiative.

For these reasons, a behavioral view of business modeling has to deal with the perception of (1) the current business model of the firm; and (2) the evaluation of risks and rewards associated with different changes on this model. In line with these two, the discussion of business modeling starts by assuming that a firm is established because there is a business model enabling it to perform some truncations in a way markets cannot do. This business model is, at core, a cognitive reference point. Business funders use it by virtue of their bounded rationality to develop a mental model or a representation of the way they want to perform business transactions in the market.

At this stage, a business model is simply a simplified representation of reality. One would ask how a business funder adopts a business model. Behavioral view suggests that based on existing knowledge of the business, experience and mental maps of the industry one could develop a number of alternative representations of reality (Porac & Thomas, 1990). Depending on different cognitive filters rooted in skills, competencies, and values of individuals one representation becomes ideal. Two behavioral assumptions are of key importance here. First, the choice of a business model is guided by the satisficing principle. That is, an executive/business owner or the funder chooses the first option that satisfies his/her idea of a feasible business. The second principle is that, due to bounded rationality and limited search capacity, this option is sought in familiar or proximate contexts yet superior ideas tend to be in cognitively distant contexts (Gavetti, 2012) where very few dare to penetrate and search for business models. Therefore, the first proposition is:

> **Proposition 1:** *The first business model of the firm is most likely found within cognitively proximate/familiar contexts and is adopted if it satisfices the funder/business owner's idea of a feasible business.*

Then, this ideal model becomes the business model of the firm. Executives use this model to direct their attention in desired directions. At this stage, the business model resembles the dominant logic of the firm (Prahalad & Bettis, 1986) and strategic reference points (Bamberger & Fiegenbaum, 1996; Fiegenbaum et al., 1996). Despite this resemblance, business model is different from the dominant logic and strategic reference points of the firm in terms its scope. The business model of the firm focuses on three specific aspects of the business: nature of the value offering, creating the vale offering and commercializing it. So, business model of the firm serves as a logic that is composed of three dimensions: what value is being offered, how it must be created and how it should be commercialized. Being held in the mind of managers, these three shape three cognitive reference points (Rosch, 1975). According to Rosch, "to be a reference point within a category, a stimulus must be shown to be one which other stimuli are seen in relation to" (p. 532). Therefore, the main criterion in use of cognitive reference points is the perceived asymmetry between a cognitive reference point (CRP) and a non-CRP (Tribushinina, 2008). That being said, a business model represents mental pictures of ideal value offering, ideal processes to create this offering and ideal ways to commercialize it.

Being ideal in the mind of executives, the above cognitive reference points of a business model shape aspirations. Since ideal value should be enacted two goals are assigned to these three reference points: goal for value creation and goal for value capture. In the behavioral view of the firm, goals consist of aspirations level on a measurable outcome and the realized outcome called performance (Greve, 2008). Value creation goal consists of operational measurable outcomes and value capture goals consist of financial measurable outcomes.

Of course, different firms operating in different industries adopt various operational and financial goals. For instance, service firms may measure their operation in terms of service heterogeneity, quality and inherent attributes of service value offerings whereas manufacturing firms could consider raw-material costs, production costs, etc. With respect to financial goals, literature suggests that executives adopt measures such as return on investment, profitability, etc. (Brown & Perry, 1994; Capon, Farley, & Hoenig, 1990). In addition, privately held firms, family firms and publicly listed firms have varying goals based on their governance structure.

To adopt these three goals, executives use a variety of perceptual tools that help them simplify complexities surrounding goals setting and emergence of conflicting goals. Literature suggests at least three types of these tools. Shared general rules of industry known as an industry's recipe (Spender, 1989), key technological features of an industry—also known and the industry's dominant design—(Abernathy & Utterback, 1978) and key preference of customers followed by majority of firms known as the performance trajectory of the industry (Christensen & Raynor, 2003). These three provide general guidelines for executives to determine the scope of different goals and aspiration levels that capture the essence of each goal. As noted, behavioral view suggests that, executives use social comparison with similar firms which are easily available and viewed as relevant sources of information for evaluating goals (Greve, 2008).

Here, another aspect of these three goals is explained. Being part of the same business model implies that these three goals are complementary. It means that only the combined outcome of these three matters in evaluating the overall performance of the business model (Teece, 1986, 2006). This reasoning leads to:

> **Proposition 2:** *Executives enact business model of the firm by setting three complementary goals: value-description goal, value creation goal, and value capture goal.*

This conception is in line with a long-held belief that executives develop multiple cognitive representations in pursuit of different goals to reduce uncertainty and enhance decision making (Hodgkinson, 1997; Hodgkinson & Johnson, 1994). These complementarities motivate executives to search for a different bundle of resources which enables their firm to pursue these goals. The consistency between each goal and its respective set of activities can be captured in distinct designs possessed by different firms operating in the same industry (Amit & Zott, 2001, 2012).

At this stage, a business model becomes a performative entity (Perkmann & Spicer, 2010) guiding the way executives perform their choice-making tasks. Particularly with respect to goal-driven activities, executives engage in searching for and acquiring new resources from strategic actor markets (Barney, 1986; Makadok & Barney, 2001) internal development

(Knott, Bryce, & Posen, 2003). According to the behavioral view, the limited cognitive capacity of executives prevents them from pursuing multiple goals simultaneously (Gavetti et al., 2012). A quasi-resolution is to attend to goals sequentially in order of their importance (Argote & Greve, 2007; Greve, 2008). Consequently, some executives prioritize value conception over creation and capture, some pay more attention to value creation at the expense of underemphasizing value capture and conception, and some may commit more resources to capture profit from value offerings. The sequential attention to dimensions of business models creates asymmetries in capabilities of the firm to execute its business model. March recognized this problem and captured its essence in the notion of exploratory and exploitative logics (March, 1991). According to this postulate, executives tend to focus on either creating new value (i.e., exploration) or capturing value (i.e., exploitation). Therefore, there is reason to assume that;

> **Proposition 3:** *Executives tend to develop asymmetrical sets of activities around their business models in pursuit of either value creating or capturing goals.*

By performing these activities a firm becomes part of business ecosystems (i.e., markets and industries). Consequently, uncertainty surrounding business model activities increases and the likelihood of unexpected competitive attacks rises. Since knowledge of these circumstances of time and place is neither available to executives not will be given to them in its totality (Hayek, 1945), executives strive to constantly evaluate realized outcomes of business activities. According to the behavioral perspectives, three sources will be used in this evaluation: historical feedback, subjective evaluation of competitors across same attributes, and future expectations. Again, it is important to consider which set of activities and their respective goals are foci of attention. The next proposition simplifies this notion:

> **Proposition 4:** *Executives tend to evaluate the realized outcome of their value creating activities through a combination of (a) their firm's historical value creating performance; (b) current value creating performance of similar firms; and (c) value creating expectations. Similar analogy applies to value capturing activities.*

Having posited that, realized outcomes of the firm in the market will be attributed to activities performed for respective goals and will be associated with the priory given to the goals. In other words, performance above the aspiration level on one goal triggers executives to shift the attention to the other goal. On the other hand, realized outcomes below each aspiration level trigger more attention to the goal and initiate problemistic search for solutions (Augier & March, 2008; Gavetti, 2012). In light of this understanding the following are proposed:

Proposition 5: *Perceived performance above the aspiration levels on value creating goals would shift emphasis of executives to evaluating outcomes of value capturing activities and vice versa.*

Proposition 6: *Perceived performance below the aspiration levels on value creating goals would increase the existing emphasis of executives on value creating activities and vice versa.*

Executives' perception of low performance in a dimension of business model could be responded to by making different changes to the activities that are believed to have caused low performance. This reasoning is rooted in a psychological tendency of executives to protect their business model. This tendency is due to the fact that executives get accustomed to their business models and develop an emotional attachment to its underlying assumptions (Hodgkinson, 1997; Hodgkinson & Johnson, 1994). This attachment is caused by cognitive efforts made over time as business models act as a filter through which executives search for information, interpret their business landscape, and organize their resources. So, re-arranging easy-to-change activities is the first option with minimal cognitive effort sought by executives to adjust the business model.

Proposition 7: *Business models causing below aspirations level outcomes will be adjusted by changing the structure of activities. Depending on the scope of attention, these adjustments are made to either value creating activities or value capturing activities.*

The proposition above is consistent with Winter and Szulanski's (2001) argument that, business models are a set of routines (purposeful activities) which are improvised through learning by doing.

Satisficing principle and perception of the potency of existing resources—the internal organization of the activities—are key factors behind these adjustments because a problemistic search is bound within the limited attention and availability of resources (Gavetti, et al., 2012). More specifically, slack resources allow executives to make more specific and carefully targeted adjustments; and amongst different options the first promising one is most likely undertaken. Hence, it can be stated that:

Proposition 8: *Adjustments to business models are subject to inefficiencies caused by lack of potent resources and satisficing available options.*

Following these adjustments feedback on realized outcome of changes are sought. New performance feedback will be evaluated against historical performance, performance of competitors and expectations. These evaluative efforts show executives whether these changes have made the business model more effective or not. Two predictions can be made here. First, if changes are perceived as effective, new aspiration levels (goals) will be chosen and then attention will be shifted to other areas of business model; for example, from value creation (e.g., product design, inventory, etc.) to value capture (cost management, etc.). Second, if they have not resulted in above aspiration outcomes, new changes will be planned.

The behavioral view suggests that repeated failure to meet an aspiration level would lead executives to accept greater risk (Gavetti et al., 2012) and undertake more drastic courses of action. Therefore, it can be assumed that perception of prolonged performance below aspirations would result in radical changes to the business model which takes the form of business model reinvention (Johnson et al., 2008) or transformation (Aspara et al., 2011). In light of this behavioral assumption it can be stated that business model reinvention is triggered by problemistic search and failures of minor adjustments to value creating or capturing activities leading to propose:

> **Proposition 9:** *Executives tend to respond to a prolonged low performance of value creating/value capturing activities by making radical changes to configuration of resources driving those activities.*

Although performance below aspiration levels triggers change, radical changes to the business model are not solely based on realized low performance. As it was noted, aspirations are evaluated against performance of competitors and future expectations. More importantly, in situations where competition intensifies, uncertainty around activities increases. In view of this, although deliberate adjustments can be made regularly in the light of circumstances not known before (Hayek, 1945) but uncertainty make it increasingly difficult to evaluate outcomes of adjustments (Greve, 2008). It hence will trigger mimetic behavior in executives (Greve, 1998a). Therefore, there is reason to predict that:

> **Proposition 10:** *In dynamic contexts, business model transformation can also be initiated through mimetic behavior of executives.*

Research on responding disruptive business models through business model transformation (Dewald & Bowen, 2010) offers evidence supporting this behavioral prediction (Najmaei, 2012). In addition, the behavioral view suggests (if executives perceive that pursuing current goals lead them away from future expectations) they tend to respond by changing goals and resources committed to them (Lant & Shapira, 2008). Therefore, it can be proposed that:

> **Proposition 11:** *Business model transformation can also be initiated when executives predict that the current business model fails to meet future expectations.*

These propositions portray an outline of a behavioral view of business modeling. This view is far from a comprehensive behavioral theory of business modeling and must be taken as an early attempt to capture basics of behavioral business modeling and an entry into to the realm of psychological and cognitive picture of how and why executives do what they do. In light of this, next sections shed light on some of the theoretical and managerial implications of this attempt and present few directions for future research on this nascent field.

DISCUSSION AND IMPLICATIONS

As it has been argued throughout this chapter, business modeling is a key task of executives. While the importance of this task has been recognized, little is known about its behavioral dimensions. Therefore, this chapter portrayed a behavior view of this task and discussed its dimensions. This view was based on three assumptions. First, individual executives are different in terms of their skills, knowledge, and cognitive capacities. Second, firms are also different in terms of their governance structure (i.e., how they perform different transactions) and their resources (i.e., possession of different bundles of heterogeneous resources/capabilities). Third, neither individual executives nor the environment where their firms operate remain stable over time. These changes generate an impetus for executives to learn and adjust their courses of action. This study highlighted that business modeling of executives offers a new integrative view by which individuals' and firms' difference come together to create a more nuanced view of firms' performance variations. The description of this view has a variety of implications some of which for theory and practice of management will be discussed in this section.

Theoretical Implications

For years strategic management scholars have argued that executives matter in emergence, survival, success and failure of firms (Hambrick & Quigley, 2014). Dynamic managerial capabilities (DMC) are "capabilities with which managers build, integrate, and reconfigure organizational resources and competences" Adner and Helfat, (2003, p. 1012). This chapter highlights that business modeling is essentially a dynamic managerial capability with which executives adjust their business models which in turn, generates incentives and directions for new configuration of resources and capabilities. In light of this, another important implication of this research for this line of thinking derives from the view of first- and second-order dynamic managerial capabilities. Literature on capabilities (Collis, 1994; Danneels, 2002) indicates existence of two types of capabilities; first-order capabilities are simple activities performed by different configuration of resources. Whereas second-order or higher order capabilities are those capabilities that are required for developing or managing first order capabilities (Danneels, 2012). This study posits that executives' business modeling is a second-order or higher-order dynamic managerial capability with which executives adopt the logic and formulate activities required for reconfiguring their resources. As a result, this chapter adds to and extends dynamic managerial capabilities by delineating the concept of business modeling and its behavioral dimensions.

In a similar vein, scholars (Achtenhagen et al., 2013; Dewald & Bowen, 2010; George & Bock, 2011) have argued that managing business models and particularly developing new business models is a fundamental entrepreneurial capability which allows individuals to induce game-changing strategies to render entrepreneurial wealth. Drawing on this reasoning, research suggests that, business modeling capability lies at the heart of corporate entrepreneurship (Wolcott & Lippitz, 2007). From this point of view, a behavioral view of business modeling appears to have far-reaching implications for entrepreneurial activities of individuals and corporates. Hence, by incorporating the behavioral view of business modeling into entrepreneurial capabilities and strategies, scholars can gain a deeper understanding of how business models emerge and change to create wealth.

Finally, it was discussed that business modeling is path-dependent because the initial business model of the firm acts as a reference point by which future business model deviations along new paths will develop. This would add to the behavioral side of the debate between path-creation and path-dependence in organization theory (Garud, Kumaraswamy, & Karnøe, 2010). More specifically, as long as a business model is viewed as being able to generate above-aspiration outcomes, path-reinforcement is behaviorally sought and persistence on the current paths will be expected. Further to this point, the discussion offered here helps researchers design empirical investigations into dynamism of organizational paths from a new perspective.

These theoretical implications seem to have sufficient resonance with practice. The next section discusses these managerial implications.

Managerial Implications

This chapter broadly favors the idea that business modeling is a multidimensional behavioral phenomenon. The discussion developed in this chapter contributes to the understanding of this phenomenon and can serve as a tool for investigating how executives engage in different business modeling activities. This section illuminates some aspects of this issue.

First, at core, the above does not imply that executives can always manage their business models. The nature of this ability is contingent upon the extent to which managers are free to choose (Finkelstein & Peteraf, 2007). In other words, managerial discretion or latitude of action is limited by factors such as legal and political constraints which in turn impair their ability to manage their business models effectively. An important takeaway for managers from this issue is that, lobbying, negotiation and political skills and ties would enable managers to increase their latitude of action. Therefore, a deep understanding of the task environments and developing ties are requisite behaviors that complement behavioral view of business modeling. Without freedom of action the behavioral view of business modeling is invalid and incapable of explaining dynamism of business modeling.

Second, recent studies on executives have revealed that although business modeling has become a top priority of executives (IBM, 2007; Pohle & Chapman, 2006), there is a lack of consensus among executives about both the concept of business model (George & Bock, 2011) and dimensions of managing business models (Govindarajan & Trimble, 2011; Gulati, 2004; McAfee, 2011). This chapter helps executives gain new insight into both the business model of the firm and its management. In particular, it shows that business modeling consists of a set of behavioral elements which can be learned, trained and practiced. Learning to manage business models is triggered by an accurate understanding of both the current business model of the firm and that of competitors. Given this, this chapter equips executives with insights into how business model unlearning and consequent rigidities could emerge in a firm especially in situations where they find themselves confused about their business model.

Finally, the proposed behavioral view of business modeling suggests that bounded rationality and satisficing principle play key roles in the dynamism of business models. An important implication of this issue for managers is that learning to harness intuitive thinking, understanding reasoning by analogy and self-regulatory practices are cognitive skills which can help managers turn limited cognitive capacity into effective behavior. Recent research on these skills (Chiaburu, 2010; Heatherton, 2011) provides more detailed discussion on how executives can develop and excel at these skills and then deploy them in managing their business models.

SUGGESTIONS FOR FUTURE RESEARCH

Future research can advance the foregoing discussion in three ways: empirical examination, conceptual extension, and empirical extension. This section sheds light on a few potential directions for these three areas of future research.

First, as this is a conceptual chapter, the validity of ideas and propositions developed here needs to be empirically tested. These empirical examinations can be carried out qualitatively, quantitatively, or through mixed-methods designs. For example, qualitatively, longitudinal case studies of firms which have undergone different changes in their business model appear to be an appropriate starting point. Strategy process methodology (Pettigrew, 1990) and case-study methodology (Eisenhardt, 1989) offer a robust methodological basis for this endeavor. Furthermore, recently Achtenhagen et al. (2013) probed into activities involved in the management of small firm's business model. Although their research is not within the behavioral domain, it offers valuable insights into business modeling of firms.

Propositions developed in this research can also be examined through quantitative studies. Literature in strategy and entrepreneurship contain valid scales for a number of constructs used in our discussion. For example, the works of Greve and colleagues (Greve, 1998b, 2008; Mezias, Chen, & Murphy, 2002) contain numerous ways to measure aspirations as well as social and historical comparison performed by managers. In addition, scale development in the business model literature has been underemphasized and is a major shortcoming of this literature. So, quantitative researchers interested in examining the behavioral side of business modeling may need to develop new scales capturing the essence of this issue. Existing scale on the design of the business model (Zott & Amit, 2007, 2008) can be a ground based on which new scales develop.

Alternatively, insights from other behavioral theories such as prospected theory (Kahneman & Tversky, 1979), threat-rigidity theory (Staw, Sandelands, & Dutton, 1981) and attention-based view (Ocasio, 1997) can be incorporated into the proposed model to extend the conceptual boundaries of a behavioral view of business modeling. Although the time is ripe for such attempts, these conceptual extensions are surrounded by competing assumptions. This issue goes beyond the scope of this research. However, there have been several attempts to dismantle these perplexities. For instance, the recent study of Dewald and Bowen (2010) presents a detailed discussion on the differences between assumptions of prospect theory and threat-rigidity thesis in the context of business model disruptions, which can be used in future investigations on business modeling of different firms.

Finally, as noted in the previous section, business modeling of firms is directly related to entrepreneurial and managerial dynamic capabilities.

In addition, it is believed to directly influence firms' survival and growth. Therefore, a behavioral view of business modeling can be empirically linked to the entrepreneurial and managerial capabilities of executives. Then, the impact of these integrative models on firms performance outcomes (i.e., survival, growth and competitiveness) can be investigated using longitudinal (Ployhart & Vandenberg, 2010) or agent-based simulation modeling (Fioretti, 2012).

CONCLUSION

The chapter explained how executives adopt and adjust the business model of the firm. To do so, a behavioral view of the business modeling of the firm based on a synthesis of insights from strategic cognition and the behavioral theory of the firm such as managerial cognitive reference points, aspiration adjustments, performance attributed to the current business model of the firm, attainment of past goals as well as future expectations was developed. Implications of this approach for several fields of research were discussed and a few directions for future research were illuminated.

REFERENCES

Abernathy, W. J., & Utterback, J. (1978). Patterns of industrial innovation. *Technology Review, 80*(7), 40–47.

Achtenhagen, L., Melin, L., & Naldi, L. (2013). Dynamics of business models—strategizing, critical capabilities and activities for sustained value creation. *Long Range Planning, 46,* 427–442.

Adner, R., & Helfat, C. E. (2003). Corporate effects and dynamic managerial capabilities. *Strategic Management Journal, 24,* 1011–1025.

Amit, R., & Zott, C. (2001). Value creation in e-business. *Strategic Management Journal, 22,* 493–520.

Amit, R., & Zott, C. (2012). Creating value through business model innovation. *MIT Sloan Management Review, 53*(3), 41–49.

Ansoff, I. H. (1987). The emerging paradigm of strategic behavior. *Strategic Management Journal, 8*(6), 501–515.

Argote, L., & Greve, H. R. (2007). A behavioral theory of the firm—40 years and counting: Introduction and impact. *Organization Science, 18,* 337–349.

Aspara, J., Lamberg, J.-A., Laukia, A., & Tikkanen, H. (2011). Strategic management of business model transformation: Lessons from Nokia. *Management Decision, 49,* 622–647.

Audia, P. G., & Greve, H. R. (2006). Less likely to fail: Low performance, firm size, and factory expansion in the shipbuilding industry. *Management Science, 52,* 83–94.

Augier, M., & March, J. G. (2008). A retrospective look at a behavioral theory of the firm. *Journal of Economic Behavior & Organization, 66*(1), 1–6.

Augier, M., & Teece, D. J. (2009). Dynamic capabilities and the role of managers in business strategy and economic performance. *Organization Science, 20,* 410–421.

Bamberger, P., & Fiegenbaum, A. (1996). The role of strategic reference points in explaining the nature and consequences of human resource strategy. *Academy of Management Review, 21,* 926–958.

Barney, J. B. (1986). Strategic factor markets: Expectations, luck, and business strategy. *Management Science, 32,* 1231–1241.

Bock, A. J., Opsahl, T., George, G., & Gann, D. M. (2012). The effects of culture and structure on strategic flexibility during business model innovation. *Journal of Management Studies, 49,* 279–305.

Bougon, M., Weick, K., & Binkhorst, D. (1977). Cognition in organizations: An analysis of the Utrecht jazz orchestra. *Administrative Science Quarterly, 22,* 606–639.

Bowman, C., & Ambrosini, V. (2000). Value creation versus value capture: Towards a coherent definition of value in strategy. *British Journal of Management, 11,* 1–15.

Brown, B., & Perry, S. (1994). Removing the financial performance halo from fortune's "most admired" companies. *Academy of Management Journal, 37,* 1347–1359.

Capon, N., Farley, J. U., & Hoenig, S. (1990). Determinants of financial performance: A meta-analysis. *Management Science, 36,* 1143–1159.

Chatterjee, S. (2013). Simple rules for designing business models. *California Management Review, 55*(2), 97–124.

Chen, W. R., & Miller, K. D. (2007). Situational and institutional determinants of firms' R&D search intensity. *Strategic Management Journal, 28*(4), 369–381.

Chesbrough, H. (2010). Business model innovation: Opportunities and barriers. *Long Range Planning, 43*(2–3), 354–363.

Chesbrough, H., Minin, A. D., & Piccaluga, A. (2013). Business model innovation paths. In L. Cinquini, A. D. Minin, & R. Varaldo (Eds.), *New business models and value creation: A service science perspective* (Vol. 8, pp. 25–44). Milan, Italy: Springer-Verlag.

Chiaburu, D. S. (2010). Chief executives, self-regulation and strategic orientation: A theoretical model. *European Management Journal, 28,* 467–478.

Christensen, C. M., & Raynor, M. E. (2003). *The innovator's solution: Creating and sustaining successful growth.* Boston, MA: Harvard Business School Press.

Collis, D. J. (1994). Research note: How valuable are organizational capabilities? *Strategic Management Journal, 15*(Special Issue), 143–152.

Cyert, R. M., & March, J. G. (1963). *A behavioral theory of the firm.* Englewood Cliffs, NJ: Prentice-Hall.

Cyert, R. M., & Williams, J. R. (1993). Organizations, decision making and strategy: Overview and comment. *Strategic Management Journal, 14,* 5–10.

Danneels, E. (2002). The dynamics of product innovation and firm competences. *Strategic Management Journal, 23,* 1095–1121.

Danneels, E. (2012). Second-order competences and Schumpeterian rents. *Strategic Entrepreneurship Journal, 6,* 42–58.

Demil, B., Lecocq, X., Ricart, J. E., & Zott, C. (2013). Business models: Call for papers for a special issue. *Strategic Entrepreneurship Journal.* Retrieved from sej.strategicmanagement.net/conf-dl/SEJ-Business_Models.pdf

Demil, B., & Lecocq, X. (2010). Business model evolution: In search of dynamic consistency. *Long Range Planning, 43*(2–3), 227–246.

Desyllas, P., & Sako, M. (2013). Profiting from business model innovation: Evidence from pay-as-you-drive auto insurance. *Research Policy, 42*(1), 101–116.

Dewald, J., & Bowen, F. (2010). Storm clouds and silver linings: Responding to disruptive innovations through cognitive resilience. *Entrepreneurship Theory and Practice, 34*(1), 197–218.

Dickinson, Q. T. (2000). Can you patent your business model? *Harvard Business Review, 78*(4), 16.

Doz, Y. L., & Kosonen, M. (2010). Embedding strategic agility: A leadership agenda for accelerating business model renewal. *Long Range Planning, 43*, 370–382.

Eisenhardt, K. M. (1989). Building theories from case study research. *Academy of Management Review, 14*, 532–550.

Fiegenbaum, A., Hart, S., & Schendel, D. (1996). Strategic reference point theory. *Strategic Management Journal, 17*, 219–235.

Finkelstein, S., & Peteraf, M. A. (2007). Managerial activities: A missing link in managerial discretion theory. *Strategic Organization, 5*, 237–248.

Fioretti, G. (2012). Agent-based simulation models in organization science. *Organizational Research Methods, 16*, 227–242.

Gambardella, A., & McGahan, A. M. (2010). Business-model innovation: General purpose technologies and their implications for industry structure. *Long Range Planning, 43*, 262–271.

Garbuio, M., King, A. W., & Lovallo, D. (2011). Looking inside: Psychological influences on structuring a firm's portfolio of resources. *Journal of Management, 37*, 1444–1463.

Garud, R., Kumaraswamy, A., & Karnøe, P. (2010). Path dependence or path creation? *Journal of Management Studies, 47*, 760–774.

Gavetti, G. (2012). Toward a behavioral theory of strategy. *Organization Science, 23*, 267–285.

Gavetti, G., Greve, H. R., Levinthal, D. A., & Ocasio, W. (2012). The behavioral theory of the firm: Assessment and prospects. *Academy of Management Annals, 6*, 1–40.

Gavetti, G., Levinthal, D., & Ocasio, W. (2007). Neo-Carnegie: The Carnegie school's past, present, and reconstructing for the future. *Organization Science, 18*, 523–536.

George, G., & Bock, A. J. (2011). The business model in practice and its implications for entrepreneurship research. *Entrepreneurship Theory and Practice, 35*(1), 83–111.

Govindarajan, V., & Trimble, C. (2011). The CEO's role in business model reinvention. *Harvard Business Review, 89*(1–2), 108–114.

Greve, H. R. (1998a). Managerial cognition and the mimetic adoption of market positions: What you see is what you do. *Strategic Management Journal, 19*, 967–988.

Greve, H. R. (1998b). Performance, aspirations, and risky organizational change. *Administrative Science Quarterly, 43*, 58–86.

Greve, H. R. (2008). A behavioral theory of firm growth: Sequential attention to size and performance goals. *Academy of Management Journal, 51,* 476–494.

Greve, H. R. (2011). Positional rigidity: Low performance and resource acquisition in large and small firms. *Strategic Management Journal, 32,* 103–114.

Greve, H. R., & Taylor, A. (2000). Innovations as catalysts for organizational change: Shifts in organizational cognition and search. *Administrative Science Quarterly, 45,* 54–80.

Gulati, R. (2004). How CEOs manage growth agendas. *Harvard Business Review, 82*(4), 124–132.

Hambrick, D. C. (1989). Guest editor's introduction: Putting top managers back in the strategy picture. *Strategic Management Journal, 10,* 5–15.

Hambrick, D. C., & Mason, P. A. (1984). Upper echelons: The organization as a reflection of its top managers. *Academy of Management Review, 9,* 193–206.

Hambrick, D. C., & Quigley, T. J. (2014). Toward more accurate contextualization of the CEO effect on firm performance. *Strategic Management Journal, 35,* 473–491.

Hayek, F. A. (1945). The use of knowledge in society. *American Economic Review, 35,* 519–530.

Heatherton, T. F. (2011). Neuroscience of self and self-regulation. *Annual Review of Psychology, 62,* 363–390.

Hodgkinson, G. P. (1997). The cognitive analysis of competitive structures: A review and critique. *Human Relations, 50,* 625–654.

Hodgkinson, G. P., & Johnson, G. (1994). Exploring the mental models of competitive strategists: The case for a processual approach. *Journal of Management Studies, 31,* 525–552.

IBM. (2007). Path to success: Three ways to innovate your business model. *Somers, NY: IBM Global Services.*

Johnson, M. W., Christensen, C. M., & Kagermann, H. (2008). Reinventing your business model. *Harvard Business Review, 86*(12), 50–59.

Kahneman D, & Tversky, A. (1979). Prospect theory: Analysis of decision under risk. *Econometrica, 47,* 263–291.

Katkalo, V. S., Pitelis, C. N., & Teece, D. J. (2010). On the nature and scope of dynamic capabilities. *Industrial and Corporate Change, 19,* 1175–1186.

Knott, A. M., Bryce, D. J., & Posen, H. E. (2003). On the strategic accumulation of intangible assets. *Organization Science, 14,* 192–207.

Lant, T., & Shapira, Z. (2008). Managerial reasoning about aspirations and expectations. *Journal of Economic Behavior & Organization, 66*(1), 60–73.

Lant, T. K. (1992). Aspiration level adaptation: An empirical exploration. *Management Science, 38,* 623–644.

Levinthal, D. A. (2011). A behavioral approach to strategy—what's the alternative? *Strategic Management Journal, 32,* 1517–1523.

Lovallo, D., & Sibony, O. (2010). The case for behavioral strategy. *McKinsey Quarterly* (2), 30–43.

Makadok, R., & Barney, J. B. (2001). Strategic factor market intelligence: An application of information economics to strategy formulation and competitor intelligence. *Management Science, 47,* 1621–1638.

March, J. G. (1991). Exploration and exploitation in organizational learning. *Organization Science, 2,* 71–87.

March, J. G., & Shapira, Z. (1992). Variable risk preferences and the focus of attention. *Psychological Review, 99*(2), 172–183.

March, J. G., & Simon, H. A. (1958). *Organizations.* New York, NY: Wiley.

McAfee, A. (2011). What every CEO needs to know about the cloud. *Harvard Business Review, 89*(11), 124–132.

McGrath, R. G. (2010). Business models: A discovery driven approach. *Long Range Planning, 43,* 247–261.

McKenney, J. L., & Keen, P. G. W. (1974). How managers mind's work. *Harvard Business Review, 50*(2), 83–85.

Mezias, S. J., Chen, Y. R., & Murphy, P. R. (2002). Aspiration-level adaptation in an American financial services organization: A field study. *Management Science, 48,* 1285–1300.

Mintzberg, H. (1976). Planning on the left side and managing on the right. *Harvard Business Review, 54*(4), 49–58.

Moussetis, R. (2011). Ansoff revisited: How Ansoff interfaces with both the planning and learning schools of thought in strategy. *Journal of Management History, 17*(1), 102–125.

Najmaei, A. (2012). Business model: Strategic logic of disruptive innovation. In K. Rezaul (Ed.), *Strategic and pragmatic E-business: Implications for future business practices* (pp. 100–131). Hershey, PA: IGI Global Publishing.

Ocasio, W. (1997). Towards an attention-based view of the firm. *Strategic Management Journal, 18*(S1), 187–206.

Penrose, E. T. (1959). *The theory of the growth of the firm.* Oxford, UK: Basil Blackwell.

Perkmann, M., & Spicer, A. (2010). What are business models? Developing a theory of performative representations. In N. Phillips, G. Sewell, & D. Griffiths (Eds.), *Technology and organization: Essays in honor of Joan Woodward* (Vol. 29, pp. 265–275). Bingley, UK: Emerald Group Publishing Limited.

Pettigrew, A. M. (1990). Longitudinal field research on change: Theory and practice. *Organization Science, 1,* 267–292.

Pierce, J. L., Boerner, C. S., & Teece, D. J. (2008). Dynamic capabilities, competence and the behavioral theory of the firm. In D. J. Teece (Ed.), *Technological know-how, organizational capabilities, and strategic management business strategy and enterprise development in competitive environments* (pp. 53–68). Singapore: World Scientific Publishing.

Pitelis, C. (2009). Edith Penrose's theory of the growth of the firm: Fifty years later. *Available at SSRN 1477885*

Pitelis, C. N. (2007). A behavioral resource-based view of the firm: The synergy of Cyert and March (1963) and Penrose (1959*). Organization Science, 18,* 478–490.

Pitelis, C. N., & Teece, D. J. (2009). The (new) nature and essence of the firm." *European Management Review, 6*(1), 5–15.

Ployhart, R. E., & Vandenberg, R. J. (2010). Longitudinal research: The theory, design, and analysis of change. *Journal of Management, 36,* 94–120.

Pohle, G., & Chapman, M. (2006). IBM's global CEO report 2006: Business model innovation matters. *Strategy & Leadership, 34*(5), 34–40.

Porac, J. F., & Thomas, H. (1990). Taxonomic mental models in competitor definition. *Academy of Management Review, 15*, 224–240.

Powell, T. C., Lovallo, D., & Fox, C. R. (2011). Behavioral strategy. *Strategic Management Journal, 32*, 1369–1386.

Prahalad, C. K., & Bettis, R. A. (1986). The dominant logic: A new linkage between diversity and performance. *Strategic Management Journal, 7*, 485–501.

Rhee, M. (2009). Does reputation contribute to reducing organizational errors? A learning approach. *Journal of Management Studies, 46*, 676–703.

Rosch, E. (1975). Cognitive reference points. *Cognitive Psychology, 7*, 532–547.

Rumelt, R. P., Schendel, D., & Teece, D. J. (1991). Strategic management and economics. *Strategic Management Journal, 12*, 5–29.

Sako, M. (2012). Business models for strategy and innovation. *Communications of the ACM, 55*(7), 22–24.

Shinkle, G. A. (2011). Organizational aspirations, reference points, and goals: Building on the past and aiming for the future. *Journal of Management, 38*, 415–455.

Simon, H. A. (1957). *Models of man*: Social and rational. New York, NY: Wiley.

Simon, H. A. (1961). *Administrative behavior* (2nd ed.). New York, NY: Macmillan.

Simon, H. A. (1987). Satisficing. In J. Eatwell, M. Millgate, & P. Newman (Eds.), *The New Palgrave: A dictionary of economics* (Vol. 4, pp. 243–245). New York, NY: Stockton Press.

Simon, H. A. (1991). Bounded rationality and organizational learning. *Organization Science, 2*, 125–134.

Sinfield, J. V., Calder, E., McConnell, B., & Colson, S. (2012). How to identify new business models. *MIT Sloan Management Review, 53*(2), 85–94.

Spender, J. C. (1989). *Industry recipes: An inquiry into the nature and source of managerial judgment* Cambridge, MA: Blackwell.

Spieth, P., Tidd, J. O. E., Matzler, K., Schneckenberg, D., & Vanhaverbeke, W. I. M. (2013). Editorial note: Special issue on business model innovation. *International Journal of Innovation Management, 17*(01), 1–3.

Staw, B. M., Sandelands, L. E., & Dutton, J. E. (1981). Threat rigidity effects in organizational behavior: A multilevel analysis. *Administrative Science Quarterly, 26*, 501–524.

Teece, D. J. (1986). Profiting from technological innovation: Implications for integration, collaboration, licensing and public policy. *Research Policy, 15*, 285–305.

Teece, D. J. (2006). Reflections on "profiting from innovation." *Research Policy, 35*, 1131–1146.

Teece, D. J. (2007). Explicating dynamic capabilities: The nature and microfoundations of (sustainable) enterprise performance. *Strategic Management Journal, 28*, 1319–1350.

Teece, D. J. (2010). Business models, business strategy and innovation. *Long Range Planning, 43*, 172–194.

Tribushinina, E. (2008). *Cognitive reference points: Semantics beyond the prototypes in adjectives of space and color.* Utrecht, Netherlands: LOT.

Williamson, O. E. (1981). The economics of organization: The transaction cost approach. *American Journal of Sociology, 87*, 548–577.

Winter, S. G. (2000). The satisficing principle in capability learning. *Strategic Management Journal, 21*, 981–996.

Winter, S. G., & Szulanski, G. (2001). Replication as strategy. *Organization Science, 12*, 730–743.

Wolcott, R. C., & Lippitz, M. J. (2007). The four models of corporate entrepreneurship. *MIT Sloan Management Review, 49*(1), 75–82.

Zott, C., & Amit, R. (2007). Business model design and the performance of entrepreneurial firms. *Organization Science, 18*, 181–199.

Zott, C., & Amit, R. (2008). The fit between product market strategy and business model: Implications for firm performance. *Strategic Management Journal, 29*, 1–26.

Zott, C., & Amit, R. (2010). Business model design: An activity system perspective. *Long Range Planning, 43*, 216–226.

Zott, C., Amit, R., & Massa, L. (2011). The business model: Recent developments and future research. *Journal of Management, 37*, 1019–1042.

CHAPTER 9

TOWARD A FRAMEWORK FOR BEHAVIORAL STRATEGY

What We Can Learn from Austrian Economics

Per L. Bylund

ABSTRACT

The Austrian school of economics has recently made inroads into and appears to be an emerging important perspective in the study of strategic management and entrepreneurship. Yet, we see little of the prediction two decades ago that a specifically "Austrian school of strategy" would emerge (Jacobson, 1992). This chapter summarizes the measurable influence of "Austrian economics" in strategy to date, and notes core insights from the Austrian school that are yet to be discovered by strategy and entrepreneurship scholars. I argue that our field has much to gain from looking closer at the uniquely integrated framework, perspective, and approach of the Austrian school, rather than to just incorporate individual Austrian concepts, and illustrate the argument with a discussion on the distinctively Austrian conception of time and implications thereof for strategy and entrepreneurship.

Behavioral Strategy: Emerging Perspectives, pages 205–232

INTRODUCTION

Modern strategy research has increasingly shown interest in the concepts and theoretical constructs of the Austrian school of economics. This should not be surprising, since a "variety of strategic frameworks share commonalities with Austrian perspectives" (Jacobson, 1992, p. 802). But despite the 150+-year tradition of theory-building in the Austrian school, it has only recently been rediscovered and adopted by business scholars. Two decades ago, Jacobson (1992) identified a then-emerging stream of research that "is distinctly Austrian in nature" (Jacobson, 1992, p. 802) and therefore appeared to be forming an Austrian school of strategy (for early adopters, see e.g., Bhide, 1986; Itami & Roehl, 1987; Jacobson, 1990; Levitt, 1986; Peters, 1987; Rumelt, 1984; Wensley, 1982).

Jacobson showed that this new stream of strategy research utilizing Austrian thinking is distinct from the traditional approach, based on the "neoclassical" Bain/Mason paradigm of industrial organization (IO) (Bain, 1951; see also, e.g., Porter, 1980, 1981, 1985), along at least four dimensions: Strategic Objective, Market Conditions, Profitability Modeling, and Nature of Success Factors (Jacobson, 1992, p. 785). But while some of the Austrian concepts have already been incorporated in strategy research, Jacobson (1992) suggests that more explicitly adopting the Austrian perspective is an opportunity for further advancement. He consequently predicts (and endorses) an increasing—and increasingly conscious—adoption of the Austrian perspective, its approach as well as theoretical framework. Its real value, he argues, lies in deliberately adopting and applying concepts from the Austrian school in an Austrian manner. He cautions that "inconsistencies can arise when attempting to integrate other frameworks with Austrian paradigms" (Jacobson, 1992, p. 803) and therefore doing so is not advisable. Indeed, Austrian economics is a complete whole that due to its deductive logic is greater than the sum of its parts.

This chapter briefly summarizes the influence of the Austrian school in strategy and entrepreneurship research to date along Jacobson's dimensions, and argues that there is still much to gain from looking closer at what the distinct perspective of the Austrian school has to offer. I further argue that great advances are possible, following Jacobson (1992), by consciously adopting the fundamental and uniquely Austrian conception of time as a factor of production, which offers a sound foundation for different yet interdependent levels of behavioral analysis; the particularly Austrian approach to this concept, which has only minimally been studied by management scholars (Das, 1993), also indicates the function of entrepreneurship in the practical functioning and study of markets, organizations, and strategy.

The next section illustrates the Austrian influence looking at publication data from the *Academy of Management Review* (AMR). I thereafter discuss the Austrian view and analytic use of the concept of time and the necessary future-orientedness of action, especially its implications for subjective value, production plans, and time preference. I then elaborate on the implications for research in strategic management and entrepreneurship, and conclude by summarizing the potential of an Austrian approach to strategy, and discuss opportunities for future research.

AUSTRIAN INFLUENCE IN STRATEGY RESEARCH

Originally called "causal-realist" economics due to its focus on causality in social reality (studying processes and cause-effect relationships between events and actions in society) and economic realism (studying the market as it is rather than streamlined models of it), the Austrian school[1] is today rather unique in its approach to analyzing real-world social phenomena. While the school's theoretical framework is purely deductive, which means all its expositions are ultimately logically derived from a fundamental premise in the "action axiom" (L. v. Mises, [1949] 1998), Jacobson (1992) seems unaware of its methodological peculiarity. Instead, he focuses on four dimensions that delineate what he believes are the school's "distinct features" in contrast to traditional IO. He therefore discusses how strategy based on Austrian thinking would adopt a perspective based on entrepreneurial discovery, disequilibrium, heterogeneity, and unobservable factors, and how this perspective stands in stark contrast to IO-based, "traditional" strategy's perspective based on success through restricting competitive forces, the equilibrium assumption, focus on empirical regularities, and observed strategic factors, respectively.

The contrast should be clear, and judging from the contemporary literature in strategy and entrepreneurship it indeed seems Jacobson's prediction (or perhaps recommendation) was perceptive—we appear to have taken decisive steps toward an Austrian approach to the study of strategy and entrepreneurship: Entrepreneurial discovery is at the core of the entrepreneurship literature (e.g., Alvarez & Barney, 2007a, 2008; Shane, 2003; Shane & Venkataramen, 2000); the observation of heterogeneity is core to the resource-based view (e.g., Barney, 1986, 1991; Dierickx & Cool, 1988; Wernerfelt, 1984); and analyses of unobservable factors like knowledge and information occur frequently on the pages of top management journals (e.g., Foss, 1996a, 1996b; Grant, 1996; Spender, 1996; Tsoukas, 1996).

Looking specifically at the aforementioned dimensions and papers published in the *Academy of Management Review* (AMR) in the two decades following the publication of Jacobson's article (1993–2012), we find that there are a large number of articles relying on Austrian-type concepts. However, only a few are consciously using them in an Austrian way, which we here

TABLE 9.1 Articles in the *Academy of Management Review* (1993–2012) That Use Austrian Concepts

Dimension	Use Austrian Concepts	Consciously Austrian
Strategic Objective	363	6
Market Conditions	128	8
Profitability Modeling	165	1
Nature of Success Factors	419	2

operationalize as being backed up by direct citations to the Austrian literature or that related Austrian concepts are used in conjunction or in a typically "Austrian" way. As shown in Table 9.1, the concepts in the four dimensions have been used in several hundred articles[2].

However, while there are indeed hundreds of articles with Austrian-style concepts, a mere 12 of the total 716 articles published in AMR during this period are decidedly and consciously Austrian in their theorizing. This amounts to only 1.68% and may seem negligible and unimportant. Yet, seen in light of the common and widespread use of Austrian *concepts* during the same period, and the fact that their use appears to be increasing over time (see Table 9.2) in all four dimensions (Figures 9.1 to 9.4), the ostensible (though perhaps indirect or inadvertent) influence of Austrian strategy may be quite significant.

Indeed, the use of Austrian concepts have during this time period (1993–2012) increased in each of the four dimensions (Figures 9.1 to 9.4). However, the consciously Austrian use of these concepts has increased only in the market condition (disequilibrium) dimension (Figure 9.2). In the strategic objectives (entrepreneurial discovery) dimension the trend is clearly decreasing (Figure 9.1), while the success factors (unobservable factors) dimension shows little change (though, if any, decreasing) and the trend for the profitability modeling (heterogeneity) dimension is inconclusive

TABLE 9.2 Articles in the *Academy of Management Review* That Use Austrian Concepts, by Year

	1993	1994	1995	1996	1997	1998	1999	2000	2001	2002
Austrian Concepts	23	27	30	33	27	40	48	40	28	26
Consciously Austrian	0	0	1	2	0	0	1	2	0	0

	2003	2004	2005	2006	2007	2008	2009	2010	2011	2012
Austrian Concepts	33	32	42	53	59	47	34	28	38	28
Consciously Austrian	0	0	0	2	0	0	0	0	1	2

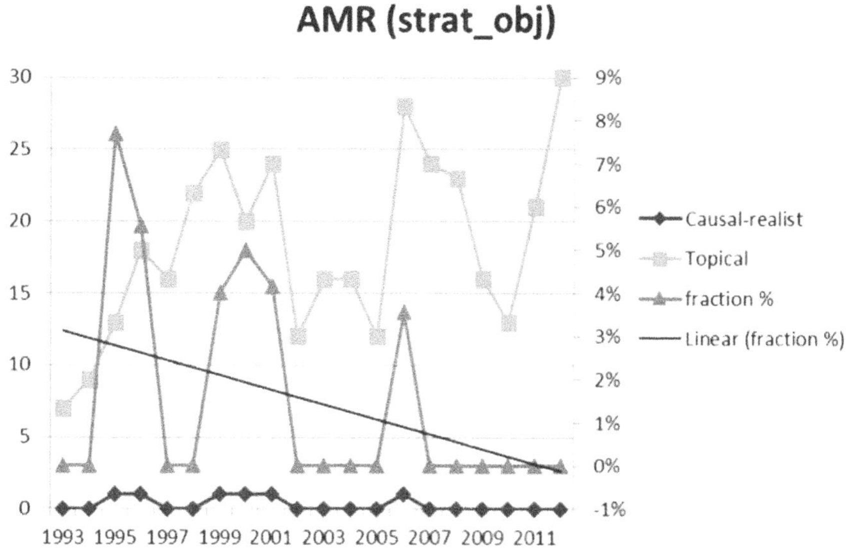

Figure 9.1 The influence of entrepreneurial discovery, topically and decidedly Austrian use, in the *Academy of Management Review* 1993–2012 as percentage of total published articles.

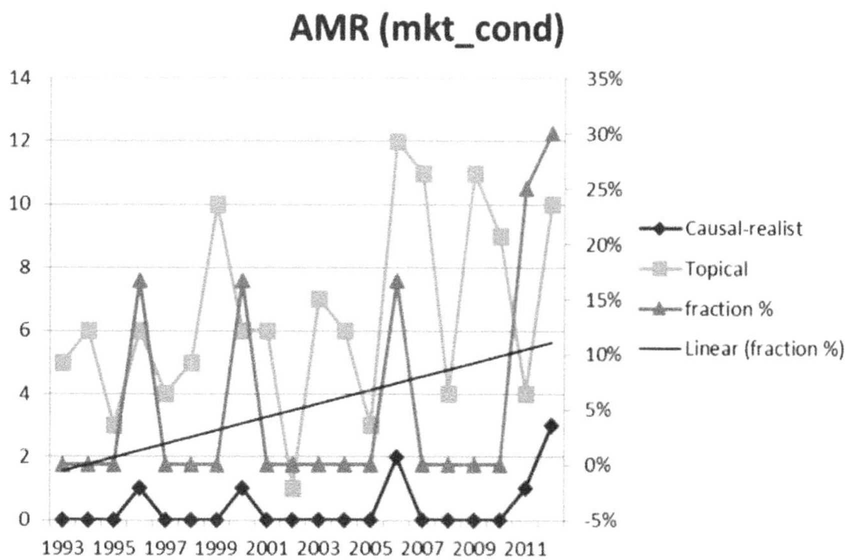

Figure 9.2 The influence of disequilibrium, topically and decidedly Austrian use, in the *Academy of Management Review* 1993–2012 as percentage of total published articles.

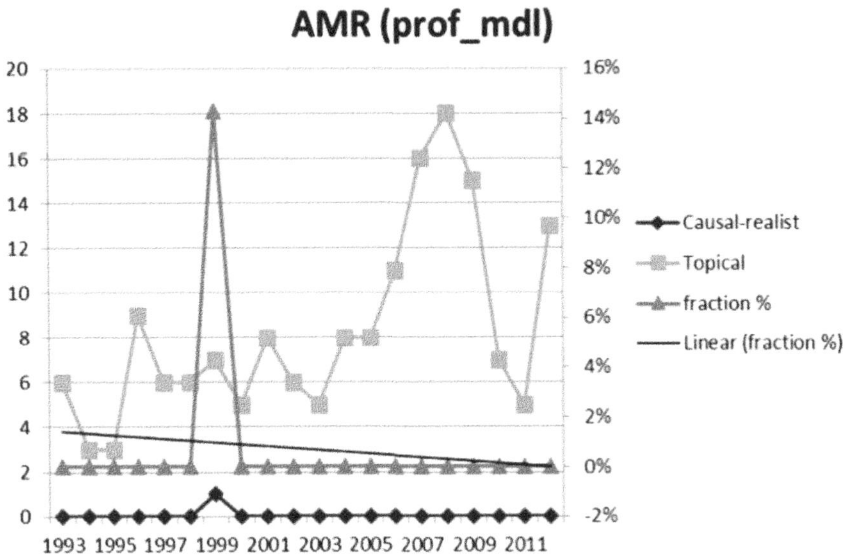

Figure 9.3 The influence of heterogeneity, topically and decidedly Austrian use, in the *Academy of Management Review* 1993–2012 as percentage of total published articles.

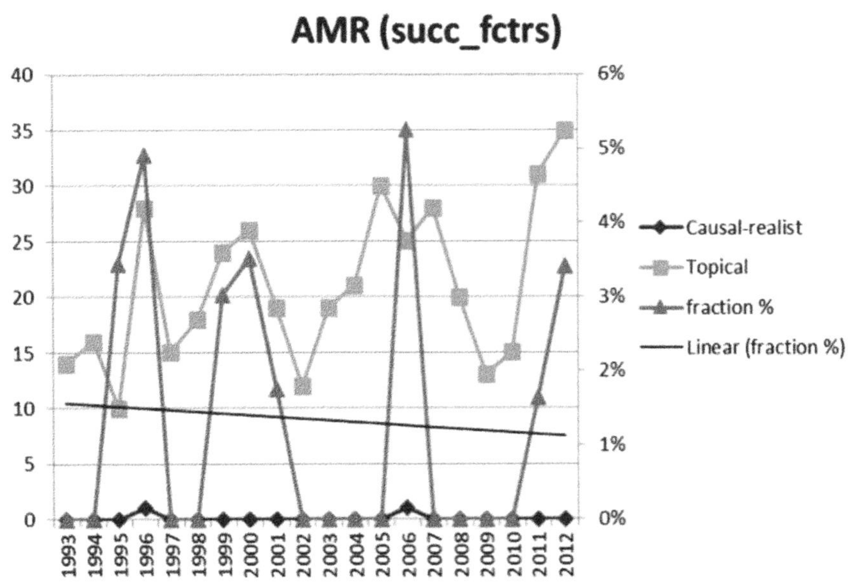

Figure 9.4 The influence of unobservable factors, topically and decidedly Austrian use, in the *Academy of Management Review* 1993–2012 as percentage of total published articles.

due to too few data points (Figures 9.4 and 9.3, respectively). The data thus suggest that management scholars have acted in direct contrast to Jacobson's recommendation and, consequently, have not heeded his warning. Since the concepts have become so widely used and, on the face of it, seem to have become core to theorizing in our field, their adapted or expanded uses and the reinterpretations of well-defined concepts that have long been used in Austrian economics may have exposed our theories and analytical frameworks to potentially severe latent "inconsistencies." The eventual implications of such conceptual inconsistencies, should they prove to exist and have the serious repercussions Jacobson seems to forebode, may undermine and prove shaky the very foundations of management theory.

It may at this point be premature to "cry wolf" in this matter, but the tendencies we have identified in the AMR data are, in light of Jacobson's warning, potentially troubling. To the extent reinterpretations of and continued use of these concepts deviate, whether wittingly or unwittingly, from their Austrian interpretations, their value in analysis may diminish. In fact, due to the deductive nature of Austrian theory, theorizing about these concepts in ways that deviate from the Austrian model may prove problematic and even counterproductive.

One way of determining the impact of such potential problems, as well as acting along the lines of Jacobson's original recommendation, is to further consider the potential Austrian contributions—especially such concepts that are fundamental to the Austrian perspective and hence create a substructure and provide support and deeper understanding for the concepts in Jacobson's dimensions. It also includes ascertaining whether there are additional opportunities in using, and hence value in adopting, the Austrian *perspective*, which is inseparable from its fundamental conceptions. In the next section, we will look into a core Austrian concept that is recurrent throughout and core to Austrian thinking and thus also (though perhaps only implicitly) in Jacobson's dimensions, and that provides a fundamentally important and—in its scope—potentially novel perspective in the study of strategy and entrepreneurship.

TIME IN AUSTRIAN ECONOMICS

Rather than studying the making of an individual decision or choice between known alternatives, as appears to often be the case in neoclassical economic models, the unit of analysis in Austrian economics is *action*. By action is meant purposeful human behavior that aims toward the attainment of a valued end. Austrians hold that "[a]ction is will put into operation and transformed into an agency, is aiming at ends and goals, is the ego's meaningful response to stimuli and to the conditions of its environment, is a person's conscious adjustment to the state of the universe that determines his life" (L. v. Mises, [1949] 1998, p. 11).

The study of action suggests that value (valuation) is subjective, which means that it is considered of value by the individual him- or herself. Action thus implies that a subject chooses to act in accordance with his or her own will toward an imagined and valued end along the path and using the technology that appears, to his or her understanding, most likely to achieve this end. That which is deemed an appropriate action to attain the chosen end is fundamentally based on an assessment of the actor's spatial, temporal, and relative position. For this reason, anything that facilitates, affects, limits, or otherwise influences the individual actor and his or her specific assessment of the state of the world, such as culture, norms, other unobservable institutions and types of influence, is also important for understanding the action taken and the choices made (Jacobson, 1990, 1992, pp. 795–797).

Furthermore, human action is possible only by making several conscious choices in conjunction, of both means and ends: it requires some degree of accuracy in how the acting person understands the world so that the individual has (or perceives) a real chance of attaining the end; and it necessitates perceived availability, by direct ownership or indirectly by being able to procure through trade or exchange, of those resources deemed required to carry out the action. As any individual has several alternative valued courses of actions, he or she necessarily chooses that which is subjectively held as most valuable at the time the decision is made. Action therefore implies subjective maximizing of available and procurable scarce resources, but does not denote ultimate correctness in interpreting available market data. Indeed, any course action can turn out to be wrong for a number of reasons—including exogenous changes to the person's situation and endogenous changes of preferences, values, etc.—but what matters for the decision to act is what is known or perceived prior to or at the time of deciding to act. Action, summarized, is "purposeful behavior directed toward the attainment of ends in some future period which will involve the fulfillment of wants otherwise remaining unsatisfied" (Rothbard, [1962] 2004, p. 7). It is, in other words, production.

Actions are never carved in stone but may naturally be revised or canceled before completed if the individual deems another course of action more valuable. This is true for all acting since it necessarily has a temporal dimension: any outcome of an action must come about in the (immediate or more distant) *future.* The past and present are "sunk" and unchangeable and acting must always follow the decision to act—and thus takes place in the future. Similarly, the result of the action, the change toward which the actor aims, can appear only after it has been taken, which suggests the necessary temporal nature of action as a process. Indeed, "[a]ll change consists of nothing but differences through time" (Menger, [1871] 2007, p. 122), and since all people act in order to cause such differences the conditions to each individual's actions change over time, which may require a change in the chosen course of action (or even the end).

It is consequently an undeniable fact that "*production takes time*" (Kirzner, [1963] 2007, p. 190), since it entails the process of changing the state of the world from that of the present to a future more highly valued state. Action and production are thus inseparable, though the latter may in the specialized exchange economy be seen as a process consisting of multiple serially executed and interdependent actions. It is also the case that "the more complex the production process the more time must be taken" (Rothbard, [1962] 2004, p. 337) to complete the process. For this reason, action entails both production and change, and one cannot take action without considering the passing of time and the change that it entails.

The Austrian school of economics identifies, as do most schools of economic thought, production as the core economic problem (Rothbard, [1962] 2004, pp. 319–628; Menger, [1871] 2007; Strigl, [1934] 2000). The production process implies the use of scarce (productive), heterogeneous resources for the attainment of subjectively held consumer wants and thus the issue of how to best allocate resources to maximize the attainment of valued ends. The concept of time, both perceiving and economizing on it, is therefore central to the analysis.

Subjective Valuation and Society

Adam Smith notably described how the economy, though it lacks centralized planning and top-down coordination (cf. L. v. Mises, [1936] 1951), brings about or tends toward a state of resource use and allocation that is most beneficial for society as a whole. This is due to the individual actor and producer, who "by directing [his] industry in such a manner as its produce may be of the greatest value, he intends only his own gain, and he is in this, as in many other cases, led by an invisible hand to promote an end which was no part of his intention" (Smith, [1776] 1976, p. 477). The tendency toward the maximizing wants-satisfaction equilibrium is an inherent quality of the structure of the specialized market economy, in which any individual can profit only by satisfying the wants of others. This is the case since production under the division of labor, which is the case in any modern and productive economy, is interdependent and therefore one action cannot be taken or valued without the actions of others.

Consumer wants can only be satisfied on the consumer's own terms and therefore in his or her own subjective judgment—only if the consumer perceives that a good or service is beneficial, by serving a recognized and valued end, will he or she engage in exchange in order to gain ownership or control over it. The market value of producers' actions is therefore fundamentally subject to the sovereignty of consumers (L. v. Mises, [1949] 1998, pp. 270–273), and producers thus compete for profit by contributing as much as possible to the satisfaction of consumers. Likewise, consumers produce in order to afford consumption (Say, [1821] 2008).

Consumers consider as value "the importance that individual goods or quantities of goods attain for us because we are conscious of being dependent on command of them for the satisfaction of our needs" (Menger, [1871] 2007, p. 115). They act in accordance with their perception of what will be or become most valuable to them: "In the value of goods . . . we always encounter merely the significance we assign to the satisfaction of our needs—that is, to our lives and well-being" (Menger, [1871] 2007, pp. 121–122). This value placed in goods and services is directly related to the satisfaction expected from using them for a specific purpose, whether this purpose itself entails the direct or indirect attainment of a valued end. The conclusion is that

> Value is thus nothing inherent in goods, no property of them, nor an independent thing existing by itself. It is a judgment economizing men make about the importance of the goods at their disposal for the maintenance of their lives and well-being. (Menger, 2007, pp. 120–121)

For this reason, any individual's behavior, and thus his or her chosen actions, is fundamentally based on choosing between valuable ends by ranking them based on the actor's personal judgment (that is, subjective value assessment) of their expected potential for wants satisfaction, considering each end's timeliness, the duration of the good's serviceableness, and its period of provision (Rothbard, [1962] 2004, p. 17). In cases where "a quantity of goods stands opposite needs of varying importance to men, they will first satisfy, or provide for, those needs whose satisfaction has the greatest importance to them" (Menger, [1871] 2007, p. 131; cf. Böhm-Bawerk, [1889] 1959, pp. 143–147). In other words, any person will ultimately rank the values or satisfactions that he or she identifies, and act accordingly. As any individual will always choose to attain the more highly valued end over the less valued, the market consequently tends toward greater overall want satisfaction through voluntary exchange of the means toward valuable ends. The market process must thus be equilibrating, but is not at any time *in* equilibrium.

Furthermore, in a market society based on social cooperation under the division of labor (L. v. Mises, [1949] 1998), an individual's wants are satisfied only by means of serving others in their aims to attain subjectively valued ends. It is this indirect social cooperation that Adam Smith was referring to in his well-known statement about the "invisible hand" (quoted above).

Even though Smith was unaware of the subjectivity of values as well as the marginal analysis simultaneously introduced by Menger ([1871] 2007), Jevons (1871), and Walras ([1874] 1954), the social coordination of the decentralized market was correctly identified. As later economists, including the Austrians, show, the indirect generation of social benefit through the market creates an intricate web of loosely held interdependencies where individuals, in order to satisfy their own wants, assist others in the attainment of their ends for the sake of procuring the means of production necessary for attaining their own. In this sense, the market consists of implicitly coordinated, mutually supporting—but subjectively valued—production plans that create wealth for society as a whole.

Production Plans and Value

In order to produce, by which we mean the process consisting of multiple actions that jointly generate economic value through ultimately satisfying consumer wants, whether by use of material or immaterial means, any individual must choose the course of action that is best suited to attain his or her most highly valued end. Naturally, what is considered "best" is as subjectively assessed, based on the person's appreciation of his or her current and potential future position, as the end itself. By choosing an action all other opportunities to act in order to satisfy alternative wants are necessarily forsaken, which makes the most highly valued alternative *not* chosen the real, subjective cost of the action. This cost—the value of what is forgone by taking the action—is referred to as the economic or opportunity cost of acting in order to attain the more highly valued end. As valuations are always subjective and therefore directly known only by the individual himself, any person will at any time and without exception maximize the potential outcome of their actions. In this sense, any action is always rational in the sense that it aims toward attaining the end most highly valued using the best possible means as identified by the individual him- or herself.

The value of the outcome of an action is derived from its serviceableness to the ends chosen by the individual. A person can choose to satisfy a want through the production of goods that are directly serviceable to him or her, or produce goods that are *in*directly serviceable (Rothbard, [1962] 2004, p. 8). The former are consumers' goods, defined as those goods that "serve our needs directly" (Menger, [1871] 2007, p. 56). The aim in any endeavor is always the eventual production of directly serviceable goods as that is what individuals value. In fact, as Rothbard ([1962] 2004, p. 966) notes, production "makes no sense whatever except as a means to *consumption*". This is, in essence, the reason why production is the core problem of economic analysis, since consumption always happens if the price (opportunity cost) is right; production, in contrast, must allocate scarce resources and coordinate individual actions to facilitate consumption.

Production may not be limited to a direct action but often tends to require a whole set of activities carried out in sequence. This sequence constitutes a production process, which by definition consists of all "the actions that eventually result in the attainment of consumers' goods" (Rothbard, [1962] 2004, p. 319). Also, the ultimate products, the "goods of the lowest order," are commonly produced using capital goods and other factors of production, what Austrians refer to as "goods of higher orders" (Menger, [1871] 2007, pp. 56–57). Capital goods, the produced means of production, are created because they contribute value to production and thus indirectly contribute to the satisfaction of wants. Investments in capital goods increase output through facilitating the use of tools and machinery (Böhm-Bawerk, [1889] 1959, pp. 95-96; L. v. Mises, [1949] 1998, pp. 480–490). This, in effect, makes the production process more roundabout (indirect) by adding stages of production of goods of higher orders to the original production process (Böhm-Bawerk, [1889] 1959). In other words, using machinery to replace certain tasks carried out by manual labor increases the indirect nature of the production process since the machine itself needs to be produced. The process as a whole, including the "production for production," is thus *longer*. But while the total production process is lengthened, the increased output constitutes a net gain.

As "capital resources are scarce resources *with alternative uses*" (Lachmann, [1956] 1978, p. 8), their specific uses in production are always subject to a choice in face of alternatives. As capital resources are heterogeneous and used together in production structures (Barney, 1986, 1991), it follows that their specific "uses must 'fit into each other' [and that each resource] has a function which forms part of a plan" (Lachmann, [1956] 1978, p. 8). They are therefore highly complementary (Lewin, 2011, pp. 134-136; Lachmann, 1947), and the totality of capital constitutes "an intricate, delicate, interweaving *structure* of capital goods" (Rothbard, [1962] 2004, p. 967). In order to facilitate the attainment of a valued future end, a production plan is formulated that includes the anticipated process for how this end will be attained, the resources and orders of goods used, and the necessary stages of production. The plan also estimates the time production will take.

While production plans are necessary to initially set the production process in motion, plans may need revisions as time passes. Human action in general, and roundabout production processes in particular, are always future-oriented and thus subject to a severe "uncertainty about future events [that] stems from two basic sources: the unpredictability of human acts of choice, and insufficient knowledge about natural phenomena" (Rothbard, [1962] 2004, p. 7). As we noted above, the actions of others necessarily (and intentionally) change the state of the world, which means we "are living in a world of unexpected change" (Lachmann, [1956] 1978, p. 13). It follows that capital structures too "will be ever changing, will be dissolved and re-formed" (Lachmann, [1956] 1978, p. 13). As a result of this continuous change "there are typically a number of opportunities to make production decisions, to revise them, to carry them forward, or to abandon them" (Kirzner, [1963] 2007, p. 190). Plans may be continuously revised and re-coordinated, but these actions only add to the uncertainty of the market's future state.

This uncertainty poses a fundamental problem to production—as well as its planning—since the actions of others may change future availability of resources as well as consumer demand. Production plans must therefore be based on estimates about the future state of the market, including the changes brought about by actions of others, as well as what consumers will demand, for which there is only very incomplete knowledge, and this state then requires an estimate of economic value (Knight, [1921] 1985). As this is the case for production of consumers' goods, the market value of yet-to-be-produced capital goods is also uncertain and, due to the longer period of production and only indirect contribution to want satisfaction, increasingly so. This has important implications for factor markets.

Austrians hold that only direct wants satisfaction can be inherently valued by actors, and therefore that there is direct valuation only of goods of the lowest order. As production is intended to produce consumer goods, capital goods and production processes can be valued only through their ultimate contribution to want satisfaction. The relative values of capital goods are therefore "imputed" from their expected (future) contribution to the value to consumers (Bilo, 2005; Hayek, [1926] 1984; Rothbard, [1962] 2004, pp. 453–464, Rothbard, 1987). As Menger ([1871] 2007, p. 152) notes, "the factor that is ultimately responsible for the value of goods of higher order is merely the importance that we attribute to those satisfactions with respect to which we are aware of being dependent on the availability of the goods of higher order whose value is under consideration."

This "importance" attributed to specific capital goods is necessarily derived (imputed) from the direct valuation of the satisfaction gained from using specific consumer goods; it is assessed through market prices established by entrepreneurs bidding for those resources in order to provide (future) value to consumers. Factor prices therefore indirectly reflect the social value of the factors' use in production toward the directly valued want satisfaction of consumers. Entrepreneurs bidding for these resources can only to a very limited degree rely on existing factor prices, however. They must rely on their judgment when imagining future demand and how to profit from it, and then in investing towards this end and thus bearing the uncertainty of production. Entrepreneurial judgment is the only basis on which subjective valuation of productive resources can be made, due to the "ever changing" and "dissolved and re-formed" capital structure. It is in "this activity [that] we find the real function of the entrepreneur," which involves "to *specify* and make decisions on the concrete form the capital resources shall have" (Lachmann, [1956] 1978, pp. 13, 16).

Time Preference

Austrians identify that individuals have different "time preferences" that help them choose between the outcomes of imagined production processes, and therefore to assess the value of production plans of different times to maturity. That is, individuals place different value on the time of waiting before wants are satisfied. We have already seen that all actions aim for the attainment of ends (want satisfactions) and that these ends are expected at some future point in time. How do individuals choose between them? Since more roundabout production processes, where the completion of goods of the lowest order is postponed for the production of goods of higher orders to increase output of the former at a later time, provide actors with greater wants satisfaction overall, we would expect actors to consistently forsake immediate satisfactions for future greater satisfaction if values attained at different times can be compared as is. Yet, this is not what we see in the real world and it also would not be a possible state of affairs: it suggests that no production would ever be concluded as there are always more elaborate and productive ways to increase output. Consequently, we would all starve to death.

We do not postpone want satisfaction to ever more distant futures. Individuals discount future want satisfaction based on the *urgency* of the need they feel in the present, the need they expect to feel in the future, and the assessment of the satisfaction they will feel when the end is attained at some time in the future. A person's time preference is this sense of urgency that the individual feels (L. v. Mises, [1949] 1998, pp. 480–487), the relative valuations of sooner versus later want satisfaction. This subjective cost of waiting for the sake of removing future uneasiness is a "categorical requisite of human action" (L. v. Mises, [1949] 1998, p. 486). It is a perdurable fact of human action that the "[s]atisfaction of a want in the nearer future is, other things being equal, preferred to that in the farther distant future" (L. v. Mises, [1949] 1998, pp. 480–481). An individual's time preference is thereby the means by which he or she estimates the subjective present value of want satisfactions at future times, and therefore the means by which the value of different actions and production plans of differing maturities can be compared. It is thus only under time preference that an individual can choose between future ends and therefore decide whether to postpone consumption in the present in order to invest in capital goods.

The nature of the capital structure, and therefore also the existing market for factors of production, is reflective of the social (or aggregated) time preference of market actors. On a societal level, the market price for waiting—the social value of postponing consumption into the future—is appraised through the market interest rate, itself a consequence of individuals' economic actions (Herbener, 2011; Rothbard, [1962] 2004, pp. 445–450). The magnitude of the rate of interest, based on individuals' time preferences, ultimately determines the social value of productive investments and for this reason the interest rate is essential for what Austrians call the "time-structure of production," society's combined capital structure.

It should be clear that the time preference expressed through individual actions depends on the availability of goods that satisfy wants, and therefore that relative scarcities affect the individual's sense of urgencies. Or, rather, that the urgency felt for the presently most highly valued end naturally depends on the attainment of more urgently felt needs. In prosperous societies therefore, where the immediate and basic wants are regularly and comparatively easily satisfied (cf. Maslow, 1954), we should expect to find overall lower social time preference as the time horizons for people acting in face of relative abundance is longer. In other words, they have more to gain, relatively speaking, from investing in production or capital goods that will bring about want satisfaction in the distant future; they can to a greater extent "afford" to forego consumption in the present in order to increase output in the future.

On both the social and individual levels, the time preference phenomenon connects the physical reality, and the necessity of considering time (or waiting) a factor in production, with the subjectivity of valuation. While cost of waiting is itself subjective, it is at the same time subject to the ontological state of the world and the physical resistance that any endeavor to bring about change meets. It provides a bridge between the physical and temporal scarcity of the real world and the limitlessness (insatiability) of human wants, and thereby brings structure to the human condition, guidance in valuation, and facilitates actions taken for the sake of production. Without considering time, therefore, we cannot understand the market.

IMPLICATIONS FOR STRATEGY

While Jacobson's (1992) dimensions only implicitly include the future-orientedness of human action and, consequently, the implication of the passing and valuation of time, it is an aspect that is implied in each of them. Entrepreneurial discovery suggests new ways to satisfy wants will be found, which may pertain to the satisfaction of previously unknown or unsatisfiable wants or the sooner satisfaction of already existing wants. Indeed, discovery of new means-ends frameworks (Kirzner, 1973; Shane, 2003) improves production and therefore improves or enhances the potential for overall want satisfaction. Disequilibrium implies a state where all wants are not satisfied for those willing and able to procure the means to do so, and therefore the existence of unexploited opportunities to act on for betterment, which suggests a process view of the market. It also implies the emergence of new or changing wants, which increases the complexity of the market place. Heterogeneity is necessary to appreciate the intricate problems of society's capital structure and therefore the problem of production as well as the valuation of the means of production. As we can easily see in the discussion above, the subjective formulation of wants and thus valuation of ends, as well as the many influences exercised on any individual embedded in the social cooperation of a market under the division of labor, suggests that unobservable factors play an important role in how individuals see the world and thus also in their assessment, decision-making, and acting.

Even so, Jacobson does not discuss time or even the temporal aspect of strategy in the sense Austrians would. But it is an important part of the dimensions he discusses, and it is difficult to argue for the use of them without considering the fundamental influence of time on human behavior and, consequently, the deeper understanding and contextualization of the dimensions. Indeed, one can argue that Jacobson's omission is a devastatingly important one, which may itself contribute to the inconsistency of which he warns others. The implications of this central concept for human behavior in general and especially in temporal production—and therefore necessarily strategic management—consequently remain to be discussed and analyzed in the strategy and entrepreneurship literatures. Time plays an important role in the complexity of market action, which cannot be understood if time is only implicitly considered. This section provides a draft and initial discussion on the implications of time with emphasis on decision-making, opportunities, and strategic factor markets, respectively.

Decision Making and Time

As we have noted above, in a world of change and subjective valuations the facts are ever changing since actors are constantly revising their plans and are, indeed, shooting for a seemingly moving target: predictions of future consumer wants. All action is therefore inherently uncertain, since the exact outcome of any endeavor under the passing of time cannot be known. Whereas it may seem less difficult to foresee the immediate future than the distant, only because fewer facts about the world may change, it is not possible to predict whether the impending or immediate change is of little or great magnitude for the outcome of one's action. This is especially the case considering how even a small change in the market data may be detrimental for certain production plans or actions, since even small changes may radically alter resource use, availability of resources, and consumer demand through shifting preferences. The introduction of the iPod was not in itself a major event, but the ripple effects thereof (the introduction and breakthrough for the iPhone, the consequent surge in streamed music, etc.) have fundamentally changed how people communicate and work—and their expectations of products as well as everyday behavior.

The social world, due to the subjectivity of valuation and constant individual reinterpretation of market data, consists of an immensely complex constant flow of changing parameters. This means everything is always in a flux in the sense that any past, present, or future situation is unique. Learning and experience change actors' preferences and therefore their relative valuations of satisfactions; the constant flux and fundamental unforeseeability of the market are a consequence of the fact that "human action … is characterized by the absence of constant relations" (L. v. Mises, [1949] 1998, p. 58). Action in the market hence faces Knightian uncertainty rather than mere probabilistic risk (Knight, [1921] 1985), which means any endeavor is subject to the inherently incalculable "case" (not "class") probability (R. v. Mises, [1939] 1957).

It should therefore be clear that all decision-making and strategizing must be dependent on a fundamentally qualitative or subjective component—an *understanding* of the world. Quantitative or statistical models may provide guidance by informing decision-makers of historical facts, but can never predict the true future state of the market; decision-makers must rely on their perception of the present as well as their judgment of what may change between the present and the future point in time at which the planned undertaking is estimated to come to fruition. Decision-making is necessarily based on incomplete knowledge about the world, and is always subject to uncertainty in outcomes (Klein, 2009).

While this is a complication that managers must deal with yet are unable to fully overcome, it also suggests that the responsibility and task of management must be to bear uncertainty through exercising the art of estimating the business value of the estimated future (Das, 1991). In this sense, managers are entrepreneurs (Cantillon, [1755] 2010), or what Foss, Foss, and Klein (2007) call *proxy*-entrepreneurs, though their responsibility and thus uncertainty-bearing can be limited to only part of the production process or its supporting functions and they may not have an ownership stake in the organization. The final decision-making power and thus the uncertainty of the enterprise is always borne by the original entrepreneur-investor on whose judgment the business endeavor ultimately rests (Bylund, 2011; Foss & Klein, 2012).

This discussion is neither comprehensive nor complete, but shows how adopting an Austrian perspective opens new venues for research into management and decision-making. Furthermore, the thick and realistic conception of the market that is employed in Austrian economics can greatly improve our understanding for the market process in general as well as the complex problems of top level management and organizational issues. It also suggests new ways of understanding organizational forms and strategic choices, and—as we will now see—sheds light on the ongoing discussion on the nature of entrepreneurial opportunities.

Implications for Opportunities

The modern entrepreneurship literature is centered on the concept of entrepreneurial opportunity. A dividing line is whether the opportunities are discovered by alert entrepreneurs (Kirzner, 1973, 1979; Shane, 2003, 2012; Shane & Venkataraman, 2000) or created by innovative entrepreneurs who shape or bring about their preferred market situation (Alvarez & Barney, 2007a, 2004, 2007b, 2002, 2008; Alvarez & Busenitz, 2001; Schumpeter, [1911] 1934, 1942, 2000). Both arguments hold that an entrepreneurial opportunity ontologically exists in the market and that an entrepreneur is needed to exploit it.

The discovery view holds that entrepreneurs are comparatively alert to the opportunities that exist in the market (Kirzner, 1973), and for this reason they are able to respond to their discovery and profit from it. However, as we have seen in the discussion above, it appears impossible for anyone to foresee a future state of the market in such detail that he or she can acquire only the necessary resources to exploit an opportunities that will (at some point) exist. If even the outcome of a single-actor action is fundamentally uncertain and temporal, how can entrepreneurs "discover" and exploit opportunities? Such reasoning seems to give the successful entrepreneur the status of omniscient divinity or the quality of perfect prediction.

The creation story may seem more acceptable, since it opens for uncertainty and change. But even if an entrepreneur brings about change according to a previously devised plan—which in itself is quite a feat, especially in a complex, specialized modern exchange economy—the problem lies in the assumed objectivity of the market opportunity. There are certainly opportunities for profit in the market, and entrepreneurs can prepare for what they expect to be a profit opportunity by acquiring or creating resources, but whether it turns out as foreseen is another matter. It is equally uncertain if satisfaction for the eventual consumers of the good of lowest order, and hence its imputed value to the acting entrepreneur, will be according to expectations. As was briefly noted above, market demand can change swiftly and without warning. Disruptive innovation can change the market literally overnight, which always takes some entrepreneurs by surprise, but whether an innovation in fact will have disruptive effect cannot be foretold. Many great innovations with potential for overturning the market were met with no or very limited consumer demand and therefore ended up having no impact.

Considering how any action is temporal and therefore implies uncertainty, it is impossible to exploit opportunities discovered in the present simply for the fact that exploitation generally requires production or use of resources (which takes time). It is also impossible to "foresee" with certainty what will be. Likewise, entrepreneurs cannot "create" opportunities, since attempting to do so is as uncertain an undertaking as any other in the market: the opportunity may or may not be realized, but this cannot be known in advance. In fact, as so many of the variables necessary to make up an opportunity cannot be controlled and there are no fixed relationships, it may be more accurate to say that opportunities "emerge" (Klein, 2008).

Whether there "are" opportunities or not, entrepreneurship is a temporal undertaking based on the production of potential future value and therefore must necessarily be exercised under Knightian uncertainty. Entrepreneurs must therefore rely on their *judgment* of the future market situation and then, based on it, estimate its potential market value (Knight, [1921] 1985, 1942). This "estimate of an estimate" (Knight, [1921] 1985, p. 227) must then be assessed by the entrepreneur through comparing it with its estimated opportunity costs using the entrepreneur's personal time preference rate of discounting. Based on this appraisement (L. v. Mises, [1949] 1998, pp. 328–332), he or she may choose to act on the perceived opportunity. If it really was an opportunity can only be identified *ex post facto*—and only if it was "exploited" and thus proved to generate profits.

Strategic Factor Markets

The "creation" perspective on entrepreneurial opportunities comes close to the problem of strategic factor markets. Indeed, based on the market-disruptive view of Schumpeterian innovation (Schumpeter, [1911] 1934, 1942), the entrepreneur is assumed to create opportunities by acquiring and creating the resources needed for "novel" profit opportunities. Yet the "new combinations" Schumpeter discusses relate to the production of new or existing goods and therefore have important consequences for the productive efforts over time.

In the case of new goods, the market value of the productive resources cannot be imputed from the price at which consumers value the product. As there are no markets for the product or the productive resources, the market price does not yet exist, and so the social value of these resources must therefore remain unknown until the production process is completed and consumers engage in exchange to acquire the product. Time, and the cost of waiting, here plays a very important role, since the return on investment is both uncertain and can only be realized in the distant future. This is an awesome problem for anyone attempting to appraise the value of a single resource to be used in production. Will the imagined production process, and the resources it is expected to utilize, ultimately create or destroy value (cf. Baumol, 1990)?

There is no basis for answering this question except for the entrepreneurial judgment on which such ventures are necessarily founded. The uncertainty facing an entrepreneur creating new productive resources (new machines, processes, or routines) is immense.

The creating of new productive resources used in the production of already marketed consumer products poses a similar but lesser problem. While the value of the "new combinations" could potentially be estimated through the social valuation of the consumer product, this is possible only under very specific circumstances. As new productive resources are not innovated to be perfect substitutes of those already in use, by which we mean that they are then *identical*, but rather more productive in some sense, their social value lies in their full contribution in the improved production of consumers' goods. An entrepreneur can possibly rely on heuristics to estimate their value should the exact contribution of the new production process be perfectly known (say, 10% increased output).

Such rules of thumb provide some guidance and may lessen the problem of calculating value contribution of resources, but do not completely solve the problem. As supply of consumers' goods increase, wants and preferences will shift as consumers' opportunity costs also change and they find new means to satisfy their desires. In other words, a productive resource that increases output, lowers cost, or improves quality in production of a certain consumers' good cannot be valued ex ante based on the previously existing market price. Its true market value will be revealed only through the working of the market's price mechanism and thus the bidding and other actions of entrepreneurs, producers, and consumers.

Also, the market demand for existing products at the time in the future when the new productive resources have been integrated in the production process remains uncertain even if new resources would not be put in use; any combinations of existing and new capital must be tried out and could potentially create problems; the real effect of the new resource may turn out to be very different from what is expected. Furthermore, there is no market for the new resource and therefore no social appraisement and thus no market price for the resource (L. v. Mises, [1936] 1951). The market price can only exist where there is already a market and thus competitive bidding for the resource.

Entrepreneurs rely on market prices to the extent possible in order to calculate whether a project will generate a profit or loss. This money price estimate provides a basis for appraisement of the endeavor as a whole and therefore provides the entrepreneur with the means to calculate estimated profit and loss of a project (L. v. Mises, 2008). Of course, these calculations are necessarily uncertain and therefore ultimately based on his or her judgment. But the existence of market prices, which approximate the social value of productive resources in the present, imputed from consumer want satisfaction through competitive entrepreneurial bidding, lessens the uncertainty through providing reliable (though time-dependent) estimates.

Without prices, production processes cannot be coordinated in an efficient manner, and therefore the risk of losses—money losses for the entrepreneur as well as value losses for society—is increased (L. v. Mises, [1936] 1951). But as other entrepreneurs notice the productive capability of the innovated resource, they attempt to imitate and reproduce it for their own gain. This leads to a situation where entrepreneurs, imitating for profit and bidding for each other's resources, create a market for productive resources between themselves and thereby relieve them of the uncertainty of their undertakings caused by a lack of market prices. In this sense, integration precedes markets (Stigler, 1951; Bylund, 2011).

DISCUSSION AND CONCLUSIONS

We have seen that many concepts recurrent in and central to Austrian economics are presently widely used in strategy and entrepreneurship research. However, as Jacobson (1992) feared, their use is only limitedly Austrian and often quite unknowingly so. Not only do they often therefore deviate from how they are used by scholars in the Austrian tradition, but they appear to also be adapted and reinvented. This may cause problems down the road due to inconsistencies, but a greater problem may be the loss of the deeper meaning and relevance of these concepts that appears only when adopting an Austrian perspective.

Indeed, concepts such as heterogeneous resources, entrepreneurial discovery, and disequilibrium are not—cannot—be used as independent concepts in the Austrian framework. Rather, they are essential components of the empirical market process and therefore indispensable for understanding the complexity of the market. While streamlined models can possibly identify potential inefficiencies due to heterogeneous resources, this is of little import in a market where such heterogeneity is a core component of a market process in disequilibrium. Likewise, studying entrepreneurial discovery without acknowledging the import of disequilibrium (a condition for real entrepreneurship) and heterogeneous resources (a fundamental complexity) comes close to what Ronald Coase disdained as "blackboard economics." The understanding and thus analysis of one concept requires the inclusion of the related concepts, and to understand the workings of a complex market process all of the aforementioned concepts are fundamental. Austrian economics provides a sophisticated theoretical framework for studying action and behavior in the "thick" market, which necessarily provides a better and more elaborate image of the real market than limited or "thin" conceptions.

Our focus on one core insight in Austrian economics—the passing of time—is intended to illustrate this point: how the Austrian concepts not only are coherent and consistent but mutually supporting. The Austrian understanding of time as a fundamental factor of action and production conveys a much deeper meaning of the aforementioned concepts already adopted in strategy; this meaning unfortunately appears to be poorly understood in the contemporary literature. The great body of literature in the Austrian tradition can provide guidance and inspiration to develop a deeper understanding of strategy and entrepreneurship.

This does not mean that Austrian economics should be adopted hook, line, and sinker. No school of thought is perfect and no theory is final, but the Austrian school's much longer tradition, the consistency of their deductive theorizing, and the cross-level understanding for human action and the market has much to offer. In this sense, Jacobson's (1992) recommendation should be taken seriously. The study of management has much to gain from adopting a framework that can offer structure to the use of common constructs and the numerous theoretical and empirical approaches employed in the literature.

In the previous section, we elaborated on the implications of the Austrian understanding of the temporal nature of the market for strategy and entrepreneurship. We stressed how this view of time and the future-orientedness of action provide new venues for research and a thicker understanding for strategic and entrepreneurial decision-making, entrepreneurial opportunities, and strategic factor markets. These are only three distinct areas of research in which the adoption of an Austrian perspective appears to break new ground and can provide greater understanding. As time is a universally present and important concept—indeed, it is a scarce resource—there should be many more areas and applications where the temporal aspect of human behavior should prove important and may provide theoretical advances.

I have only summarily drafted how the Austrian understanding of time may impact our thinking. The discussion up to this point has therefore been general and unspecific in order to not unnecessarily restrict the potential applications and implications of this understanding. There are a vast number of specific applications that should be further studied, but this author is unable to foresee even a fraction of them. For this reason, it would be equally naïve and presumptuous to attempt to list these areas of study or provide a guide for where the Austrian perspective is most valuable.

Some research has already been done in line with what I here recommend (see e.g., Chiles, Bluedorn, & Gupta, 2007; McMullen & Dimov, 2013; McMullen & Shepherd, 2006), but whereas these contributions are indeed both important and illustrative much remains to be done. The three areas discussed above seem to this author to be of great importance and present active streams of research that can gain much from adopting parts of the Austrian framework. Indeed, it is quite possible that an Austrian approach can shed light on and potentially solve some of the problems that have emerged in the present approaches to these topics in the literature.

Decision-making and strategizing in the market, whether in corporations or "atomistically," has an obvious temporal component that introduces Knightian uncertainty. The role of managers is therefore much more difficult, elaborate, and intuitive than is commonly asserted in economic models. Rather than being simple maximizers of known production functions using existing market prices, managers deal with and attempt to overcome market uncertainty in a sense that is fundamentally entrepreneurial. They must bear uncertainty in every decision and must utilize heuristics and judgment to produce a "mental image" of the future firm, its place in the market, and the future state of the market in which it is embedded. In this sense, the entrepreneurial manager must provide the organization with and maintain a "cognitive leadership" that resonates with internal resources as well as market opportunities (Witt, 1998).

This view of the manager as proxy-entrepreneur, who plays a role that appears to be as much of an art as it is a science, integrates strategy and entrepreneurship, and includes behavioral aspects that are at present understudied, while providing a new basis for understanding a firm's strategy, its internal organizing, and its function in the market place. The potential implications of this view are vast, but there are many minor differences between this Austrian-inspired behavioral perspective and the strategy literature that need teasing out. Perhaps a way forward and toward greater understanding for strategic management and entrepreneurship lies in taking such baby steps to refine our theories rather than revolutionizing the field. One should be weary to throw out any babies with the bath water.

This may be the case also with the consequences of introducing the temporal perspective in the study of entrepreneurship. Others have argued that the opportunity concept is impotent (Klein, 2008) and should be replaced by a more subjectively held view based on judgment. There are many reasons to accept this criticism and the recent shift in the literature toward creation rather than semi-passive discovery of opportunities appears to be in the right direction. But our discussion above raises fundamental questions about the study of the entrepreneurial opportunity *per se*, which appears too limiting in a world of subjective values and temporal action. It may not be the case that the Austrian view of time offers conclusive evidence for the nature of opportunities, be they objective or not, but whether the opportunity should be the unit of analysis. If we adopt the Austrian view of entrepreneurship as the exercise and acting on judgment under uncertainty, then the opportunity concept appears to be mostly a shorthand for describing historical entrepreneurial successes. It may therefore offer no value for research attempting to understand the entrepreneurial function and process in the market. Should we rather study investments as the measurable outcome of entrepreneurial judgment?

These investments always take place in the factor markets for the sake of improving or establishing new structures of production. Our time-perspective therefore establishes an explicit connection or relationship between the firm, its strategy, entrepreneurship, and strategic factor markets. This connection introduces the Austrian concept of economic calculation and provides an important role for market prices, which are, for capital goods, market expressions of the social value of productive resource use, and, for consumer's goods, an estimation of the social valuation of relative wants satisfaction. As Jacobson (1992) alludes to in his seminal article, the Austrian view is an integrated theoretical framework where the explanatory power of the whole is greater than the sum of its parts. While Jacobson argued that the use of Austrian concepts without an Austrian understanding may create inconsistencies, it may also be the case that Austrian concepts are mutually dependent and that the value of adopting the concepts rather than the perspective is of much lesser worth or scholarly significance than relying on the underlying structure of the Austrian perspective.

The question then arises: to what extent can we as strategy and entrepreneurship scholars borrow from the Austrian school without adopting the whole framework? We have seen in this chapter how the deeper understanding of Austrian concepts can provide new venues for interesting and potentially important research. But where does one draw the line? In order to make the most out of our use of Austrian concepts it appears we would benefit from adopting parts of the Austrian perspective, such as their identification and use of the concept of time. But one must tread carefully not to discard of all non-Austrian advances our field has made to date.

Perhaps the best way is found in Jacobson's discussion of establishing an Austrian school of strategy. This need not be an all-or-nothing deal in the sense of restructuring and fundamentally changing the field. Rather, such a stream of research could easily be adopted as one of several possible and competing points of view. Strategy indeed has much to benefit from adopting Austrian perspectives, but we may have more to gain from allowing an Austrian school of strategy to develop and make theoretical advances side by side with alternative perspectives.

NOTES

1. The Austrian school was founded by Carl Menger with his groundbreaking 1871 treatise *Grundsätze der Volkswirtschaftslehre* (Menger, [1871] 2007), and

developed by three generations of scholars based in the University of Vienna (Schulak & Unterköfler, 2011). While Menger called his approach causal-realist, the school was disdainfully referred to as "Austrian" by German scholars during the great controversy in the late 19th century on economic method—the *Methodenstreit*—between the deductive Vienna-based economists, primarily Menger (Menger, 1884, [1883] 1985), and the inductive, anti-theory German Historical School (Schmoller, 1883).

2. Note that an article may be counted more than once if its Austrian concept use fits in more than one dimension.

REFERENCES

Alvarez, S. A., & Barney, J. B. (2002). Resource-based theory and the entrepreneurial firm. In M. A. Hitt, R. D. Ireland, S. M. Camp, & D. L. Sexton (Eds.), *Strategic entrepreneurship: Creating a new mindset* (pp. 89–105). Malden, MA: Blackwell Publishers.

Alvarez, S. A., & Barney, J. B. (2004). Organizing rent generation and appropriation: Toward a theory of the entrepreneurial firm. *Journal of Business Venturing, 19,* 621–635.

Alvarez, S. A., & Barney, J. B. (2007a). Discovery and creation: Alternative theories of entrepreneurial action. *Strategic Entrepreneurship Journal, 1*(1–2), 11–26.

Alvarez, S. A., & Barney, J. B. (2007b). The entrepreneurial theory of the firm. *Journal of Management Studies, 44,* 1057–1063.

Alvarez, S. A., & Barney, J. B. (2008). Opportunities, organizations, and entrepreneurship. *Strategic Entrepreneurship Journal, 2,* 265–267.

Alvarez, S. A., & Busenitz, L. W. (2001). The entrepreneurship of resource-based theory. *Journal of Management, 27,* 755.

Bain, J. S. (1951). Relation of profit rate to industry concentration: American manufacturing, 1936–1940. *Quarterly Journal of Economics, 65,* 293–324.

Barney, J. B. (1986). Strategic factor markets: Expectations, luck, and business strategy. *Management Science, 32,* 1231–1241.

Barney, J. B. (1991). Firm resources and sustained competitive advantage. *Journal of Management, 17,* 99–120.

Baumol, W. J. (1990). Entrepreneurship: Productive, unproductive, and destructive. *Journal of Political Economy, 98,* 893–919.

Bhide, A. (1986). Hustle as strategy. *Harvard Business Review, 64*(5), 59–65.

Bilo, S. (2005). *Imputation and value in the works of Menger, Böhm-Bawerk and Wieser.* E-Logos. University of Economics. Prague, Czech Republic.

Böhm-Bawerk, E. v. ([1889] 1959). *Positive theory of capital* (Vol. 2). South Holland, IL: Libertarian Press.

Bylund, P. L. (2011). Division of labor and the firm: An Austrian attempt at explaining the firm in the market. *Quarterly Journal of Austrian Economics, 14*(2), 188–215.

Cantillon, R. ([1755] 2010). *An essay on economic theory* (C. Saucier, Trans.). Auburn, AL: Ludwig von Mises Institute.

Chiles, T. H., Bluedorn, A. C., & Gupta, V. K. (2007). Beyond creative destruction and entrepreneurial discovery: A radical Austrian approach to entrepreneurship. *Organization Studies, 28*, 467–493.

Das, T. K. (1991). Time: The hidden dimension in strategic planning. *Long Range Planning, 24*(3), 49–57.

Das, T. K. (1993). Time in management and organizational studies. *Time & Society, 2*, 267–274.

Dierickx, I., & Cool, K. (1988). *Competitive advantage: A resource based perspective.* Fontainebleau, France: INSEAD.

Foss, K., Foss, N. J., & Klein, P. G. (2007). Original and derived judgment: An entrepreneurial theory of economic organization. *Organization Studies, 28*, 1–20.

Foss, N. J. (1996a). Knowledge-based approaches to the theory of the firm: Some critical comments. *Organization Science, 7*(5), 470–476.

Foss, N. J. (1996b). More critical comments on knowledge-based theories of the firm. *Organization Science, 7*(5), 519–523.

Foss, N. J., & Klein, P. G. (2012). *Organizing entrepreneurial judgment: A new approach to the firm.* Cambridge, UK: Cambridge University Press.

Grant, R. M. (1996). Toward a knowledge-based theory of the firm. *Strategic Management Journal, 17*, 109–122.

Hayek, F. A. v. ([1926] 1984). Some remarks on the problem of imputation. In R. McCloughry (Ed.), *Money, capital & fluctuations: Early essays* (pp. 33–54). Chicago, IL: University of Chicago Press.

Herbener, J. M. (2011). *The pure time-preference theory of interest.* Auburn, AL: Ludwig von Mises Institute.

Itami, H., & Roehl, T. W. (1987). *Mobilizing invisible assets.* Cambridge, MA: Harvard University Press.

Jacobson, R. (1990). Unobservable effects and business performance. *Marketing Science, 9*(1), 74–85.

Jacobson, R. (1992). The "Austrian" school of strategy. *Academy of Management Review, 17*, 782–807.

Jevons, W. S. (1871). *The theory of political economy.* London, UK: Macmillan and Co.

Kirzner, I. M. (1973). *Competition and entrepreneurship.* Chicago, IL: University of Chicago Press.

Kirzner, I. M. (1979). *Perception, opportunity, and profit: Studies in the theory of entrepreneurship.* Chicago, IL: University of Chicago Press.

Kirzner, I. M. ([1963] 2007). *Market theory and the price system.* Auburn, AL: Ludwig von Mises Institute.

Klein, P. G. (2008). Opportunity discovery, entrepreneurial action, and economic organization. *Strategic Entrepreneurship Journal, 2*, 175–190.

Klein, P. G. (2009). Risk, uncertainty, and economic organization. In J. G. Hülsmann & S. Kinsella (Eds.), *Property, freedom, & society: Essays in honor of Hans-Hermann Hoppe* (pp. 325–337). Auburn, AL: Ludwig von Mises Institute.

Knight, F. H. (1942). Profit and entrepreneurial functions. *Journal of Economic History, 2*(2), 126–132.

Knight, F. H. ([1921] 1985). *Risk, uncertainty and profit.* Chicago, IL: University of Chicago Press.

Lachmann, L. M. (1947). Complementarity and substitution in the theory of capital. *Economica, 14,* 108–119.

Lachmann, L. M. ([1956] 1978). *Capital and its structure.* Kansas City, MO: Sheed Andrews and McMeel.

Levitt, T. (1986). *The marketing imagination.* New York, NY: Free Press.

Lewin, P. (2011). *Capital in disequilibrium: The role of capital in a changing world.* Auburn, AL: Ludwig von Mises Institute.

Maslow, A. (1954). *Motivation and personality.* New York, NY: Harper.

McMullen, J. S., & Dimov, D. (2013). Time and the entrepreneurial journey: The problems and promise of studying entrepreneurship as a process. *Journal of Management Studies, 50,* 1481–1512.

McMullen, J. S., & Shepherd, D. A. (2006). Entrepreneurial action and the role of uncertainty in the theory of the entrepreneur. *Academy of Management Review, 31,* 132–152.

Menger, C. (1884). *Die irrthümer des historismus in der deutschen nationalökonomie* [The errors of historicism in German economics]. Vienna, Austria: Alfred Hölder.

Menger, C. ([1883] 1985). *Investigations into the method of the social sciences with special reference to economics* (F. J. Nock, Trans.). New York, NY: New York University Press.

Menger, C. ([1871] 2007). *Principles of economics* (J. Dingwall & B. F. Hoselitz, Trans.). Auburn, AL: Ludwig von Mises Institute.

Mises, L. v. ([1936] 1951). *Socialism: An economic and sociological analysis* (J. Kahane, Trans.). New Haven, CT: Yale University Press.

Mises, L. v. ([1949] 1998). *Human action: A treatise on economics. The scholar's edition.* Auburn, AL: Ludwig von Mises Institute.

Mises, L. v. (2008). Profit and loss. In Mises, L. v. *Planning for freedom: Let the market system work* (pp. 143–172). Indianapolis, IN: Liberty Fund.

Mises, R. v. ([1939] 1957). *Probability, statistics and truth.* New York, NY: Dover Publications.

Peters, T. (1987). *Thriving on chaos: Handbook for a management revolution.* New York, NY: Knopf.

Porter, M. E. (1980). *Competitive strategy: Techniques for analyzing industries and competitors.* New York, NY: Free Press.

Porter, M. E. (1981). The contributions of industrial organization to strategic management. *Academy of Management Review, 6,* 609–620.

Porter, M. E. (1985). *Competitive advantage: Creating and sustaining superior performance.* New York, NY: Free Press.

Rothbard, M. N. (1987). Imputation. In *The new Palgrave: A dictionary of economics* (Vol. 2, pp. 738–739). London, UK: Macmillan Press.

Rothbard, M. N. ([1962] 2004). *Man, economy, and state with Power and market. Scholar's edition.* Auburn, AL: Ludwig von Mises Institute.

Rumelt, R. P. (1984). Towards a strategic theory of the firm. In R. Lamb (Ed.), *Competitive strategic management* (pp. 556–570). Englewood Cliffs, NJ: Prentice-Hall.

Say, J.-B. ([1821] 2008). *A treatise on political economy or the production, distribution and consumption of wealth* (C. R. Prinsep, Trans.). Auburn, AL: Ludwig von Mises Institute.

Schmoller, G. v. (1883). *Schmollers jahrbuch für gesetzgebung, verwaltung und volkswirtschaft (Vol. 7): Zur methodologie der staats- und sozialwissenschaften* [Schmoller's yearbook for legislation, administration and economics (Vol. 7): Methodology of the political and social sciences]. Berlin, Germany: Duncker & Humblot.

Schulak, E. M., & Unterköfler, H. (2011). *The austrian school of economics: A history of its ideas, ambassadors, and institutions* (A. Oost-Zinner, Trans.). Auburn, AL: Ludwig von Mises Institute.

Schumpeter, J. A. ([1911] 1934). *The theory of economic development: An inquiry into profits, capital, credit, interest, and the business cycle.* Cambridge, MA: Harvard University Press.

Schumpeter, J. A. (1942). *Socialism, capitalism and democracy.* New York, NY: Harper and Bros.

Schumpeter, J. A. (2000). Entrepreneurship and innovation. In R. Swedberg (Ed.), *Entrepreneurship: The social science view* (pp. 51–75). Oxford, UK: Oxford University Press.

Shane, S. (2003). *A general theory of entrepreneurship: The individual-opportunity nexus.* Cheltenham, UK: Edward Elgar.

Shane, S. (2012). Reflections on the 2010 AMR decade award: Delivering on the promise of entrepreneurship as a field of research. *Academy of Management Review, 37,* 10–20.

Shane, S., & Venkataraman, S. (2000). The promise of entrepreneurship as a field of research. *Academy of Management Review, 25,* 217–226.

Smith, A. ([1776] 1976). *An inquiry into the nature and causes of the wealth of nations.* Chicago, IL: University of Chicago Press.

Spender, J. C. (1996). Making knowledge the basis of a dynamic theory of the firm. *Strategic Management Journal, 17,* 45–62.

Stigler, G. J. (1951). The division of labor is limited by the extent of the market. *Journal of Political Economy, 59*(3), 185–193.

Strigl, R. v. ([1934] 2000). *Capital & production.* Auburn, AL: Ludwig von Mises Institute.

Tsoukas, H. (1996). The firm as a distributed knowledge system: A constructionist approach. *Strategic Management Journal, 17*(S2), 11–25.

Walras, L. ([1874] 1954). *Elements of pure economics, or the theory of social wealth* (W. Jaffé, Trans.). Paris, France: Richard D. Irwin.

Wensley, R. (1982). Pims and bcg: New horizons or false dawn? *Strategic Management Journal, 3,* 147–158.

Wernerfelt, B. (1984). A resource-based view of the firm. *Strategic Management Journal, 5,* 171–180.

Witt, U. (1998). Imagination and leadership: The neglected dimension of an evolutionary theory of the firm. *Journal of Economic Behavior & Organization, 35,* 161–177.

ABOUT THE CONTRIBUTORS

Sandip Basu is an Assistant Professor of Management at the Zicklin School of Business, Baruch College, City University of New York. He received his PhD in Management from the Foster School of Business at the University of Washington, Seattle, WA, and has previously taught at the California State University, East Bay, in Hayward, California. Professor Basu's research interests are in the areas of entrepreneurship and innovation, strategic change, organizational capabilities, and new venture creation. He has published articles in the *Journal of Business Venturing, Journal of Product Innovation Management, Strategic Entrepreneurship Journal, Frontiers of Entrepreneurship Research*, and *Proceedings of the Academy of Management*. E-mail: sandip.basu@baruch.cuny.edu

Christophe Boone is a Professor of Organization Theory and Behavior at the Department of Management, Faculty of Applied Economics, University of Antwerp, Belgium, and founding member of the Antwerp Centre of Evolutionary Demography ([A]CED). Current research topics include the dynamics of top management team composition in relationship to organizational effectiveness and market structure, organizational ecology and the neuroeconomics of cooperative behavior. His recent work has been published in international scholarly journals such as *Academy of Management Review, Academy of Management Journal, Management Science, Journal of Management Studies, Hormones and Behavior, Journal of Economic Psychology*, and *Evolution and Human Behavior*. E-mail: christophe.boone@uantwerpen.be

Behavioral Strategy: Emerging Perspectives, pages 233–237

Tine Buyl is a postdoctoral researcher at the Antwerp Centre of Evolutionary Demography (ACED), Department of Management, Faculty of Applied Economics, University of Antwerp, Belgium. She received her PhD from the University of Antwerp. Her research focuses on the composition, cognition, and dynamics of top management teams and their relation to organizational processes and outcomes. Recent work has been published in academic journals such as *Journal of Management Studies, Strategic Organization,* and *British Journal of Management.* E-mail: tine.buyl@uantwerpen.be

Per L. Bylund is the John F. Baugh Center Research Professor in the Department of Management and Entrepreneurship in the Hankamer School of Business at Baylor University, TX. He has a PhD in Applied Economics from the University of Missouri, MO, as well as master's degrees in Political Science from Lund University in Sweden and in Informatics from Jönköping International Business School in Sweden, and is an associated scholar with the Ludwig von Mises Institute in Auburn, AL. E-mail: Per_Bylund@baylor.edu

T. K. Das is Professor of Strategic Management at the Zicklin School of Business, Baruch College, City University of New York. He is concurrently a member of the University's Doctoral Faculty. Professor Das received his PhD in Organization and Strategic Studies from the Anderson Graduate School of Management, University of California at Los Angeles (UCLA). He also has degrees in Physics, Mathematics, and Management, and a Professional Certification in Banking. Prior to entering the academic life, Professor Das had extensive experience as a senior business executive. He has research interests in strategic alliances, strategy making, organizational studies, temporal studies, and executive development. Professor Das has published over a dozen books and monographs, and his research has appeared in over 45 journals, of which some of the later ones include *Academy of Management Executive, Academy of Management Review, British Journal of Management, Journal of International Management, Journal of Management, Journal of Management Studies, Organization Science, Organization Studies,* and *Strategic Management Journal.* Professor Das was formerly a Senior Editor of *Organization Studies* and has served, or is currently serving, on the editorial boards of a number of scholarly journals. He is the founding (and current) Series Editor of the two book series, *Research in Behavioral Strategy* and *Research in Strategic Alliances* (Information Age Publishing). E-mail: TK.Das@baruch.cuny.edu

Gjalt de Jong is an Associate Professor of Strategy at the Faculty of Economics and Business, University of Groningen. His research interests related to and publications on strategy concern: the management of strategic alliances; business ethics in transition economies; the structure and organization of multinational enterprises; and the causes and consequences of national rules. He is responsible for the design and coordination of courses in the fields of international business, international economics, and public administration. Prior to his current position, he was affiliated with PricewaterhouseCoopers and KPMG as a senior management consultant, and as such responsible for large-scale strategy programs at Dutch multinational firms in industry and the financial sector, as well as for educational institutes. E-mail: g.de.jong@rug.nl

Rick M.A. Hollen is a PhD Candidate at the Department of Strategic Management and Entrepreneurship of the Rotterdam School of Management, Erasmus University. He obtained a Master's degree (2009) in Strategic Management (cum laude) and a Bachelor's degree in Business Administration at the same university. Before starting his PhD trajectory, he worked as Project Manager Business Development for a global technology and services company. His PhD research mainly focuses on managerial and organizational factors that increase and sustain international competitiveness of established firms. Interrelated key topics include management innovation, industrial ecosystems, interorganizational interdependence, ambidexterity and strategic value creation. Much of his research is conducted in the Port of Rotterdam, Europe's largest seaport and one of the world's largest petrochemical complexes, which provides an interesting empirical research context for studying these topics. One of his papers, which examines the role of management innovation in enabling technological process innovation, recently appeared in *European Management Review*, while other papers have been presented at international conferences such as the Academy of Management Annual Meeting in Orlando and Strategic Management Society conferences in Atlanta, Lausanne and Tel Aviv. E-mail: rhollen@rsm.nl

Suresh Kotha is the Douglas E. Olesen/Battelle Excellence Chair in Entrepreneurship and a professor of management and organization at the Michael G. Foster School of Business, University of Washington, Seattle, WA. He received his PhD in strategic management from the Lally School of Management & Technology, Rensselaer Polytechnic Institute, NY. His research interests focus on entrepreneurship, technology and innovation management, and competitive strategy. He was also a faculty member at New York University prior to joining the Foster School of Business. E-mail: skotha@uw.edu

Arash Najmaei is a doctoral candidate at the Macquarie Graduate School of Management, Sydney, Australia. His research interests include business modeling, managerial cognition, dynamic capabilities and growth of the firm. His doctoral project focuses on the business modeling of Australian manufacturing firms. He has published a number of book chapters and has an article forthcoming in *International Journal of Strategic Information Technology and Applications.* E-mail: arash.najmaei@mq.edu.au

Bing-Sheng Teng is an Associate Professor of Strategic Management and Associate Dean for MBA at Cheung Kong Graduate School of Business in Beijing, China. He was previously an Associate Professor of Strategic Management with tenure at George Washington University (GWU). Professor Teng's research has been published in such top academic journals as *Academy of Management Review* and *Organization Science.* Professor Teng's expertise on Chinese management led to frequent interviews by the popular media such as *Wall Street Journal* and *Business Week.* Email: bsteng@ckgsb.edu.cn

Jiulin Teng is working on his PhD degree at the Department of Strategy and Business Policy at HEC Paris (France). Previously, he earned his MSc from Karolinska Institute, Stockholm, Sweden. His primary research interests concern the dynamic aspects of inter-firm relationships, in particular shifts of characteristics that define such relationship that lead to the evolution of contracts, and how such shifts may relate to the micro-foundation for dynamic capabilities. He is also interested in the topic of institutions as an exogenous force that effect inter-firm relationships. E-mail: jiulin.teng@hec.edu

Frans A. J. Van Den Bosch is Professor of Management Interfaces between Organizations and Business Environment at the Department of Strategic Management and Business Environment, Rotterdam School of Management (RSM), Erasmus University. He holds a BA in Mechanical Engineering from the Polytechnic of Rotterdam (with distinction), received his Master's degree in Economics (cum laude) from the Erasmus University Rotterdam and his PhD in Law from Leiden University, Netherlands. He has published several books and over 165 articles in scientific journals including *Academy of Management Journal, Management Science, Organization Science* and *Strategic Management Journal,* supervised 35 PhD theses and is board member of several top scientific journals. His major research interests are the development of integrative strategy frameworks incorporating both the externally and internally focused view of strategy, and the application of these frameworks to general management issues such as management innovation, organizational ambidexterity, strategic renewal processes and corporate governance. Professor Van Den Bosch has been actively involved in the business community and the public sector, e.g., as chairman of the Board of Non-executive Directors of Dutch companies, vice-chairman of the Rotterdam Chamber of Commerce, member of the Rotterdam City Council (including the Port Committee) and advisor of a Dutch trade union association. At present, his main activities concern conducting and supervising scientific research. E-mail: fbosch@rsm.nl

Jan Veijer is a research master's student at the Faculty of Economics and Business, University of Groningen, Netherlands. He was awarded a Bachelor of Science degree in business economics by the University of Groningen. In his studies, he has specialized in economic development, international cooperation, energy, international trade and behavioral aspects that underlie economic decision-making. E-mail: j.veijer@student.rug.nl

Henk W. Volberda is Professor of Strategic Management and Business Policy and Director Knowledge Transfer at the RSM Erasmus University. He obtained his doctorate in Business Administration (cum laude) from the University of Groningen. He has been a visiting scholar at the Wharton School at the University of Pennsylvania and Cass Business School, London. Professor Volberda has worked as a consultant for many large European corporations. His research on organizational flexibility and strategic renewal received the NCD Grant, ERASM Research Award, Erasmus University Research Award, ERIM Impact Award and the prestigious Igor Ansoff Strategic Management Award. His work has been published in many refereed books and scientific journals, for which he received among others the ROA Publication Prize, SAP Best Strategy Paper Award and the SMS McKinsey honourable mention. His book *Building the Flexible Firm: How to Remain Competitive* (1998) received wide acclaim, and his book together with Tom Elfring 'Rethinking Strategy' (2001) was awarded with the ERIM Best Book Award. Recently he published *Strategic Management: Competitiveness and Globalization* (2011), a new strategy textbook. Professor Volberda is director of the Erasmus Strategic Renewal Centre, Coordinator of the ERIM Strategy Research Program and Scientific Director of the top institute INSCOPE: Research for Innovation. He is a member of the Editorial Board of among others the *Global Journal of Flexible Systems Manag*ement, *Journal of Management Studies*, *Journal of Strategic Management Education*, *Journal of Strategy and Management*, *Long Range Planning*, *Management Executive*, and *Organization Science*. E-mail: hvolberda@rsm.nl

INDEX

Behavioral Strategy: Emerging Perspectives, pages 239–251

B

C

D

I

J

K

L

M

N

O

P

Q

R

S

T

U

V

W

Y

Z

Printed and bound by CPI Group (UK) Ltd, Croydon, CR0 4YY

15/09/2026

14962370-0003